JAY ALAN SEKULOW

ROBERT WESTON ASH, CECE HEIL & MARSHALL H. GOLDMAN

SHARIAH
IN AMERICA

ISLAMIC SHARIAH'S THREAT TO AMERICAN LIBERTY

American Center
for Law & Justice
P.O. Box 90555
Washington, D.C. 20090-0555
www.ACLJ.org

ISBN 978-0-9836855-0-0

Printed in the United States by Dickinson Press, Grand Rapids, Michigan
Cover design by American Center for Law and Justice

PREFACE

The fundamental principle underlying our system of government is the principle of individual liberty. The genius of the American system is that our Forefathers chose to bequeath to us a system of government that limited the reach of government officials so that individual Americans could control their own lives and destinies. Americans were not to be controlled by their rulers; instead, the rulers of the United States were to serve only with the consent of the governed. Moreover, all Americans, whether rulers or the ruled, are governed by the rule of law. It is for this reason that the American system and the blessings that we enjoy as Americans are anathema to many around the world.

The attack on the United States of America on September 11, 2001, was committed by those who despise the freedoms we enjoy and who seek to bring the entire world under theocratic rule reflecting values derived from desert tribes living in the Arabian Peninsula in the seventh century. On September 11th, the true face of radical Islamic ideology was exposed for the world to see. Prior U.S. Administrations had dismissed warnings—the first Twin Towers attack, the attack on the USS Cole, the attacks on the barracks in Saudi Arabia—as being isolated incidents. However, September 11th changed that. On that day, we came face-to-face with a rabid Islamic ideology committed to destroying our way of life and imposing upon us (and the entire Western world) Islamic *Shariah*, which demands total submission to Allah.

The principles of *Shariah* are wholly incompatible with U.S. law and legal tradition. While the Western world has foresworn medieval punishments for centuries, *Shariah* continues to demand them. Countries governed by *Shariah* routinely amputate limbs for minor offenses and stone victims to death. Due process, as we know it, does not exist under *Shariah*. A woman's testimony only counts as half of a man's. A woman who is raped will herself be charged with criminal sexual conduct unless she can produce four righteous Muslim men to testify that they witnessed the rape. Adherents of fundamental Islam frequently take it upon themselves to execute those who they allege have offended Islam or Muhammad and then publicly pride themselves for having acted righteously. As such, Islamic *Shariah* represents a grave danger to the United States, our values, and our way of life.

In *Shariah in America: Islamic Shariah's Threat to American Liberty*, the American Center for Law and Justice (ACLJ) has exposed the dangers of Islamic *Shariah* to our essential liberties. We have explained the basic rules and principles of *Shariah* using the words of its practitioners and scholars. We have used primary Islamic sources and cited real examples to show the breadth and serious nature of the threat posed by *Shariah*. Please pay special attention to our inclusion of *Appendix C*, the Muslim Brotherhood Memorandum, which lays out the Muslim Brotherhood's strategy for destroying our system of law and government in favor of a system based on *Shariah*.

This book exposes not only the incompatibility of *Shariah* with U.S. law, but also the attempts by fundamentalist Muslims—both in the United States and abroad—to subvert our legal system in favor of a system that would destroy individual liberty. Each of us should take heed to what this book reveals in order to protect and defend the Constitution of the United States against all enemies, be they foreign or domestic.

ABOUT THE AUTHORS

Jay Alan Sekulow is the Chief Counsel of the American Center for Law and Justice (ACLJ), Washington, D.C., and the Chief Counsel of the European Centre for Law and Justice (ECLJ), Strasbourg, France. Sekulow has presented oral arguments in numerous cases before the Supreme Court of the United States on an array of constitutional issues and has filed several briefs with the Court on issues regarding national security and the law of war. Several of his landmark cases have become part of the legal landscape in the area of religious liberty litigation. He was twice-named one of the "100 Most Influential Lawyers" in the United States by the *National Law Journal*, and was listed as "one of the 90 Greatest Washington Lawyers of the Last 30 years" by the *Legal Times*. Sekulow has served as a faculty member for the Office of Legal Education at the United States Department of Justice. He received a B.A. (*cum laude*) and J.D. (*cum laude*) from Mercer University, and a Ph.D. from Regent University with a dissertation on American Legal History. Sekulow has authored numerous books, law review articles, and other publications.

Robert Weston Ash serves as Senior Litigation Counsel for National Security Law at the ACLJ. Ash is responsible for matters involving national security issues, religious liberties of those in uniform, and the law of armed conflict. Ash is also an Associate Professor of Law at the Regent University School of Law. He teaches courses on national security law, international law, comparative law, First Amendment law, and business associations. Ash is a graduate of the U.S. Military Academy and served 22 years on active duty as a U.S. Army officer, which included serving as a military strategist for the Secretary of Defense in the Office of the Assistant Secretary of Defense for Strategy and Requirements in the Pentagon.

CeCe Heil is a Senior Counsel with the ACLJ. Heil specializes in public policy and global legal matters, including issues at the United Nations. She heads a team of lawyers handling cases in defense of life, protecting U.S. national security interests, and dealing with

Islamic extremism. Before joining the ACLJ, Heil worked in private practice in Missouri and Tennessee, serving as counsel to many internationally recognized clients, and is currently on the board of several national ministries. She is a recognized leader in her work to have pro-family, pro-life, and pro-free enterprise policies enacted, including being a candidate for Congress. Heil is a 1992 graduate of Regent University School of Law. She is admitted to practice law in California, Missouri, and Tennessee.

Marshall H. Goldman is an Associate Counsel with the ACLJ whose area of expertise is international matters. Goldman is a graduate of Oral Roberts University (*cum laude*). He also graduated from Regent University School of Law and the Robertson School of Government, where he was the recipient of the Outstanding Research Award for Distinction in Scholarship. At the ACLJ, Goldman works on international legal issues, including *Shariah*-related issues. Before joining the ACLJ, he worked in private practice. Goldman is admitted to practice law in Virginia.

TABLE OF CONTENTS

AN INTRODUCTION TO **ISLAMIC LAW**

In the West, we generally divide the world into regions consisting of nation-states. Based on where they reside, people are identified as "Westerners," "Asians," "Americans," "Britons," "Germans," etc. Within regions and nation-states live peoples of different races and religions, yet, for purposes of nationality, they are identified as residents of a given nation-state.

Islam, one of the major world religions, represents approximately 1.6 billion people. While Muslims make up about twenty-three percent of the world's population and live in both Islamic and non-Islamic countries, their national identity is not only represented by the respective nation-states in which they reside, but also by their religion, as one global community—the Islamic world.

The Islamic world, which includes fifty-six Islamic countries, is governed (or expected to be governed) by a religiously-based law that covers not only religious matters, but also civil and secular matters. Secular matters, such as traffic laws, contracts, financial transactions, or crime and punishment, are matters that are usually regulated and governed in the West by the state. Islam, however, does not distinguish between the religious and the secular. As a result, all Muslim countries and all Muslims living in non-Muslim countries consider themselves to be members of one supra-national community. It is this political nature of Islam that requires its adherents to be governed by one law wherever they reside.

Not only do Muslims carry Islamic law with them when they move to other areas of the world, they also bring the belief that Islamic law, because it is revealed by Allah, is superior to all other law and must ultimately replace all non-Islamic law, whether by acquiescence or by compulsion.

CHAPTER ONE

SHARIAH AND THE WEST

Liberty is one of the principal hallmarks of American society.[1] It is an unalienable right recognized in the Declaration of Independence and protected under the United States Constitution.[2] This liberty includes freedom to believe (or not believe), to express religious (and other) sentiments as one wishes, and to practice one's faith (or philosophy) according to one's own conscience.[3] Such liberties, however, are not absolute and must operate within the bounds of law.[4] Therefore, when disagreements and controversies arise in the United States, they are debated in the free marketplace of ideas or resolved in courts of law that are committed to implementing and upholding the laws enacted by the U.S. Congress and state legislatures.[5] These laws indiscriminately govern people of all races, religions, and social classes in the United States[6] and must be in accordance with the U.S. Constitution, which is "the supreme Law of the Land."[7]

[1] THE DECLARATION OF INDEPENDENCE pmbl. (U.S. 1776) ("We hold these truths to be self-evident, that all men are created equal, that they are endowed by their Creator with certain unalienable Rights, that among these are Life, Liberty and the pursuit of Happiness.").

[2] *Id.*; *see also* U.S. CONST. amend. XIV ("[N]or shall any State deprive any person of life, liberty, or property, without due process of law . . . .").

[3] U.S. CONST. amend. I ("Congress shall make no law respecting an establishment of religion, or prohibiting the free exercise thereof; or abridging the freedom of speech . . . or the right of the people peaceably to assemble . . . .").

[4] *See* Reynolds v. United States, 98 U.S. 145, 162–67 (1878) (recognizing that citizens of the United States are free to subscribe to any religious belief but that actions that emanate from that religious belief and are deemed harmful to society may legitimately be restricted by the government).

[5] *See* Abrams v. United States, 250 U.S. 616, 630 (1919) (Holmes, J., dissenting) ("[T]he best test of truth is the power of the thought to get itself accepted in the competition of the market, and that truth is the only ground upon which their wishes safely can be carried out."); *see also* U.S. CONST. arts. I, III (establishing the legislative and judicial branches and setting forth their proper functions and concomitant obligations to uphold the United States Constitution).

[6] U.S. CONST. amend. XIV ("[N]or shall any State deprive any person of life, liberty, or property, without due process of law; nor deny to any person within its jurisdiction the equal protection of the laws.").

[7] U.S. CONST. art. VI, cl. 2 ("This Constitution, and the Laws of the United States which shall be made in Pursuance thereof . . . shall be the supreme Law of the Land; and the Judges in every State shall be

Immigrants to the United States historically have assimilated themselves into the population and, despite their different countries of origin, have learned to respect and abide by the laws of the land they have come to call "home." Some segments of the Muslim population in the United States, however, now are seeking to be governed by a wholly different set of laws[8]—laws that are not only foreign to this country and its legal traditions and not enacted by the proper authorities, but are also incompatible with the existing laws of this land and contrary to natural justice.

Capitalizing on the American values of life, liberty, freedom, and religious accommodation, both so-called radical and moderate Islamic groups have begun establishing large Muslim communities in the United States[9] with the goal of implementing their religious

---

bound thereby . . . ."); While article IV lists the Constitution, Laws, and Treaties as supreme law, it has long been understood that the Constitution itself is the supreme source of law in the U.S. system and that other sources of law must give way when they are inconsistent with the Constitution; Marbury v. Madison, 5 U.S. (1 Cranch) 137, 178 (1803) ("If then the courts are to regard the constitution; and the constitution is superior to any ordinary act of the legislature; the constitution, and not such ordinary act, must govern the case to which they both apply.").

[8]*E.g.*, *House Protests Calling for Muslims to 'Rise up and Establish Islamic State in America'*, DAILYMAIL.CO.UK (Feb. 20, 2011), http://www.dailymail.co.uk/news/article-1358792/Anjem-Choudary-lead-White-House-protest-calling-Muslims-rise-up.html (British Imam Anjem Choudary described a planned Islamic rally outside the White House and organized by the Islamic Thinkers Society as "'a rally, a call for the Sharia, a call for the Muslims to rise up and establish the Islamic state in America.'"); *Video: Muslim Cleric Plans White House Protest in Attempt to Spread Sharia Law in America*, FOX NEWS (Feb. 20, 2011), http://www.foxnews.com/us/2011/02/20/muslim-cleric-plans-protest-outside-white-house-attempt-spread-sharia-law/ (Muslim cleric Anjem Choudary told Sean Hannity that "Americans are the biggest criminals in the world today. . . The Sharia will come to America . . . and it will remove the corruption . . . of democracy and freedom and all of your exploitation. You are worried because you know Islam is coming to your backyard."); The Jersey Journal, *Bayonne Man Convicted of Raping His Wife Seeks New Trial*, NJ.COM (Dec. 17, 2010), http://www.nj.com/bayonne/index.ssf/2010/12/bayonne_man_convicted_of_rapin.html (A Muslim man convicted of raping his wife claimed that his religious beliefs, founded in *Shariah*, trumped state statutes against rape.); Chris Serres, *On the Job, Their Way*, STAR TRIBUNE (June 15, 2008), http://www.startribune.com/business/19934184.html?page=1&c=y (noting that twenty-two Muslim workers filed a class action lawsuit for religious discrimination against Celestica manufacturing plant after Celestica fired them for taking unauthorized prayer breaks that were disruptive to the assembly line).

[9]*See, e.g.*, Cathy Lynn Grossman, *Number of U.S. Muslims to Double*, USA TODAY (Jan. 27, 2011), http://www.usatoday.com/news/religion/2011-01-27-1Amuslim27_ST_N.htm (predicting that the Muslim population in the United States will grow from 2.6 million people in 2010 to 6.2 million in 2030 and that Muslims will account for more than a quarter of the world's projected 8.3 billion people by 2030); Richard Kerbaj, *Muslim Population 'Rising 10 Times Faster Than Rest of Society'*, SUNDAY TIMES (Jan. 30, 2009), http://www.timesonline.co.uk/tol/news/uk/article5621482.ece (documenting the extraordinary growth rate of the Muslim population in Great Britain from 2004 to 2008).

and political agenda. This is not to say that Muslims are not welcome in the United States; they are. But it is imperative to understand the motivation of fundamentalist Muslims in establishing such detached and intransigent communities. The goal of these Islamic groups is *not* to peaceably assimilate into American society on equal footing with other religious (or non-religious) persons and groups.[10] Rather than peacefully assimilating into American society and readily submitting to American laws, such Muslims press for official recognition of their beliefs, enforcement of their religious laws with the force and funding of the state, and, ultimately, the adoption of an Islamic system of government.[11]

The theories driving political Islam are no longer abstract,

---

[10]*E.g.*, TAWFIK HAMID, INSIDE JIHAD: UNDERSTANDING AND CONFRONTING RADICAL ISLAM 111 (2007), *available at* http://www.potomacinstitute.org/attachments/862_INSIDE_JIHAD.pdf (Omar M. Ahmad, Chairman of the Board on the Council on American-Islamic Relations, has been recorded as saying that "Islam isn't in America to be equal to any other faith but to become dominant. The Koran, the Muslim book of scripture, should be the highest authority in America, and Islam the only accepted religion on Earth."); *see also* AHMAD IBN NAQIB AL-MISRI, RELIANCE OF THE TRAVELLER 603 (Nuh Ha Mim Keller, trans., Amana Publications rev. ed. 2008) (1368) [hereinafter RELIANCE OF THE TRAVELLER] ("The caliph fights all other peoples until they become Muslim . . . ([T]hough according to the Hanafi school, peoples of all other religions, even idol worshippers, are permitted to live under the protection of the Islamic state if they either become Muslim or agree to pay the poll tax . . . .)." (citation omitted)).

[11]The *Qur'an* commands Muslims to fight until Allah's *Din* (religion) is established on the earth. ABDULLAH YUSUF 'ALI, THE MEANING OF THE HOLY QUR'AN, *Surah* 2:193, n. 207 (10th ed. 2001) [hereinafter QUR'AN]. Because *Qur'an* is transliterated from Arabic into English, it can be spelled in various ways. We generally use "*Qur'an*" throughout this book, unless directly quoting from another source. This is true of other Arabic terms used in this book, such as, *Shariah*, which is also spelled Shari'ah or Sharia. We will use Shariah throughout this book, unless quoting from another source. Because *Shariah* is derived from purely religious texts and there is no distinction between religion and state in Islam, Muslims demand application of *Shariah* in United States courts based on the right to freedom of religion guaranteed by the First Amendment to the United States Constitution. Most recently, when Oklahoma voters approved the "Save Our State Amendment" to the Oklahoma Constitution, restricting the application of *Shariah* and other foreign laws in Oklahoma courts, a Muslim U.S. citizen challenged the amendment, claiming violation of his right to freedom of religion. *See* Awad v. Ziriax, No. CIV-10-1186-M, 2010 U.S. Dist LEXIS 125612 (W.D. Okla. Nov. 29, 2010); *see also supra* note 8. This is not unique to the United States. Recently, in Australia, the Australian Federation of Islamic Councils called for Muslims in Australia to be offered "legal pluralism," i.e., that Australian Muslims be permitted to apply *Shariah*. *Attorney-General Robert McClelland says there is 'no place' for sharia law in Australia*, THE AUSTRALIAN (May 17, 2011), http://www.theaustralian.com. au/national-affairs/muslims-use-multiculturalism-to-push-for-sharia/story-fn59niix-1226057476571. Australian Attorney General Robert McClelland rejected the call for "legal pluralism," stating, "As our citizenship pledge makes clear, coming to Australia means obeying Australian laws and upholding Australian values." *Id.* He noted that "Australia's brand of multiculturalism promotes integration. If there is any inconsistency between cultural values and the rule of law then Australian law wins out." *Id.*

but are becoming reality. Muslims have already begun implementing their political-religious ideology (submission to Allah at all costs) in America and other parts of the Western world. In fact, the British Prime Minister, the President of France, and the Chancellor of Germany have all acknowledged that their respective nations' acquiescence to Muslim immigrants' demands to maintain separate cultural and legal systems has failed.[12] Furthermore, the United States now has documented evidence proving that Islamic fundamentalist organizations have been actively working to impose *Shariah* (Islamic religious law)[13] throughout North America (including the United States) for the past twenty to twenty-five years.[14]

In 2004, the revelation of terrorist funding based in the United States made headlines when a federal grand jury in Dallas, Texas, returned a 42-count indictment against the Holy Land Foundation for Relief and Development (Holy Land Foundation or HLF) and seven of its senior leaders for providing and conspiring to provide material financial support to the international terrorist organization, Hamas.[15] The Department of Justice's (DOJ) investigation of HLF

[12]*See, e.g.*, John F. Burns, *Cameron Criticizes 'Multiculturalism' in Britain*, N.Y. TIMES (Feb. 5, 2011), http://www.nytimes.com/2011/02/06/world/europe/06britain.html (declaring that the "'hands-off tolerance' . . . that had encouraged Muslims and other immigrant groups 'to live separate lives, apart from each other and the mainstream,'" had failed Britain, just as it had failed all other European nations that have subscribed to it); *French President Nicolas Sarkozy Blasts Multiculturalism*, FOX NEWS (Feb. 14, 2011), http://www.foxnews.com/on-air/special-report/transcript/french-president-nicolas-sarkozy-blasts-multiculturalism (declaring that "in all our democracies, we've been too concerned about the identity of the new arrivals and not enough about the identity of the country receiving them" (internal quotation marks omitted)); Matthew Weaver, *Angela Merkel: German Multiculturalism Has 'Utterly Failed'*, THE GUARDIAN (Oct. 17, 2010), http://www.guardian.co.uk/world/2010/oct/17/ angela-merkel-german-multiculturalism-failed (lamenting that "this approach [of living side-by-side] has failed, utterly failed" (internal quotation marks omitted)).

[13]*Shariah* is an Arabic term that means "law." *Al-Shariah* is "the revealed, or canonical, law of Islam" or "the law of God." *See* WEHR, *infra* note 52. Thus, the phrase "*Shariah* law" would be redundant. For the meaning and detailed discussion of *Shariah*, *see* discussion *infra*, Chapter 2.

[14]*See generally* MOHAMED AKRAM, MUSLIM BROTHERHOOD, AN EXPLANATORY MEMORANDUM ON THE GENERAL STRATEGIC GOAL FOR THE GROUP IN NORTH AMERICA, SHURA COUNCIL (May 22, 1991) [hereinafter AKRAM, EXPLANATORY MEMORANDUM], *available at* http://www.investigativeproject.org/ documents/misc/20.pdf (exhibit of the U.S. DEP'T OF JUSTICE). The Memorandum is also available in this book as Appendix C.

[15]John Ashcroft, Attorney General, United States Dep't of Justice, Prepared Remarks of Attorney General John Ashcroft — Holy Land Foundation Indictment (July 27, 2004), *available at* http://www. justice.gov/archive/ag/speeches/2004/72704ag.htm.

resulted in a highly-publicized list of terrorist co-conspirators and joint venturers, as well as a mountain of evidence exposing the true purpose underlying fundamentalist Muslim organizations that had been posing as non-profit charitable organizations. In a national press release, then-Attorney General John Ashcroft announced, "Today, a U.S.-based charity, that claims to do good works, is charged with funding works of evil."[16]

One set of documents discovered by the DOJ and produced at trial specifically revealed the *Ikhwan al-Muslimin*'s plans for North America. The *Ikhwan al-Muslimin*, commonly known as the Muslim Brotherhood (Brotherhood), is a fundamentalist Islamic movement dedicated to resurrecting the true Islamic caliphate (divinely instituted Islamic government)[17] based on *Shariah*.[18] During the *Holy Land Foundation* litigation,[19] the U.S. Government offered evidence of the original document in Arabic and its English translation. The document's title translated into English is "An Explanatory Memorandum On the General Strategic Goal for the Group in North America"; the document was dated May 22, 1991.[20] The memo was written by Mohamed Akram, a leader of the Brotherhood's Shura Council (strategic/consultative body).[21]

Inspired by the "new stage of Islamic activism" in North

---

[16]*Id.*

[17]*See* BERNARD LEWIS, THE POLITICAL LANGUAGE OF ISLAM 55 (1991) ("In the early Islamic centuries, it became customary to contrast kingship with caliphate. While the latter represented Islamic government under God's law, kingship was taken to mean arbitrary personal rule, without this religious and legal basis and sanction.").

[18]*See* BYLAWS OF THE MUSLIM BROTHERHOOD art. 2(E), (F) (on file with authors) ("The need to work on establishing the Islamic State, which seeks to effectively implement the provisions of Islam and its teachings."). For a description of this powerful, religious-political organization, see OLIVER GUITTA, CTR. FOR EUROPEAN STUDIES, MUSLIM BROTHERHOOD PARTIES IN THE MIDDLE EAST AND NORTH AFRICA (MENA) REGION, (Sept. 2010), *available at* http://www.thinkingeurope.eu/images/dbimages/docs/CESMuslimBrotherhoodParties.pdf.

[19]Holy Land Found. for Relief & Dev. v. Ashcroft, 333 F.3d 156 (D.C. Cir. 2003), *cert. denied*, 124 S. Ct. 1506 (2004).

[20]AKRAM, EXPLANATORY MEMORANDUM, *supra* note 14, at 16.

[21]*Id.* at 17.

America, Akram described a long-term strategic plan that the Shura Council had approved and adopted in 1987.[22] The 1991 memo was an effort by the Brotherhood to supplement the 1987 plan in anticipation of the group's upcoming meeting.[23] The Brotherhood's plan began as the "Enablement of Islam in North America" with the priority of "Settlement."[24] In developing the Brotherhood's ten-year strategic plan for Islam's implementation in North America,[25] Akram recalled a number of the Brotherhood's general strategic goals: "Establishing an effective and stable Islamic Movement led by the Muslim Brotherhood"; "[p]resenting Islam as a *civilization alternative*"; and "[s]upporting the establishment of the *global Islamic State* wherever it is."[26] Akram further stressed the agreement among all the members of the Muslim Brotherhood that the organization must "'settle' or 'enable' Islam and its Movement in this part of the world (North America)."[27]

Furthermore, Akram wrote that the concept of settlement includes Islam's "becoming a part of the homeland it lives in" and that in the process of settlement, Muslims must shoulder the responsibility for carrying out the grand mission as "Civilization Jihadist[s]"[28] (i.e., soldiers engaged in a holy war designed either to convert or to destroy unbelievers).[29] After emphasizing the importance of what the Muslim Brotherhood had already achieved in North America, Akram called for the additional construction of mosques, Islamic centers, Islamic organizations, and schools to propagate Islamic ideals to Americans and prepare the way for absolute submission

[22]*Id.*

[23]*Id.*

[24]*Id.* at 18.

[25]*See id.* at 18 (declaring that the question Islamic strategists faced is, "How do you like to see the Islam Movement in North America in ten years?" (internal quotation marks omitted)).

[26]*Id.* at 18–19 (emphasis added).

[27]*Id.* at 19.

[28]*Id.*

[29]*E.g.*, QUR'AN, *supra* note 11, at *Surah* 9:29 ("Fight those who believe not in Allah nor the last day"); *see also infra* Chapter 6.

to Islam.[30] Akram's description of the Brotherhood's role in North America is quite revealing:

> The [Muslim Brotherhood] must understand that their work in America is a kind of grand Jihad in *eliminating and destroying the Western civilization from within* and "sabotaging" its miserable house by their hands and the hands of the believers so that it is eliminated and [Allah's] religion is made victorious over all other religions . . . . It is a Muslim's destiny to perform Jihad and work wherever he lands until the final hour comes, and there is no escape from that destiny . . . .[31]

To the Brotherhood, "success . . . in America in establishing an observant Islamic base with power and effectiveness will be the best support and aid to the global Movement project."[32]

The North American Muslim Brotherhood's strategic plan also called for the creation of "The Islamic Center" in every city.[33] Akram described the Islamic Center as a place for study, family, *battalions*, courses, seminars, visits, sports, schools, social clubs, female gatherings, kindergarten for male and female children, and an office of domestic political resolution, among other things.[34] The proposed $100 million mosque and cultural center near the tragic site of the September 11th terrorist attacks in New York City reflects this description of "The Islamic Center."[35]

---

[30]*See* AKRAM, EXPLANATORY MEMORANDUM, *supra* note 14, at 20.
[31]*Id.* at 21.
[32]*Id.* at 22.
[33]*Id.* at 25.
[34]*Id.* (emphasis added). This description mirrors article 3(D) of the Muslim Brotherhood's Bylaws.
[35]Joe Jackson & Bill Hutchinson, *Plans for Mosque Near World Trade Center Site Moves Ahead*, N.Y. DAILY NEWS (May 6, 2010), http://www.nydailynews.com/ny_local/2010/05/06/2010-05-06_ plan_for_mosque_near_world_trade_center_site_moves_ahead.html. The Ground Zero Mosque does not quite resemble the typical house of worship that most would have in mind when they picture an Islamic mosque. The so-called "Park 51" center will not only include a religious house of worship, but will also feature in its glass-and-steel building a 500-seat performing arts venue, a swimming pool, and a basketball court, to name just a few amenities. *Id.*

Finally, after describing the Muslim Brotherhood's internal educational, political, economic, cultural, and legal goals, Akram listed twenty-nine affiliate organizations with which the Brotherhood would work to achieve its strategic goals for North America.[36] This list included the following U.S. charities and other non-profit organizations: the Islamic Society of North America (ISNA), the Muslim Students' Association (MSA), Islamic Medical Association (IMA), North American Islamic Trust (NAIT), Muslim Youth of North America (MYNA), Muslim Arab Youth Association (MAYA), and the Occupied Land Fund (OLF).[37] In fact, the OLF, which later became the Holy Land Foundation,[38] was found guilty of funding Hamas, and many of the remaining groups were identified as unindicted co-conspirators in the *Holy Land Foundation* cases.[39]

This important evidence uncovered by the DOJ reveals the Brotherhood's true aspirations and its extensive cooperation with other Islamic groups throughout the United States. It further demonstrates that the ultimate objective is to "make Almighty [Allah's] word"—and by implication, its emanating legal system, *Shariah*—the "highest" authority in the land.[40] This aim unavoidably conflicts with the U.S. Constitution's Supremacy Clause, which declares that the "Constitution, and the Laws of the United States which shall be made in Pursuance thereof" are "the supreme Law

---

[36]AKRAM, EXPLANATORY MEMORANDUM, *supra* note 14, at 32.

[37]*Id.* at 15.

[38]*Holy Land Found. for Relief & Dev.*, 333 F.3d at 160 ("HLF was originally established as the Occupied Land Fund and incorporated as a tax-exempt organization in California in 1989. In 1991 it changed its corporate name to the Holy Land Foundation for Relief and Development and moved to Texas.").

[39]United States v. Holy Land Found. for Relief and Dev., No. 3:04-CR-240-G, ATTACHMENT A List of Unindicted Co-conspirators and/or Joint Ventures 5, 8 [hereinafter Unindicted Co-conspirators], *available at* http://www.investigativeproject.org/documents/case_docs/423.pdf.

[40]AKRAM, EXPLANATORY MEMORANDUM, *supra* note 14, at 23. This objective is also cited in the Brotherhood's Bylaws. BYLAWS OF THE INTERNATIONAL MUSLIM BROTHERHOOD art. 2 (establishing that one of the Brotherhood's main objectives is to "establish Allah's law in the land"); *see also* HAMID, *supra* note 10, at 111.

of the Land."[41] The contrary view of *Shariah*'s supremacy is held not only by fundamentalist Islamic groups, but also by all Islamic countries, which identify *Shariah* as supreme and maintain that no rights or freedoms exist other than those provided under Islamic *Shariah*.[42]

Moreover, the evidence presented in the *Holy Land Foundation* cases indicates that fundamentalist Islamic networks in the United States exploit the political freedom available in the West to organize and fund their extremist activities.[43] Muslim organizations linked to terrorist groups have set up operations in the United States, masquerading as legitimate, "moderate" groups on record as opposing "'extremism,' 'oppression,' and 'terrorism.'"[44] Yet, in reality, many of these organizations serve as foreign-funded training grounds for radical Islamic militants.[45]

---

[41]U.S. CONST. art. VI, cl. 2 ("This Constitution, and the Laws of the United States which shall be made in Pursuance thereof; and all Treaties made . . . shall be the supreme Law of the Land; and the Judges in every State shall be bound thereby . . . .").

[42]*See generally* World Conference on Human Rights, April 19–May 7, 1993, *Addendum: Contribution of the Organisation of the Islamic Conference*, U.N. Doc. A/CONF.157/PC/62/Add.18 (June 9, 1993) [hereinafter CAIRO DECLARATION], *available at* http://www1.umn.edu/humanrts/instree/cairodeclaration.html (document submitted by the fifty-six Member States of the Organisation of the Islamic Conference for and setting forth *Shariah* definitions of and limitations on human rights).

[43]Jamie Glazov, *Radical Islamic Networks in America*, FRONTPAGE MAGAZINE (Jan. 13, 2009), http://archive.frontpagemag.com/readArticle.aspx?ARTID=33699.

[44]*Id.* According to the Investigative Report on Terrorism (a study published by the Investigative Project), the Muslim Students Association (MSA) in America is primarily responsible for the rise of Islamic extremism and spread of radical Islam to a new generation of Islamic activists and sympathizers. Under the guise of a moderate faith club, the MSA advances its true agenda of militant Islamic ideology through 600 MSA chapters on college campuses throughout the United States and Canada. *See* THE INVESTIGATIVE PROJECT ON TERRORISM, MUSLIM STUDENTS ASSOCIATION 1 (2008), http://www.investigativeproject.org/documents/misc/31.pdf.

[45]The Pakistan-based Jamaat al-Fuqra is organized in the United States as "The Muslims of America." This Islamic group, led by an anti-Semitic extremist, Sheikh Mubarak Gilani, is dedicated to training terrorists in the United States for an Islamic *jihad* (holy war) and is generally thought to be responsible for training a number of the past two decades' most notorious terrorists, including those involved in the first World Trade Center bombing, the beltway sniper attacks, and the attempted shoe-bombing. Douglas J. Hagmann, *Exclusive Report: Hurricane Katrina Charity Tied to Islamic Terrorist*, NE. INTELLIGENCE NETWORK (Feb. 19, 2007), http://homelandsecurityus.com/archives/1613; *see also* Yasser Latif Hamdani, *Faisal Shahzad's Radicalisation*, DAILY TIMES (May 10, 2010), http://www.dailytimes.com.pk/default.asp?page=2010%5C05%5C10%5Cstory_10-5-2010_pg3_4 (alleging that other Islamic university societies, with a particular reference to a chapter at Rutgers University, are similarly responsible for the extremist indoctrination of Muslim (including foreign-born) Americans, including the foiled New York Times Square bomber, Faisal Shahzad).

With such significant threats escalating throughout the Western world, it has become readily apparent that we in the West must understand the nature of fundamentalist Islam and its agenda of advancing and implementing *Shariah* in Western society. Guarding against the infiltration of fundamentalist Islam is vital because its ultimate goal is to destroy Western society by establishing an Islamic theocracy operating under *Shariah*, which would subject all people—both willing and unwilling—to the laws of Allah and Muhammad.[46] It is crucial that we, as freedom-loving Americans, are not deceived by increasing cries that we must officially recognize and permit *Shariah* or else be guilty of denying freedom and reasonable accommodation of religion to the Muslim population among us.

To permit even the most basic principles of *Shariah* to co-exist with American law would clash with American notions of law and justice. Islamic *Shariah*, the divine law according to Muslims, arose in the Middle East 1,400 years ago. *Shariah*, both then and now, embraces numerous laws and punishments that are contrary to long-held Western ideals of justice and dignity of the human person. Nonetheless, as shown above, the foundation for *Shariah* in the West is already being laid.[47] Wolves have come among us wearing sheep's

---

[46]*See* discussion *infra* Chapters 3–5; *see also* HADITH OF SAHIH MUSLIM, Bk. 020, No. 4717 [hereinafter SAHIH MUSLIM], *available at* http://www.usc.edu/schools/college/crcc/engagement/resources/texts/muslim/hadith/muslim/ (Muhammad said: "This religion will continue to exist, and a group of people from the Muslims will continue to fight for its protection until the Hour is established.").

[47]Irshad Abdal-Haqq, in an article providing an overview of Islamic law, declares that in the United States, it is not a matter of whether Muslims will seek to implement *Shariah*, but when. He attributes this to the all-encompassing nature of *Shariah*:

> Islamic law is likely to become the intellectual focus in the American Muslim community as it synthesizes and matures . . . . The all-encompassing law of Islam, emanating from the Qur'an itself, embraces every aspect of human activity, defines Islamic values, and dictates standards of behavior. Therefore, it must command the attention of any Muslim community seeking to preserve and assert itself. The question then is not whether Islamic law will become the intellectual focus of American Muslims, but rather when will it become the focus and how Islamic legal principles will be implemented . . . .
>
> That Islamic law will play an increased role in the affairs of American Muslims appears inevitable. As disputes resulting from Islamic religious obligations and agreements entered under Islamic principles work themselves through arbitration and into the courts, the legal, business and political

clothing. Because *Shariah* is incompatible with U.S. law even at its most fundamental levels, *Shariah* (and similar legal systems opposed to liberal democratic rights and freedoms) must be barred from receiving recognition in the United States *if the United States is to continue to preserve liberties and freedoms protected by the U.S. Constitution and U.S. Law.*

---

communities will be asked and sometimes required to address questions of law rooted in Islamic tradition.

Irshad Abdal-Haqq, *Islamic Law: An Overview of Its Origins and Elements*, *in* UNDERSTANDING ISLAMIC LAW: FROM CLASSICAL TO CONTEMPORARY 2 (Hisham M. Ramadan et al. eds., 2006).

CHAPTER TWO

FUNDAMENTALS OF SHARIAH

Before discussing Islamic notions of justice and the imposition or incorporation of *Shariah* in the United States, it is important to note that on some level, the beliefs held by individual Muslims on specific *Shariah* principles and their interpretations of the *Qur'an* (Islam's holy book and the primary source of *Shariah*)[48] regarding the same, no matter how sincere, are largely irrelevant for the purposes of understanding Islamic teachings. This is because traditional Islamic teaching itself places strict limitations on who may speak *authoritatively* on Islam's behalf.[49] Furthermore, in the interest of fairness to all Muslims, it is equally important not to deduce Islamic teachings solely from how a particular Muslim group acts. This book, therefore, focuses on *Shariah* issues by analyzing general *Shariah* principles common to the leading schools of Islamic jurisprudence, as dictated and promulgated by the *Qur'an* and *Sunnah*[50] (the "words, actions, approvals or even silence" ascribed to Muhammad),[51] and their interpretations by Islamic scholars. The

---

[48]QUR'AN, *supra* note 11, at *Surahs* 2:142–143, 11:56, 36:1–7, 42:52 (noting various passages in which Allah confirmed that the revelation of Muhammad is true and leads men to a "straight path"); *see also* MAWIL IZZI DIEN, ISLAMIC LAW: FROM HISTORICAL FOUNDATIONS TO CONTEMPORARY PRACTICE 37 (2004) [hereinafter DIEN]; WAR AND PEACE IN THE LAW OF ISLAM 32 (Majid Khadduri, 1955) (recognizing that the *Qur'an* is "unquestionable authority").

[49]WAR AND PEACE IN THE LAW OF ISLAM, *supra* note 48, at 32 (quoting Muhammad's own statement that "'the learned are the heirs of the prophets'—they are therefore the ones who can interpret the Book"); *see also* 1 MUHAMMAD SAED ABDUL-RAHMAN, ISLAM: QUESTIONS AND ANSWERS: BASIC TENETS OF FAITH (BELIEF) 4 (2003) ("[I]t is not permissible for anyone to speak about the rulings of Islam or the tafseer [i.e., commentary] of Qur'an or the meanings of hadeeth[;] rather that should be referred to the scholars who are well-versed in knowledge."). Additionally, interpretations of *Qur'anic* revelations are subject to the interpretations Muhammad gave either directly or indirectly through his own speech and conduct (i.e., *Sunnah*). See also QUR'AN, *supra* note 11, at *Surahs* 5:101–2 ("O ye who believe! Ask not questions about things which, if made plain to you, may cause you trouble. But if ye ask about things when the Quran is being revealed, they will be made plain to you. Allah will forgive those: for Allah is oft-forgiving, most forbearing. Some people before you did ask such questions, and on that account lost their faith.").

[50]*See infra* Chapter 2.B.

[51]DIEN, *supra* note 48, at 38 (teaching that *Sunnah* includes "all practices that have been ascribed to

book does not analyze how a particular group of Muslims may practice or interpret a specific tenet or principle of Islamic law.

A. MEANING OF *SHARIAH*

Shariah is an Arabic term that means "law."[52] *Al-Shariah* is "the revealed, or canonical, law of Islam"[53] or simply "the law of God [(Allah)]."[54] According to Abdullah Yusuf Ali, the most widely accepted translator of and commentator on the *Qur'an* in the Muslim world,[55] *Shariah*, which includes more than "mere formal rites and legal provisions," is best translated as "the right Way of Religion."[56] Therefore, Islamic *Shariah* is different from other religious laws in that it covers not only the spiritual aspects of a Muslim's life, but it is also a legal system, a comprehensive code of law that must be enforced by the state and governs the total social, political, and economic lives of all Muslims.[57] It encompasses all aspects of life, from crimes and punishments[58] to the most basic civil rights and liberties of mankind.[59]

Although comparable understanding regarding divine laws can be found in other religions, Islam does not distinguish the

Muhammad, apart from the revelation of the Qur'an, in the form of words, actions, approvals or even silence . . . . [It] is a second source of law after the Qur'an, because all the principles of Islam were revealed in a general form"); *see also* NYAZEE, *supra* note 62, at 171 ("The *Sunnah* is unanimously accepted as a primary source of law and *ahkam* can be derived from it independently of any other source."); IHSAN YILMAZ, MUSLIM LAWS, POLITICS AND SOCIETY IN MODERN NATION STATES 33 (2005) ("The *Qur'an* and *Sunna* are the two most important and primary authorities and sources of Islam," and because the *Sunna* of the Prophet "interpreted, applied, explained, practiced and concretized [the values of the *Qur'an*, it] is the second material source of Islamic law."); DIEN, *supra* note 48, at 8 ("The fact that there is canonical documentation of Sunna going back to the date of 'Umar b. Abd al-Azīz is evidence by itself that there was great value given to Sunna and to all that is based upon it, and that the law cannot grow independently.").

[52]THE HANS WEHR DICTIONARY OF MODERN WRITTEN ARABIC 544 (J. Milton Cowan ed., 3d ed. 1976) [hereinafter WEHR].

[53]*Id.*

[54]LAW IN THE MIDDLE EAST 104–05 (Majid Khadduri & Herbert J. Liebesny eds., 1955) ("[T]he [*Shariah*] . . . is universally accepted by Islam as the law of God.").

[55]International Institute of Islamic Thought, *Preface to the New Edition in* QUR'AN, *supra* note 11, at ix.

[56]QUR'AN, *supra* note 11, at 1297, n.4756 (discussing *Surah* 45:18, which states, "Then we put thee on the (right) Way of religion so follow thou that (Way), and follow not the desires of those who know not"); *see also* Abdal-Haqq, *supra* note 47, at 4.

[57]*See* DIEN, *supra* note 48, at 36–37.

[58]*See* discussion *infra* Chapter 4.

[59]*See* discussion *infra* Chapter 3.

religious from the secular,[60] does not recognize territorial boundaries when implementing *Shariah*,[61] and seeks to enforce *Shariah*—with the full force and effect of the government—against every person, whether an adherent of Islam or not.

B. SOURCES OF *SHARIAH*

Shariah is comprised of several authoritative Islamic texts, the chief of which is the *Qur'an*.[62] Muslims understand the *Qur'an* to be the undisputed holy revelation of Allah to the prophet Muhammad.[63] As Dr. Mawil Izzi Dien[64] has noted in his book outlining sources of Islamic law,

> [t]he Qur'an, or the Book, *al-Kitab*, represents the most important source of Islamic law, being the ultimate word of the Divine. It is not seen by Muslims as purely a book of law, *since it is a book that includes clarification of every matter*. The word *al-Kitab* ("the book") indicates the significance of textual authority in the Islamic legal mind. It therefore also implies what was composed and given by [Allah]; this first source of Islamic law is to be respected more than any human-made law . . . . Muslims believe that the Qur'an was secured by the divine will and that the accuracy of the Qur'an as a document can be affirmed on the grounds that it was presented and recorded by oral transmission as well as script.[65]

---

[60]*See* discussion *infra* Chapter 2.D.1.

[61]*See* discussion *infra* Chapter 2.D.2.

[62]IMRAN AHSAN KHAN NYAZEE, ISLAMIC JURISPRUDENCE 158 (2000) ("The entire ummah agree[s] that the Qur'an is the primary source for the *ahkam* [commandments and/or decrees] of Allah."); DIEN, *supra* note 48, at 37 (noting that the Qur'an is "the most important source of Islamic law, being the ultimate word of the Divine").

[63]QUR'AN, *supra* note 11, at *Surahs* 2:142–43, 11:56, 36:1–7, 42:52 (teaching that Allah allegedly confirms that the revelation of Muhammad is true and leads men to a "straight path"); DIEN, *supra* note 48, at 37.

[64]Dr. Mawil Izzi Dien (PhD) is a Reader in Islamic Studies at the University of Wales, School of Theology, Religion and Islamic Studies. *School of Theology, Religion and Islamic Studies, Dr Mawil Izzi Dien B.A, PhD (Manchester)*, UNIV. OF WALES TRINITY SAINT DAVID, http://www.trinitysaintdavid.ac.uk/en/schooloftheologyreligionandislamicstudies/staff/drmawilizzidien/.

[65]DIEN, *supra* note 48, at 37 (emphasis added).

Of nearly equal import to the *Qur'an* in terms of both influence and authority is the *Sunnah*,[66] which are collected in the *hadiths* ("written record of the *Sunnah*").[67] The *Qur'an* lays the foundation for the authoritativeness of the *Sunnah/hadiths*, commanding true Muslims to obey the book and to obey Muhammad.[68] Muhammad likewise declared that obedience to the *Qur'an* and to his dictates was essential to avoid destruction. One *hadith* recounts Muhammad's stating that

> [m]y example and the example of what I have been sent with is that of a man who came to some people and said, "O people! I have seen the enemy's army with my own eyes, and I am the naked warner; so protect yourselves!" Then a group of his people obeyed him and fled . . . till they were safe, while another group of them disbelieved him and stayed . . . when the army came upon them, and killed and ruined them completely[.] So this is the example of that person who obeys me and follows what I have brought (the Quran and the Sunna), and the example of the one who disobeys me . . . .[69]

The *Sunnah* as recounted in the *hadiths*, therefore, is the second

---

[66]*Id.* at 38 (teaching that *Sunnah* includes "all practices that have been ascribed to Muhammad, apart from the revelation of the Qur'an, in the form of words, actions, approvals or even silence . . . . [It] is a second source of law after the Qur'an, because all the principles of Islam were revealed in a general form"); *see also* NYAZEE, *supra* note 62, at 171 ("The *Sunnah* is unanimously accepted as a primary source of law and *ahkam* can be derived from it independently of any other source."); IHSAN YILMAZ, MUSLIM LAWS, POLITICS AND SOCIETY IN MODERN NATION STATES 33 (2005) ("The *Qur'an* and *Sunna* are the two most important and primary authorities and sources of Islam," and because the *Sunna* of the Prophet "interpreted, applied, explained, practiced and concretized [the values of the *Qur'an*, it] is the second material source of Islamic law."); DIEN, *supra* note 48, at 8 ("The fact that there is canonical documentation of Sunna going back to the date of 'Umar b. Abd al-Azīz is evidence by itself that there was great value given to Sunna and to all that is based upon it, and that the law cannot grow independently.").

[67]NYAZEE, *supra* note 62, at 394.

[68]QUR'AN, *supra* note 11, at *Surah* 4:80 ("He who obeys the Messenger (Muhammad), obeys Allah . . . ."); *id.* at *Surah* 5:92 ("Obey Allah, and obey the Messenger.").

[69]HADITH OF SAHIH BUKHARI, Vol. 9, Bk. 92, No. 387 [hereinafter SAHIH BUKHARI], *available at* http://www.usc.edu/schools/college/crcc/engagement/resources/texts/muslim/hadith/bukhari/092.sbt.html (English translation of *hadith* of Sahih Bukhari available at http://www.usc.edu/schools/college/crcc/engagement/resources/texts/muslim/hadith/bukhari/) (official webpage of the Univ. of S. Cal.'s Center for Muslim-Jewish Engagement).

primary source of Islamic law and is a binding authority on how the principles of the *Qur'an* should be administered in Islamic society.

Hadiths recorded by Muhammad's contemporaries vary in reliability and authoritativeness[70] within the Muslim *ummah* (community).[71] Regardless of the controversial nature of some *hadiths*, which has even led to the development of a recognized science,[72] two collections are considered uniformly "sound" and authoritative ("*sahih*") by all *Sunni* schools of Islamic thought; these are the books of Bukhāri and Muslim.[73] Accordingly, the collections of *hadiths* compiled by Bukhāri and Muslim are universally authoritative for *Sunni* Muslims (but not *Shia* Muslims[74]) in establishing *Shariah* principles.[75]

The *Qur'an*'s text—even when combined with *hadiths*—does not comprehensively address every potential legal issue to arise in an Islamic state. Where the *Qur'an* and *hadiths* are silent (or where there is no consensus about the veracity, interpretation, or

[70]*See, e.g.*, IBN AL-SALĀH AL-SHAHRAZŪRĪ, AN INTRODUCTION TO THE SCIENCE OF THE HADITH 2–4 (Eerik Dickinson trans., Garnet Publ'g 1st ed. 2005) (1245) [hereinafter AL-SHAHRAZŪRĪ] (enumerating over sixty different categories of *hadiths*, with a few of the categories labeled "sound," "weak," "unsupported").

[71]WAR AND PEACE IN THE LAW OF ISLAM, *supra* note 48, at 32 (noting that while even the authority of the *Sunnah*, which is the words and actions of Muhammad, has been questioned by the *Shafi'i* school of thought, the *Shafi'i*—and all other schools of thought—view the *Qur'an* as "unquestionable authority").

[72]AL-SHAHRAZŪRĪ, *supra* note 70; *see also* Suhaib Hasan, *An Introduction to the Science of Hadith*, USC MUSLIM STUDENTS ASSOCIATION, *available at* http://www.islamic-awareness.org/Hadith/Ulum/ (discussing the science of *hadiths*, which have led to their classification into various grades of authenticity).

[73]AL-SHAHRAZŪRĪ, *supra* note 70, at 8. While Bukhāri and Muslim are the two most authoritative *hadith* collections, there are actually six major *hadith* collections; the other four in order of authority include al-Nasa'i's Sunan, Abu Dawud's Sunan, Al-Tirmidhi's Sunan, and Ibn Majah's Sunan.

[74]THE CAMBRIDGE ILLUSTRATED HISTORY OF THE ISLAMIC WORLD 211 (Francis Robison ed., 4th ed. 2005); *see also* Christopher M. Blanchard, ISLAM: SUNNIS AND SHIITES, CONG. RESEARCH SERV. (2009), *available at* http://www.fas.org/irp/crs/RS21745.pdf (providing a helpful discussion of the fundamental differences between the *Sunni* and *Shia* sects of Islam, including an historical background and basic tenets of each). Essentially, the historic debate between the two groups has centered on "whether to award leadership to a qualified, pious individual who would follow the customs of the Prophet [Muhammad] or to transmit leadership exclusively through the Prophet's bloodline." *Id.* at 1. Today, the majority of the world's Muslims are *Sunni*, and approximately 10–15% are *Shia. Id.* at 3–4; *but cf.* RAFIQ ZAKARIA, THE STRUGGLE WITHIN ISLAM: THE CONFLICT BETWEEN RELIGION AND POLITICS 304–05 (Penguin 1989) (estimating that more than 90% of Muslims were *Sunnis* in the late 1980s).

[75]AL-SHAHRAZŪRĪ, *supra* note 70, at 8 ("The books (*hadith* collections) of Bukhāri and Muslim are the soundest books after the [*Qur'an*].").

application of *hadiths*), the development of Islamic law has relied upon secondary sources. One source is *ijmā*, which is "a consensus of academic opinion on any legal issue that arose subsequent to the death of Muhammad."[76] Because the ever-evolving and -expanding Islamic world must frequently confront novel issues, often times a legal consensus among scholars is difficult to achieve. Historical *ijmā*, which emanated from the time period immediately following Muhammad's death, is "treated with great respect by various Muslim scholars, particularly when founded upon the unambiguous verses of the *Qur'an* and *hadith*."[77] Contemporary *ijmā*, however, requires more "freedom and flexibility" due to the fact that there is no centralized Islamic political leadership, making absolute consensus a virtual impossibility.[78] Historical *ijmā*, therefore, is seemingly more authoritative than modern *ijmā*.[79]

Another commonly recognized secondary source of *Shariah* is *qiyās*, analogized rationalizations of *Shariah* principles to novel legal issues made by the "highest ranked and most able" *Shariah* jurists throughout the Islamic legal tradition.[80] The final secondary source of *Shariah* is *ijtihad*—"the effort made by the [jurist] in seeking knowledge of the *ahkam* (rules) of the *shari'ah* through interpretation . . . to discover the intention of the Ultimate Lawgiver, Allah Almighty, with respect to the rules of conduct."[81] Allowing

---

[76]DIEN, *supra* note 48, at 40–41; *see also* NYAZEE, *supra* note 62, at 183 ("The consensus of *mujtahids* (independent jurists) from the *ummah* of Muhammad (peace be upon him), after his death, in a determined period upon a rule of Islamic law (*hukm shar'i*)").

[77]DIEN, *supra* note 48, at 47.

[78]*See id.* at 47–48.

[79]MOHAMMAD HASHIM KAMALI, PRINCIPLES OF ISLAMIC JURISPRUDENCE 313 (3d ed. 2003) ("The Sunni *'ulamā'* are in agreement that the consensus (*ijmā'*) of the Companions of the Prophet . . . represents the most authoritative form of *ijmā'*.")

[80]*See* YILMAZ, *supra* note 66, at 32–33 (expounding five layers of juristic activity, ranging from creating Islamic law to merely following precedent); *accord* NYAZEE, *supra* note 62, at 214 (describing *qiyas* as "the assignment of the *hukm* [law] of an existing case found in the texts of the Qur'an, the *Sunnah*, or *ijma* to a new case whose *hukm* is not found in these sources on the bases of a common underlying attribute called the '*illah of the hukm*" (internal quotation marks omitted)).

[81]NYAZEE, *supra* note 62, at 263, 265.

jurists to exercise a measure of personal judgment where the *Qur'an* and *hadiths* are silent is a practice that Muhammad himself supported.[82]

Due to the various secondary sources of *Shariah* and differing levels of acceptance of the *hadiths* among the multiple sects of Islam, *Shariah* differs from one Islamic country to another.[83] These differences of belief and practice within Islam make it a practical impossibility to incorporate Islamic *Shariah* into a foreign legal system or even to allow it to co-exist with a separate legal system.

C. SCHOOLS OF ISLAMIC JURISPRUDENCE

Islam has been divided since infancy. After Muhammad died in A.D. 632, the young religion confronted a host of novel issues as its followers rapidly conquered new territories and confronted new cultures.[84] Because Muhammad was no longer alive to apply *Shariah* to previously unaddressed or nuanced social and legal issues, "[p]rinciples for validating the derivation of law from revelation (i.e., the *Qur'an*) were needed because there were too many reports, opinions, and judgments circulating as new problems and questions constantly arose."[85] Consequently, over a 300-year period, numerous schools of jurisprudential thought arose as Islamic jurists and theologians worked to develop an appropriate

---

[82]Muhammad used personal opinion in adjudicating matters not specifically covered by the *Qur'an*, encouraged this both by his own example and by his approval of his companions who did the same. According to one account, Muhammad asked a Muslim Judge, whom he sent to Yemen,

> how he would judge between people. [The judge] responded by stating that he would refer to the Book of God and the tradition of the Prophet or Sunna. When the Prophet asked for his reaction if he might fail to find his answers there, [the judge] stated: "I will use my best judgment." The Prophet [Muhammad] was very pleased with his considered reply and begged God to bless [the judge].

DIEN, *supra* note 48, at 4–5.

[83]Its sources, however, are fixed, and the principles derived therefrom are considered to be immutable. KAMALI, *supra* note 79, at 7–8 (The sources of *Shariah*, in contrast to the sources that serve as the foundation of American law (i.e., common law), are "permanent in character and may not be overruled on grounds of either rationality or the requirements of social conditions.").

[84]*See* Abdal-Haqq, *supra* note 47, at 24.

[85]*Id.*

methodology for applying the *Qur'an* and *Sunnah*[86] to contemporary legal and social issues.[87] Five such schools remain dominant today.

The first four schools are within the *Sunni* sect of Islam, which comprises roughly eighty-five to ninety percent of all Muslims.[88] These four schools developed according to the teachings of four great *imams* (Islamic spiritual leaders), and each is named after its founder: *Hanafi, Maliki, Shafii,* and *Hanbali*.[89] The principles of the four *Sunni* schools are "substantially the same, and they differ from each other merely in matters of detail."[90] The *Hanafi* school is the most popular and purportedly takes a moderate approach in applying *Shariah* principles to contemporary legal issues, declining to apply *Shariah* strictly where the outcome would be inequitable.[91] The *Maliki* and *Shafi'i* schools similarly prioritize Islamic tenets but allow for some consideration of local customs and equitable and practical concerns.[92] The *Hanbali* school, however, stresses the "puritanical aspects of Islam" and is "uncompromising in its adherence to orthodoxy"; it is therefore the most rigid sect of *Sunni* Islam, demanding very austere lives of anyone subject to its authority.[93] Notably, it provides the basis of *Shariah* in Saudi Arabia.[94] The fifth school of jurisprudence, the *Ja'fari* school, has been adopted by the *Shia* group of Muslims (*Shi'ites*)[95] and constitutes a "heterodox

---

[86]*See supra* parenthetical text accompanying note 66.

[87]Abdal-Haqq, *supra* note 47, at 24–25.

[88]ZAKARIA, *supra* note 74, at 304–05 (estimating that more than 90% of Muslims were *Sunnis* in the late 1980s); *but cf.* Blanchard, *supra* note 74, at 3–4 (estimating that in 2009 *Shias* accounted for up to 15% of the world's Muslims).

[89]Abdal-Haqq, *supra* note 47, at 24–29.

[90]ABDUR RAHIM, MUHAMMADAN JURISPRUDENCE 23 (PLD Publishers 1988) (1911); *see also* RELIANCE OF THE TRAVELLER, *supra* note 10, at vii ("The four Sunni schools of Islamic law, Hanafi, Maliki, Shafi'i, and Hanbali, are identical in approximately 75% of their legal conclusions . . . .").

[91]*See* ZAKARIA, *supra* note 74, at 304–05.

[92]*Id.*

[93]*Id.*

[94]FRANK E. VOGEL, ISLAMIC LAW AND LEGAL SYSTEM: STUDIES OF SAUDI ARABIA 118 (2000) (explaining that the judges in Saudi courts subscribe to the *Hanbali* school).

[95]This minority school of Islamic thought holds that there is no successor to Muhammad as head of the spiritual kingdom other than Muhammad's blood descendents. Thus, Islamic leaders (*imams*) subsequent to Muhammad are religious leaders of incredible importance and power, but they are not

group" that has historically been at odds with all four schools of *Sunni* thought.[96] It provides the basis of *Shariah* in Iran.

Although the four *Sunni* schools described above are identical in roughly seventy-five percent of their legal conclusions,[97] they differ on some aspects of law and theology. Consequently, the application of *Shariah* is not consistent even among Islamic countries. For example, the Islamic Republic of Afghanistan punishes adultery with stoning or lashes,[98] but the Islamic Republic of Pakistan punishes offenders only with imprisonment.[99] Additionally, in the Kingdom of Saudi Arabia, women are prohibited from traveling without the permission of a male guardian,[100] while many other Islamic countries do not enforce such a limitation on women.[101] This dissonance creates a dilemma in interpreting a legal principle according to one school or the other, especially when a dispute involves members of two different sects who follow different interpretations of the same law. Not only are U.S. courts prohibited from choosing one interpretation of a religious law over another, but they simply are

successors to Muhammad. *See* WAR AND PEACE IN THE LAW OF ISLAM, *supra* note 48, at 38–41 ("the final authoritative interpretation of the law [is] placed in the imam").

[96] *Id.*

[97] *See supra* note 90 and accompanying text.

[98] U.S. DEP'T OF STATE, BUREAU OF DEMOCRACY, HUMAN RIGHTS, & LABOR, 2009 HUMAN RIGHTS REPORT: AFGHANISTAN (Mar. 11, 2010), *available at* http://www.state.gov/g/drl/rls/hrrpt/2009/sca/136084.htm ("The Koran does not specifically mention a punishment for rape, but under one interpretation of Shari'a, local tribal elders or religious leaders may treat rape as a form of adultery, punishable by stoning to death or 100 lashes of the whip, although there were no reports of such cases during the year. Under some interpretations of Shari'a, a woman who brings a charge of rape sometimes must produce four witnesses to prove that the rape occurred as a result of force. Accused men often claimed the victim agreed to consensual sex, which resulted in an adultery charge against the victim."); Associated Press, *Taliban Stone Couple for Adultery in Afghanistan*, FOX NEWS (Aug. 16, 2010), http://www.foxnews.com/world/2010/08/16/taliban-stone-couple-adultery-afghanistan/ ("Taliban militants stoned a young couple to death for adultery after they ran away from their families in northern Afghanistan."). Some Nigerian states also punish adultery with stoning. U.S. DEP'T OF STATE, BUREAU OF DEMOCRACY, HUMAN RIGHTS, & LABOR, 2009 HUMAN RIGHTS REPORT: NIGERIA (Mar. 11, 2010), *available at* http://www.state.gov/g/drl/rls/hrrpt/2009/af/135970.htm ("States did not carry out any death sentences (stoning) pronounced in prior years for adultery.").

[99] THE MAJOR ACTS 332 (36th ed. 2011) (Comments on PAK. PENAL CODE, ch. XX, § 497 (1860)) ("Whoever has sexual intercourse with . . . the wife of another man . . . shall be punished with imprisonment . . . .").

[100] *Saudi Arabia: Women's Rights Promises Broken*, HUMAN RIGHTS WATCH (July 8, 2009), *available at* http://www.unhcr.org/cgi-bin/texis/vtx/refworld/rwmain?page=printdoc&docid=4a55b2c112.

[101] *See generally, e.g.*, THE MAJOR ACTS (36th ed. 2011) (PAK. PENAL CODE (1860)).

not competent to adjudicate matters applying religious laws.[102]

Regardless of which school of thought a particular legal system incorporates or a Muslim population embraces, however, *Shariah* decisions and criminal sentences upheld in countries and regions representative of the varying schools of thought are strictly at odds with American notions of law and justice.[103] They thus demonstrate the incompatibility of *Shariah* with United States law.

D. THE UNIVERSALITY, SUPREMACY, AND TRANSCENDENCE OF *SHARIAH* TO THE MUSLIM

Bernard Lewis, an historian and expert on Islamic history, cautions that,

> [w]hen we in the Western world, nurtured in the Western tradition, use the words "Islam" and "Islamic," we tend to make a natural error and assume that religion means the same for Muslims as it has meant in the Western world, even in medieval times; that is to say, a section or compartment of life reserved for certain matters, and separate, or at least separable, from other compartments of life designed to hold other matters. That is not so in the Islamic

---

[102]In Watson v. Jones, 80 U.S. (13 Wall.) 679 (1872), the Supreme Court of the United States had to resolve an ecclesiastical dispute that required applying different interpretations of ecclesiastical law. The Court's response is as applicable to the question of integrating Islamic law now as it was to the question of integrating Presbyterian ecclesiastical law then:

> [I]t is a very different thing where a subject-matter of dispute, strictly and purely ecclesiastical in its character, -- a matter over which the civil courts exercise no jurisdiction, -- a matter which concerns theological controversy, church discipline, ecclesiastical government, or the conformity of the members of the church to the standard of morals required of them, -- becomes the subject of [the court's] action. . . . [I]t is easy to see that if the civil courts are to inquire into all these matters, the whole subject of the doctrinal theology, the usages and customs, the written laws, and fundamental organization of every religious denomination may, and must, be examined into with minuteness and care, for they would become, in almost every case, the *criteria* by which the validity of the ecclesiastical decree would be determined in the civil court. This principle would deprive these bodies of the right of construing their own church laws, would open the way to all [kinds of evils] . . . , and would, in effect, transfer to the civil courts where property rights were concerned the decision of all ecclesiastical questions.

Id. at 733–34 (emphasis added).

[103]*See* discussion *infra* Chapter 4.E (illustrating through case examples the incompatibility of *Shariah* with U.S. law).

world. It was never so in the past, and the attempt in modern times to make it so may perhaps be seen, in the longer perspective of history, as an unnatural aberration which in Iran has ended and in some other Islamic countries may also be nearing its end.[104]

1. No Distinction Between Religion and State

The Framers of the United States Constitution were careful to craft a bill of rights that zealously protects religious freedom but, at the same time, does not establish an official national religion. The First Amendment religion clauses provide that "Congress shall make no law respecting an establishment of religion, or prohibiting the free exercise thereof."[105] These clauses, in recognition of the far-reaching effects of volitional religious belief, are as critical now as they were at our nation's founding. Former Justice of the Supreme Court of the United States James Iredell declared the following:

> [I]t was the intention of those who formed this system to establish a general religious liberty in America . . . . [Congress] certainly [has] no authority to interfere in the establishment of any religion whatsoever; and I am astonished that any gentlemen should conceive they have . . . . If any future Congress should pass an act concerning the religion of the country, it would be an act which they are not authorized to pass, by the Constitution, and which the people would not obey . . . .[106]

Justice Joseph Story echoed Justice Iredell's sentiments in asserting that recognizing the dangers of a state religion and freedom therefrom was crucial to maintaining individual and societal freedoms:

> The framers of the constitution were fully sensible of the dangers [of establishing oneness of church and state in the national government], marked out in the

---

[104]Lewis, *supra* note 17, at 2.
[105]U.S. Const. amend. I.
[106]4 The Debates in the Several State Conventions on the Adoption of the Federal Constitution 193–94 (Jonathan Elliot ed., 2d ed. 1836) (speech of James Iredell).

history of other ages and countries; and not wholly unknown to our own. They knew that bigotry was increasingly vigilant in its stratagems, to secure to itself an exclusive ascendancy over the human mind; and that *intolerance was ever ready to arm itself with all the terrors of the civil power to exterminate those, who doubted its dogmas, or resisted its infallibility* . . . .[107]

Islam, however, recognizes no such protection from state-imposed religion.[108] Historically, "[a] mosque was [Islam's] public forum and military drill ground as well as its place of common worship. The leader in prayer (*imam*) was also to be commander in chief of the army of the faithful, who were enjoined to protect one another against the entire world."[109]

"Islam" means submission to the will of Allah[110] and mandates a comprehensive code of law, covering the total social, political, and economic life of the community, in addition to rituals of worship.[111] It covers every aspect of Muslims' lives from crimes and punishments to personal family matters to appropriate greetings. Although other religions may also require their adherents to observe their specific divine laws in every aspect of their lives, other religions do not attempt to impose their divine laws on non-adherents through man-made law and legal process. In Islam, the entire political entity is ordained "by God [(Allah)] himself, *to promote his faith and to maintain and extend his law*."[112] It is thus important to note that the real concern is not whether Muslims consider *Shariah* the divine law or whether Islam mandates Muslims to follow *Shariah* in all aspects

---

[107]JOSEPH STORY, COMMENTARIES ON THE CONSTITUTION § 1841 (1833) (emphasis added).

[108]LEWIS, *supra* note 17, at 2–3.

[109]PHILIP K. HITTI, HISTORY OF THE ARABS 121 (10th ed. 2002) (emphasis added).

[110]QUR'AN, *supra* note 11, at *Surah* 3:19 ("The religion before Allah is Islam (submission to his will) . . . ." (internal quotation marks omitted)); *id.* at *Surah* 3:85 ("If anyone desires a religion other than Islam (submission to Allah), never will it be accepted of him . . . .").

[111]*See id.* at *Surah* 6:162–63 ("Say: 'Truly, my prayer and my service of sacrifice, my life and my death, are (all) for Allah, the cherisher of the worlds; No partner hath he; this am I commanded, and I am the first of those who bow to his will.'").

[112]LEWIS, *supra* note 17, at 25 (emphasis added).

of their lives, but that *Shariah itself does not recognize territorial boundaries and is required to be applied to Muslims as well as non-Muslims, irrespective of its incompatibility with the country's civil laws.*

As noted above, in the United States, the state does not control religion but allows it to operate within its own sphere of authority. Courts apply the civil law—not religious texts—to disputes before them. On the other hand, churches, synagogues, and other religious organizations are free to govern their internal affairs and manage their congregants according to their respective religious rules, assuming such rules do not violate United States law. Furthermore, civil courts are not permitted to intermeddle with the doctrinal affairs of religious institutions: "'To permit civil courts to probe deeply enough into the allocation of power within a [hierarchical] church so as to decide . . . religious law [governing church polity] . . . would violate the First Amendment in much the same manner as civil determination of religious doctrine.'"[113] The United States Constitution protects religion from governmental control. This concept is fundamental to protecting the liberty enshrined in the Constitution because it creates an environment in which individuals are not subjected to religious mandates by the government. Under *Shariah*, however, this foundational protection would no longer exist.

2. Universality of *Shariah* to the Muslim

In the United States, laws are fundamentally territorial and are generally limited by geographical boundaries.[114] Laws promulgated in the United States are man-made, positive laws (as opposed to

---

[113]Serbian E. Orthodox Diocese v. Milivojevich, 426 U.S. 696, 709 (1976) (emphasis added) (quoting Md. & Va. Churches v. Sharpsburg Church, 396 U.S. 367, 369 (1970) (Brennan, J., concurring)).

[114]*See, e.g.*, EEOC v. Arabian Am. Oil Co., 499 U.S. 244, 248 (1991) ("It is a longstanding principle of American law 'that legislation of Congress, unless a contrary intent appears, is meant to apply only within the territorial jurisdiction of the United States.'" (quoting Foley Bros. v. Filardo, 336 U.S. 281, 285 (1949))).

divine laws), enacted by the Congress or other U.S. authorities. Further, it is a longstanding principle of legal construction that positive law is territorial in nature.[115] As Justice Oliver Wendell Holmes, Jr., wrote, "the general and almost universal rule is that the character of an act as lawful or unlawful must be determined wholly by the law of the country where the act is done."[116] This principle is axiomatic to the American legal system.[117]

In the context of state laws, this principle is even clearer. While the Full Faith and Credit Clause of the United States Constitution requires that a state recognize the judicial acts and public records of another state,[118] the corollary implication is that each state retains the power to enact and enforce its own law within its jurisdiction and may not be forced to apply the law of any other state or jurisdiction that conflicts with its laws.[119] Therefore, U.S. law is generally limited to the United States and is not enforced in other countries even if the dispute involves U.S. citizens.[120]

Shariah, on the other hand, claims to be universal, and devout Muslims are expected to enforce it worldwide.[121] Islam

---

[115]*Id.*

[116]Am. Banana Co. v. United Fruit Co., 213 U.S. 347, 356 (1909). Justice Holmes explained the importance behind the universal rule:

> For another jurisdiction, if it should happen to lay hold of the actor, to treat him according to its own notions rather than those of the place where he did the acts, not only would be unjust, but would be an interference with the authority of another sovereign, contrary to the comity of nations, which the other state concerned justly might resent.

Id.

[117]*See Arabian Am. Oil Co.*, 499 U.S. at 248.

[118]U.S. Const. art IV, § 1.

[119]*See, e.g.*, Klaxon Co. v. Stentor Elec. Mfg. Co., 313 U.S. 487, 497–98 (1941) (holding the courts of a state are free to determine whether a given matter is to be governed by the law of the forum or some other law, subject only to review by the Supreme Court of the United States on any federal question that may arise).

[120]An exception to this is found in the general legal principles of choice of law clauses in contract and conflicts of laws.

[121]*See* Qur'an, *supra* note 11, at *Surah* 2:191–93 (commanding Muslims to fight until "there prevail justice and faith in Allah"); *id.* at *Surah* 9:29 (commanding Muslims to fight Christians and Jews until they "acknowledge the Religion of Truth" or "pay the *Jizyah* [(poll tax)]"); *id.* at *Surah* 8:38–39 (commanding Muslims to slay all unbelievers until they "desist (from unbelief)"); *id.* at *Surah* 8:65 (instructing Muhammad to "rouse the believers to the fight" and to "vanquish a thousand of the unbelievers: for these are a people without understanding"); Sahih Muslim, *supra* note 46, at Bk.

is both a universal religion and a universal state,[122] representing "both a religion and a nationality for the citizen of its state."[123] This political idea of Islam as a state is implied in the concept of *ummah* (all Muslims or the global Islamic community)[124] where all Muslims belong to the "universal religion," Islam.[125] The concept of *ummah* unifies all Muslims within the Islamic world to carry out Islam's ultimate objective of converting non-Muslims to Islam.[126] This single *ummah* encompasses within its embrace everyone who professes allegiance to Muhammad, simultaneously binding them to labor toward embracing the rest of the world as well.[127] Even

020, No. 4717 (Muhammad said: "This religion will continue to exist, and a group of people from the Muslims will continue to fight for its protection until the Hour is established."); CAIRO DECLARATION, *supra* note 42, pmbl. ("[The Member States of the OIC] reaffirm[] the civilizing and historical role of the Islamic Ummah which Allah made as the *best community* and which gave humanity a universal and well-balanced civilization . . . *to fulfill the expectations from this community [Islamic Ummah] to guide all humanity* which is confused because of different and conflicting beliefs and ideologies . . . ." (emphasis added)); *see also id.* (declaring that "safeguarding" the rights enshrined in the *Qur'an* is a "collective responsibility of the entire Ummah"); Organisation of the Islamic Conference Charter art. 1 (setting forth as the first two objectives of the OIC "[t]o enhance and consolidate the bonds of fraternity and solidarity among the Member States" and "[t]o safeguard and protect the common interests . . . of the Member States in view of the challenges faced *by the Islamic world in particular* and in the international community in general" (emphasis added)).

[122] WAR AND PEACE IN THE LAW OF ISLAM, *supra* note 48, at 63 ("Islam was radically different from both [Judaism and Christianity]. It combined the dualism of a universal religion and a universal state. It resorted to peaceful as well as violent means for achieving that ultimate objective."); HITTI, *supra* note 109, at 117.

[123] WAR AND PEACE IN THE LAW OF ISLAM, *supra* note 48, at 149.

[124] The *Qur'an* refers to the Muslim community as "a distinct nation (umma) or a brotherhood, bound by common obligations to a superior divine authority." *Id.* at 3–4 (internal quotation marks omitted); *see also id.* at 158 (stating that the Muslim law "recognizes neither division in Muslim authority nor differentiation among Muslims on racial or cultural background. The law recognizes one *umma*— *ummat* Muhammad—to whom belongs everyone who professes the religion of Islam"); LEWIS *supra* note 17, at 32 ("The polity or community over which this sovereign rules is the *umma*, the single universal Islamic community embracing all the lands in which Muslim rule is established and the Islamic law prevails.").

[125] WAR AND PEACE IN THE LAW OF ISLAM, *supra* note 48, at 17.

[126] *See* QUR'AN, *supra* note 11, at *Surah* 9:29 ("Fight those who believe not in Allah nor the Last Day, nor hold that forbidden which hath been forbidden by Allah and His Messenger, nor acknowledge the Religion of Truth, from among the People of the Book, until they pay the *Jizyah* with willing submission, and feel themselves subdued."); *id.* at *Surah* 2:193 ("And fight them on until there is no more tumult or oppression, and there prevail justice and faith in Allah . . . .").

[127] *See supra* note 121; *see also* WAR AND PEACE IN THE LAW OF ISLAM, *supra* note 48, at 158. It is noteworthy that with the spread of internet access to the four corners of the world, Muslims increasingly find solidarity in a virtual, online *umma*. As Wil Van Gemert, a senior official with the Dutch Interior Ministry, acknowledged, "[c]ommunicating on the Internet leads to a virtual ideological ghetto of like-minded jihadists." Eric Schmitt, *Governments Go Online in Fight Against Terrorism*, N.Y. TIMES (Jan. 30, 2011), http://www.nytimes.com/2011/01/31/world/middleeast/31terror.html ?_r=1 &ref=europe (internal quotation marks omitted).

the testimony of Muslim leaders in U.S. courts has referred to the "Islamic nation" as the definitive body of all Muslim believers.[128]

Islam "assume[s] that mankind constitute[s] one supra-national community, bound by one law and governed by one ruler."[129] Because, according to Islam, Allah revealed all laws, both religious and secular (in a Western sense), through Muhammad to the entire *ummah*, Islam is a divine, universal "nomocracy"—a universal state that is governed by divine law.[130] Consequently, every Muslim is bound by *Shariah*, law which "binds individuals, not territorial groups."[131] The various sources of authority in Islam, discussed above,[132] transcend temporal and geographic boundaries and bind all Muslims in all places at all times.[133] *Shariah* thus travels with a Muslim wherever he goes and is expected to supersede the law of any land in which the Muslim resides. No matter the origin of *Shariah* or the difficulties in its application, one thing is certain: *Shariah "is the exclusive source of all law for the Muslims."*[134] Consequently, when *Shariah* governs, it supersedes all other laws.[135]

3. Allegiance to the "Nation" of Islam for the Muslim

The universality of Islam does not recognize contrary national or other loyalties, but demands a Muslim's full allegiance.[136] For this reason, Muslims throughout the world consider the wars

---

[128]State v. Phelps, 652 N.E.2d 1032, 1035 (Ohio Ct. App. 1995) (Muslim defendant referring to the Islamic community as the "Islamic Nation").

[129]WAR AND PEACE IN THE LAW OF ISLAM, *supra* note 48, at 17.

[130]*Id.* at 14–18.

[131]*Id.* at 147, 172.

[132]*See supra* Chapter 2.D.

[133]*See, e.g.*, KAMALI, *supra* note 79, at 7–8 ("The sources of *Shari'ah* . . . are permanent in character and may not be overruled on grounds of either rationality or the requirements of social conditions . . . . [I]n principle the *Shari'ah* and its sources can neither be abrogated nor subjected to the limitations of time and circumstance. . . . Sovereignty in Islam is the prerogative of Almighty [Allah] alone. . . . It is neither the will of the ruler nor of any assembly of men, nor even the community as a whole, that determines the values and the laws which uphold those values. In its capacity as the vicegerent of God, the Muslim community is entrusted with the authority to implement the *Shari'ah* . . . .").

[134]*Id.* at 307 (emphasis added).

[135]*Id.* at 7–8.

[136]QUR'AN, *supra* note 11, at *Surah* 6:162 ("Say: 'Truly, my prayer and my service of sacrifice, my life and my death, are (all) for Allah, the cherisher of the worlds.'").

in Afghanistan and Iraq as "crusades" against *Islam*; Muslims in Pakistan protested against cartoons published in Denmark irreverently depicting Muhammad[137]; and the pledge by a pastor in Florida to burn the *Qur'an* was met with violence and threats of violence from Muslims around the world, including in Iran, Syria, Lebanon, and even Indonesia.[138] In the legal context, the loyalty to the Islamic *ummah* (community) can be seen in the "active international grouping at the United Nations and elsewhere, [by fifty-six] Muslim governments, which together constitute the so-called Islamic Bloc."[139] Note that all fifty-six Islamic states have agreed to defend Islam's universality[140] and have made it incumbent on every Muslim of the "entire Ummah" to safeguard the "binding divine commands . . . of Allah."[141]

Because Islam distinguishes the "infidels" of the outside world from the community of believers,[142] it divides the world into two territories: *dar al-Islam*, the territory of Islam,[143] and *dar al-harb*, the "territory of war."[144] The *dar al-Islam* consists of all territories under Muslim rule, inhabited by true believers and their communities, while the *dar al-harb* includes all other states and communities not under Muslim rule.[145] According to the *Qur'an*,

[137]Associated Press, *Muslims Protest Danish Muhammad Cartoons*, MSNBC (Feb. 15, 2008), http://www.msnbc.msn.com/id/23186467/ns/world_news-europe.

[138]*See* Ian Black, *US Church's Plans to Burn Qur'an Berated Across Muslim World*, THE GUARDIAN (Sept. 8, 2010), http://www.guardian.co.uk/world/2010/sep/08/florida-church-quran-burn-threat.

[139]*See* LEWIS *supra* note 17, at 3; *see also Member States*, ORGANISATION OF THE ISLAMIC CONFERENCE, http://www.oic-oci.org/member_states.asp (listing the fifty-six states that are currently members of the Organisation of the Islamic Conference).

[140]Organisation of the Islamic Conference Charter pmbl.

[141]*See* CAIRO DECLARATION, *supra* note 42, at pmbl.

[142]The *Qur'an* frequently distinguishes between those who believe "[a] Messenger from among themselves, rehearsing unto them the signs of Allah, sanctifying them, and instructing them in scripture and wisdom," QUR'AN, *supra* note 11, at *Surah* 3:164, from those who "reject faith" and are subsequently classified as enemies who are condemned to hell. *Id.* at *Surah* 3:10–12.

[143]WAR AND PEACE IN THE LAW OF ISLAM, *supra* note 48, at 52; *see also* QUR'AN, *supra* note 11, at *Surah* 10:25 (referring to a "Home of Peace," where Allah is believed to call mankind).

[144]*See* RELIANCE OF THE TRAVELLER, *supra* note 10, at 944–47 (referring to non-Muslims in "enemy land," or *dar-al-harb*); WAR AND PEACE IN THE LAW OF ISLAM, *supra* note 48, at 52.

[145]WAR AND PEACE IN THE LAW OF ISLAM, *supra* note 48, at 52–53.

these two territories will be in constant conflict until Islam conquers the whole world and converts it through *jihad* (holy war or struggle)[146] into *dar al-Islam* to implement *Shariah* universally.[147] The goal to implement *Shariah* universally, in effect, results in "a state of warfare *permanently* declared against the outside world . . . ."[148]

Because these two territories (the territory of Islam and the territory of war) are the only distinctions that Islam recognizes, nationalities and state authorities have little significance to the individual Muslim. No matter where he resides or what sovereign claims his allegiance, every Muslim is obligated to labor in his own way toward achieving the goal of bringing the world under *Shariah*. Hence, there is an inherent tension in devout Muslims swearing loyalty to anyone besides Muhammad.[149] At the very heart of Islam is the existence of a single Islamic state, an "entirely exclusive" state that does not recognize any contrary allegiance.[150]

Consequently, a devout Muslim's allegiance to the global Islamic state is inherently in conflict with *any* oath of allegiance to any earthly authority or state. As discussed, the universal and political nature of the Islamic faith mandates that Muslim loyalty lies with the global Islamic state above the nation-state in which a Muslim resides. Because every Muslim is required to do his part in bringing the world into a state of complete *dar al-Islam* (territory of Islam), any nation that is not currently under Islamic *Shariah* is an enemy of Islam. Therefore, under *Shariah*, ultimate allegiance by

[146]*See infra* Chapter 6.

[147]*See* QUR'AN, *supra* note 11, at *Surah* 2:191–93 (commanding Muslims to fight until "there prevail justice and faith in Allah"); *id.* at *Surah* 9:29 (commanding Muslims to fight until unbelievers "acknowledge the religion of truth" or, if Christian or Jew, "until they pay the *Jizyah* (poll tax)"); *id.* at *Surah* 8:38–39 (commanding Muslims to slay all unbelievers until they "desist (from unbelief)"); *id.* at *Surah* 8:65 (instructing Muhammad to "rouse the believers to the fight" and to "vanquish a thousand of the unbelievers: for these are a people without understanding."). *See also supra* notes 121 and 127.

[148]WAR AND PEACE IN THE LAW OF ISLAM, *supra* note 48, at 63–64 (emphasis added); *see also supra* note 147 and accompanying text.

[149]*See* QUR'AN, *supra* note 11, at *Surah* 18:26 ("[N]or does [Allah] share his command with any (person) whatsoever.").

[150]*See* WAR AND PEACE IN THE LAW OF ISLAM, *supra* note 48, at 17.

devout Muslims to a non-*Shariah* nation-state is impossible.

For example, a devout Muslim cannot *truthfully*[151] swear the oath to become a citizen of the United States of America:

> I hereby declare, on oath, that I absolutely and entirely renounce and abjure all allegiance and fidelity to any foreign prince, potentate, state or sovereignty, of whom or which I have heretofore been a subject or citizen; that I will support and defend the Constitution and laws of the United States of America against all enemies, foreign and domestic; that I will bear true faith and allegiance to the same; that I will bear arms on behalf of the United States when required by the law; that I will perform noncombatant service in the armed forces of the United States when required by the law; that I will perform work of national importance under civilian direction when required by the law; and that I take this obligation freely, without any mental reservation or purpose of evasion; so help me God.[152]

Because Islam is a political religion, with the complete fusion of religion and state, Islam—in the minds of Muslims—constitutes a state or sovereignty.[153] And, as demonstrated, Muslims view themselves as permanent citizens of this universal Islamic state.[154] Thus, to become a citizen of the United States, a Muslim would have to "entirely renounce and abjure all allegiance and fidelity" to

---

[151]While many Muslims may appear to genuinely swear allegiance to the United States and its Constitution, it cannot be fully determined if the oath is genuine because Muslims are permitted to lie in *jihad* to advance Islam. *See* RELIANCE OF THE TRAVELLER, *supra* note 10, at 744–46 ("I did not hear [Muhammad] permit untruth in anything people say, except for three things: war [*jihad*], settling disagreements, and a man talking with his wife or she with him . . . ."); *see also* SAHIH BUKHARI, *supra* note 69, at Vol. 5, Bk. 59, No. 369 ("Muhammad bin Maslama got up saying, 'O Allah's Apostle! Would you like that I kill him [Ka'b bin Al-Ashraf]?' The Prophet said, 'Yes,' Muhammad bin Maslama said, 'Then allow me to say a (false) thing (i.e.[,] to deceive Kaab).' The Prophet said, 'You may say it.'"); *see infra* note 168 (taking false oath of allegiance to obtain U.S. citizenship to carry out terrorist activities).

[152]Oath of Allegiance, 8 C.F.R. § 337.1 (2010).

[153]WAR AND PEACE IN THE LAW OF ISLAM, *supra* note 48, at 63; HITTI, *supra* note 109, at 117 ("[Islam] itself became the state. Then and there Islam came to be what the world has ever since recognized it to be—a militant polity.").

[154]WAR AND PEACE IN THE LAW OF ISLAM, *supra* note 48, at 149.

the Islamic state. As such, under the traditional teachings of Islam, it is extremely challenging for a devout Muslim to truthfully take the oath to become a citizen of the United States because it would require him to repudiate his loyalty to the Islamic state—a state which requires both religious and political loyalty.[155]

A good example of this is Army Major Nidal Malik Hasan, a Muslim American[156] stationed at Fort Hood, Texas, who killed more than a dozen people in November 2009.[157] According to eye-witnesses, Major Hasan chanted the Islamic slogan, "Allahu Akbar" ("Allah is Great"), as he shot his fellow soldiers.[158] In order to receive his commission as an officer in the Army, Major Hasan would have had to sign his name to an oath requiring him to swear allegiance to "defend the Constitution of the United States against all enemies" and to "bear true faith and allegiance to the same . . . *without any mental reservations* or purpose of evasion . . . ."[159]

Nevertheless, despite having sworn to protect the United States and to remain loyal to his compatriots, Major Hasan was affected by conflicting loyalties. According to one of his former classmates, Major Hasan was unable to back the war against Islamic terrorists because he viewed it as a direct war against Islam.[160] In

---

[155]While it is admitted that many Muslims live peaceful and law-abiding lives as citizens in non-*Shariah* nation-states, the actual teaching of Islam, as interpreted by most Muslim scholars, would bar Muslims from truthfully accepting the oath in becoming U.S. citizens.

[156]Michael McAuliff, Kerry Burke, & Helen Kennedy, *Fort Hood Killer Nidal Malik Hasan Opposed Wars, So Why Did He Snap?*, N.Y. DAILY NEWS (Nov. 6, 2009), http://articles.nydailynews.com/2009-11-06/news/17938263_1_army-suicides-nidal-malik-hasan-fort-hood ("Hasan was born in Virginia to Palestinian parents who emigrated from Jordan.").

[157]*Army Honors Dead, Searches for Motive in Fort Hood Shootings*, CNN (Nov. 7, 2009) [hereinafter *Army Honors Dead*], http://www.cnn.com/2009/CRIME/11/06/texas.fort.hood.shootings/index.html.

[158]*Id.* (internal quotations omitted).

[159]ARMED FORCES OF THE UNITED STATES, OATH OF OFFICE—MILITARY PERSONNEL, DA Form 71 (1999) (emphasis added), *available at* http://armypubs.army.mil/eforms/pdf/A71.PDF ("I, _____, having been appointed an officer in the Army of the United States, as indicated above in the grade of _____ do solemnly swear (or affirm) that I will support and defend the Constitution of the United States against all enemies, foreign or domestic, that I will bear true faith and allegiance to the same; that I take this obligation freely, without any mental reservations or purpose of evasion; and that I will well and faithfully discharge the duties of the office upon which I am about to enter. So help me God."); *see also* 5 U.S.C. § 3331 (2010).

[160]Brett J. Blackledge, *Who Is Major Nidal Malik Hasan?*, ASSOCIATED PRESS (Nov. 5, 2009), http://

fact, he had even argued in favor of a conscientious-objector clause for Muslims serving in the U.S. Armed Forces.[161] At a presentation in June 2007, Major Hasan, an Army psychiatrist, cautioned his supervisors and twenty-five other mental health staff members that, to avoid "adverse events," the military should allow Muslim soldiers to be released as conscientious objectors instead of fighting in wars against other Muslims.[162] A year and a half after this presentation, the tension between Major Hasan's allegiance to Islam and his purported loyalty to the United States came to a breaking point, and he decided that his religion permitted his murdering twelve soldiers.[163]

Also, on May 3, 2010, authorities arrested Faisal Shahzad, a Pakistani-born Muslim, for attempting to detonate a car-bomb in Times Square in New York City.[164] Shahzad had visited Pakistan in 2009, allegedly to contact terrorist organizations and participate in terrorist training camps.[165] At the time, he was living in Connecticut and had become a naturalized U.S. citizen in April 2009.[166] Although Shahzad had taken the oath of allegiance to support America as a naturalized U.S. citizen,[167] that oath directly conflicted with Islam's claim to supremacy. His U.S. citizenship served as a mere tool that Shahzad used to infiltrate the United States to fight it from within. Indeed, the dialogue at trial between Judge Cedarbaum and Shahzad is quite revealing:

> Judge: "Didn't you swear allegiance to this country when you became an American citizen?"

---

www.myfoxdc.com/dpp/news/major-nidal-malik-hasan-fort-hood-shootings-110509.

[161]Dana Priest, *Fort Hood Suspect Warned of Threats Within the Ranks*, WASH. POST (Nov. 10, 2009), http://www.washingtonpost.com/wp-dyn/content/article/2009/11/09/AR2009110903618.html?hpid=topnews.

[162]*Id.*

[163]*Army Honors Dead, supra* note 157.

[164]Douglas J. Hagmann, *Muslim Terrorist Arrested in Attempted Times Square Bombing Others Being Sought*, NE. INTELLIGENCE NETWORK (May 4, 2010), http://homelandsecurityus.com/archives/3782.

[165]*Id.*

[166]*Id.*

[167]Oath of Allegiance, 8 C.F.R. § 337.1 (2010).

Shahzad: "I did swear, but I did not mean it."
Judge: "You took a false oath?"
Shahzad: "Yes."[168]

Outside the United States, Islamic terrorists have also caused horrible incidents of violence by disregarding their sworn professional loyalties out of ultimate religious and political allegiance to Allah. For instance, a number of fundamentalist Islamic physicians and other medical professionals in Britain and Australia were arrested in July 2007 following failed bombing attempts in London and Glasgow.[169]

Examples like these demonstrate that, to many Muslims, Islam demands single-minded loyalty from its adherents, a loyalty that can admit no other allegiances. The driving force behind Islamic unity will inevitably eliminate all other contenders for allegiance and will not let demands of "loyalty" to the United States stand in its way.

---

[168]*See* Michael Wilson, *Shahzad Gets Life Term for Times Square Bombing Attempt*, N.Y. TIMES (Oct. 5, 2010), http://www.nytimes.com/2010/10/06/nyregion/06shahzad.html.
[169]*Timeline: Failed Car Bomb Attacks*, BBC (July 6, 2007), http://news.bbc.co.uk/2/hi/uk_ news/6260626.stm.

SECTION TWO

ISLAMIC SHARIAH IS **INCOMPATIBLE** WITH U.S. LAW

Not only is *Shariah* incompatible with the basic concept of United States citizenship and national loyalty, but it is also fundamentally inconsistent with both U.S. civil and criminal law and the constitutional guarantees inherent in the American legal system. The Islamic principles and laws, discussed at length below, conflict in both purpose and degree with U.S. law to such an extent that there can be no reasonable expectation that the two legal systems could ever co-exist. The following sections will discuss both Islamic criminal and civil laws and compare them with their U.S. counterparts, showing the inherent conflict between U.S. and Islamic standards of justice, punishments, and dispute resolution.

Comparison between American law and *Shariah* is not always easy because many important constitutional freedoms are *protected* under American civil laws while identical conduct is *punishable* under Islamic criminal laws. For example, the freedoms of religion and speech, essentially civil matters in the United States, are considered criminal matters (apostasy and blasphemy) under *Shariah*.[170] Similarly, many values that are beloved and vigorously protected by U.S. law (e.g., the protection of women and children) are diminished or outright opposed by *Shariah* (e.g., absolute power of husbands and fathers).[171] The many differences in how the two systems view right and wrong, as well as what constitutes justice, indicate that the two legal systems are starkly incompatible.

---

[170]*See infra* Chapters 3.A, B.
[171]*See infra* Chapters 4.E, 5.

CHAPTER THREE

CIVIL RIGHTS AND LIBERTIES

The incompatibility of criminal and civil laws in the United States and criminal and civil laws under *Shariah* can be explained by the fundamentally different regard for human rights between the two. The United States and the West, in general, define human rights broadly and extend them to *all* human beings, regardless of sex, religion, or creed. In stark contrast, *Shariah* defines human rights narrowly, limiting them to Muslims and qualifying them by requiring conformity with *Shariah*.

The U.S. Declaration of Independence declares the foundational principle of the United States that "all men are created equal,"[172] and the Fourteenth Amendment to the U.S. Constitution guarantees this equality under the law.[173] The first ten amendments to the U.S. Constitution, also known as the Bill of Rights, set forth a non-exhaustive list of rights and liberties guaranteed to *all* Americans.[174] These freedoms include, *inter alia*, the free exercise of religion, freedom of speech,[175] right to due process of law,[176] and protection from cruel and unusual punishment.[177] Similarly, the law of nations, or international law, recognizes certain basic fundamental rights. The preamble to the United Nations' Universal Declaration of Human Rights (UDHR) exhibits a similar theme. The preamble begins with an unequivocal acknowledgment of "the inherent

---

[172]THE DECLARATION OF INDEPENDENCE pmbl. (U.S. 1776) ("We hold these truths to be self-evident, that all men are created equal, that they are endowed by their Creator with certain unalienable Rights, that among these are Life, Liberty and the pursuit of Happiness. That to secure these rights, Governments are instituted among Men, deriving their just powers from the consent of the governed . . . .").
[173]U.S. CONST. amend. XIV.
[174]*Id.* amends. I–X.
[175]*Id.* amend. I.
[176]*Id.* amend. V.
[177]*Id.* amend. VIII.

dignity and of the equal and inalienable rights of *all members of the human family . . . .*"[178] The UDHR further enumerates, *inter alia,* the rights to "life, liberty, and security of person";[179] freedom from torture or cruel, inhuman, or degrading treatment or punishment;[180] and rights to effective remedies under the law,[181] presumptions of innocence until proven guilty,[182] and equal protection under the law.[183] These rights, liberties, and freedoms are for all persons of all races, ethnicities, religions, and sexes simply by virtue of a person's status as a human being who is endowed with "inherent dignity" and "inalienable rights."[184]

Shariah, on the other hand, exalts the rights of only some individuals, based primarily on their religion. The *Qur'an* and *hadiths* (accounts of Muhammad's life and teachings) distinguish between the rights of Muslims and the rights of non-Muslims. The *Qur'an* likens unbelievers to cattle, goats, dogs, and donkeys.[185] Another passage declares, "[f]or the worst of beasts in the sight of Allah are those who reject him."[186] *Shariah* further promotes this distinction between Muslim believers and non-believers with the indemnity it affords a Muslim who kills a non-believer.[187]

Furthermore, even within Islam, *Shariah* discriminates

---

[178]Universal Declaration of Human Rights, pmbl., G.A. Res. 217 (III) A, U.N. Doc. A/RES/217(III) (Dec. 10, 1948) [hereinafter UDHR] (emphasis added).

[179]*Id.* art. 3.

[180]*Id.* art. 5.

[181]*Id.* art. 8.

[182]*Id.* art. 11.

[183]*Id.* art. 7.

[184]*Id.* pmbl.

[185]*See* QUR'AN, *supra* note 11, at *Surah* 25:44 (likening unbelievers to "cattle"); *id.* at *Surah* 2:171 (describing those who reject faith as a "goat-herd"); *id.* at *Surah* 7:175–76 (analogizing the man who ignores the signs of Allah and Muhammad to a "dog"); *id.* at *Surah* 62:5 (describing Jews as "donkeys"); *id.* at *Surah* 2:65 (describing Jews as "apes"); *id.* at *Surah* 5:59–60 (describing Jews and Christians as "apes and swine").

[186]*Id.* at *Surah* 8:55.

[187]*See, e.g.,* SAHIH BUKHARI, *supra* note 69, at Vol. 9, Bk. 83, No. 50; *id.* at Vol. 1, Bk. 3, No. 111; *id.* at Vol. 4, Bk. 52, No. 283; SUNAN ABU DAWUD, Bk. 39, No. 4491 (trans., Ahmad Hasan) [hereinafter ABU DAWUD], *available at* http://www.usc.edu/schools/college/crcc/engagement/resources/texts/muslim/hadith/abudawud/ (teaching that Muslims should not be punished for killing infidels, i.e., unbelievers).

against people on the basis of sex. Specifically, *Shariah* regards men as having more rights and higher status than women.[188] Illustrating this reduction of the rights of women under *Shariah*, Muhammad himself stated:

> O womenfolk, you should give charity and ask much forgiveness for I saw you in bulk amongst the dwellers of Hell. A wise lady among them said: Why is it, Messenger of Allah, that our folk is in bulk in Hell? Upon this [Muhammad] observed: You curse too much and are ungrateful to your spouses. I have seen none lacking in common sense and failing in religion but (at the same time) robbing the wisdom of the wise, besides you. Upon this the woman remarked: What is wrong with our common sense and with religion? [Muhammad] observed: Your lack of common sense (can be well judged from the fact) that the evidence of two women is equal to one man, that is a proof of the lack of common sense.[189]

In this exchange, Muhammad evidences the unequal status of women in Islam to the extent that he was willing to teach that many Muslim women will go to hell because of their supposed inherent lack of common sense and ingratitude to their husbands.

Consistent with the rights of persons under *Shariah*, all fifty-six Muslim Member States of the Organisation of the Islamic Conference (OIC)[190] disavow human rights as either "inherent" or "inalienable."[191] Instead, the OIC has adopted its own Declaration on Human Rights (the Cairo Declaration), which affirms only some

---

[188]QUR'AN, *supra* note 11, at *Surah* 2:228 (teaching that although women have "rights similar to the rights against them, according to what is equitable," men still "have a degree (of advantage) over them").

[189]SAHIH MUSLIM, *supra* note 46, at Bk. 001, No. 0142 (Abdul Hamid Siddiqui trans.).

[190]Organisation of the Islamic Conference Charter art. 3, para. 1 ("The Organisation is made up of 57 States member of the Organisation of the Islamic Conference and other States which may accede to this Charter . . . .") (The OIC's list includes Palestine as a Member State); *see also Member States*, ORGANISATION OF THE ISLAMIC CONFERENCE, http://www.oic-oci.org/member_states.asp (last visited Feb. 4, 2011) (providing a listing of all nations that are officially Member States of the OIC).

[191]*See generally* CAIRO DECLARATION, *supra* note 42 (lacking any reference to the "inherent" or "inalienable" nature of human rights).

human rights, which are qualified both in scope and application.[192] The Cairo Declaration proclaims that "all . . . rights and freedoms" are "subject to the Islamic Shari'ah"[193] and that "[t]he *Islamic Shari'ah is the only source of reference* for the explanation or clarification of any [human rights]."[194] In stark contrast to the American Declaration of Independence and the UDHR, both of which recognize the universality and inalienability of human rights and the equality of mankind, the Cairo Declaration declares that Allah has made the "Islamic Ummah . . . the *best* community," which is supposed to "guide all humanity which is confused because of different and conflicting beliefs."[195] Further, the OIC Charter declares that its purposes consist of "*defend[ing] the universality* of Islamic religion," "respect[ing] the right of . . . *non-interference* in the domestic affairs . . . , sovereignty, independence and territorial integrity of each Member State," and "safeguard[ing] and promot[ing] the rights of women and their participation in all spheres of life, [*only*] *in accordance with the laws and legislation of Member States.*"[196] The OIC Charter further states that all international human rights treaties to which any of the OIC's fifty-six members is a party will be promoted only "in conformity with Islamic values,"[197] and it reserves adjudication of alleged human rights violations to the International *Islamic* Court of Justice.[198] Accordingly, to call the Cairo Declaration "a declaration on human rights" on par with the UDHR is simply wrong, for the Cairo Declaration does not endorse

---

[192]*Id.*

[193]*Id.* art. 24.

[194]*Id.* art. 25 (emphasis added).

[195]*Id.* pmbl.

[196]Organisation of the Islamic Conference Charter pmbl. (emphasis added).

[197]*Id.* art. 15.

[198]*Id.* art. 14 (emphasis added). The International Islamic Court of Justice is one of the principle bodies of the OIC. *Organizational Structure of the OIC,* PERMANENT MISSION OF THE ORGANISATION OF THE ISLAMIC CONFERENCE, http://www.oic-un.org/oic_organs_links.asp (last visited Apr. 5, 2011). The decision to establish the Court was made by the Third Islamic Summit and "[i]t is envisioned to have 7 members elected by the Islamic Conference of Foreign Ministers and to have headquarters in Kuwait City, the State of Kuwait." *Id.*

the rights of *human beings* in general, but rather endorses the rights of only *some* humans, to wit, those who adhere to Islam.

These vast differences in defining the scope and applicability of human rights in nations that adhere to *Shariah* and those that do not are evident in the frequent, almost routine, violations of human rights that occur in virtually every nation that applies *Shariah*. Because these differences are at the most fundamental level of human rights jurisprudence, the laws and practices that emerge in nations that apply *Shariah* are often directly incompatible with those that emerge in nations that do not apply *Shariah*. Consider, for instance, Saudi Arabia and Iran, both belonging to opposing sects of Islam and which apply different interpretations of *Shariah*. The United States Commission on International Religious Freedom (USCIRF) has designated both as "countr[ies] of particular concern (CPC)" for their "systematic, ongoing, and egregious" human rights violations.[199] In fact, between 2009 and 2010, of the eight countries USCIRF prioritized due to the degree of human rights abuses on religious grounds,[200] six (seventy-five percent) are nations that apply varying degrees of *Shariah*.[201] And this figure is not anomalous. As *Shariah* continues to gain influence in legal systems around the globe, the rest of the world should expect increases in the frequency and degree of human rights abuses.

A. FREEDOM OF RELIGION

Although U.S. and other Western legal traditions view fundamental freedoms such as freedom of speech and freedom

[199]In one place, the U.S. Committee on International Religious Freedom (USCIRF) described the religious climate in Iran as follows: "The government of Iran continues to engage in systematic, ongoing, and egregious violations of religious freedom, including prolonged detention, torture, and executions based primarily or entirely upon the religion of the accused." U.S. COMM'N ON INT'L RELIGIOUS FREEDOM, ANNUAL REPORT OF THE UNITED STATES COMMISSION ON INTERNATIONAL RELIGIOUS FREEDOM 5–6, 9 (May 2010), *available at* http://www.uscirf.gov/images/annual%20report%202010. pdf.

[200]The Committee listed China, Egypt, Iran, Nigeria, Pakistan, Saudi Arabia, Sudan, and Vietnam as "priority countries." *Id.* at 2.

[201]These six are Egypt, Iran, Nigeria, Pakistan, Saudi Arabia, and the Sudan. *Id.* at 2.

of religion as civil rights and civil liberties issues, *Shariah* treats speech and religious conduct that are contrary to Islam as criminal matters.[202]

The First Amendment to the U.S. Constitution guarantees freedom of religion, which includes the right of individuals to choose, change, or deny religious belief.[203] Consequently, changing one's religious belief is not a criminal act, but rather a guaranteed individual right according to the Supreme Court's free exercise jurisprudence.[204] In interpreting the constitutional right to believe and exercise one's faith free from government entanglement, the Supreme Court has explicitly held that "[t]he free exercise of religion means, first and foremost, the right to believe and profess whatever religious doctrine one desires."[205] Even in cases where the Supreme Court has ruled that certain *conduct* of religious groups could be proscribed,[206] the Court has never refused the right of individuals to affiliate with a particular religious group or to change their religious beliefs.

In direct contrast, under *Shariah*, "apostasy" (*ridda*), the formal renunciation of the Islamic faith, is proscribed.[207] Under *Shariah*, apostasy can be committed in numerous ways, including, but not limited to, the following acts: explicitly renouncing the

---

[202]While we discuss the freedoms of religion and speech in this section (as opposed to other possible sections) because of the traditional Western classification of these topics as civil rights and civil liberties issues, we reserve a more detailed discussion of *Shariah*'s classification of criminal offenses in Chapter 4.B.1.

[203]*See* U.S. CONST. amend. I ("Congress shall make no law respecting the establishment of religion, or prohibiting the free exercise thereof . . . .").

[204]Cantwell v. Connecticut, 310 U.S. 296, 303 (1940) (The First Amendment "forestalls compulsion by law of the acceptance of any creed or the practice of any form of worship. Freedom of conscience and freedom to adhere to such religious organization or form of worship as the individual may choose cannot be restricted by law. On the other hand, it safeguards the free exercise of the chosen form of religion.").

[205]Employment Div. v. Smith, 494 U.S. 872, 877 (1990).

[206]*E.g.*, Reynolds v. United States, 98 U.S. 145 (1878) (upholding a criminal conviction of a Mormon engaging in polygamy); *see generally* Employment Div. v. Smith, 494 U.S. 872 (1990) (permitting states to prohibit the use of illegal drugs, even those traditionally used in religious ceremonies).

[207]ABDULLAH SAEED & HASSAN SAEED, FREEDOM OF RELIGION, APOSTASY, AND ISLAM 1 (2004).

Islamic faith; denying Allah's existence; sarcastically using Allah's name; blaspheming Muhammad; converting to another religion; rejecting or adding to any book or verse in the *Qur'an*; and challenging the truthfulness or legitimacy of any of Allah's prophets or messengers.[208]

Because Islam fuses religion and state, and because a Muslim's religion is also his national identity, apostasy is equated with treason.[209] Therefore, *Shariah* characterizes apostates (called *murtadd*) as enemies in war and enumerates four different potential consequences for unrepentant apostates:

> The punishment of those who wage war against Allah and His Messenger, and strive with might and main for mischief throughout the land is: execution, or crucifixion, or the cutting off of hands and feet from opposite sides, or exile from the land: That is their disgrace in this world, and a heavy punishment is theirs in the Hereafter.[210]

Apostasy is one of the most severely punished *hadd* offenses (offenses against Allah, requiring severe prescribed penalties). While the *Qur'an* explicitly sets forth a variety of punishments appropriate for apostates, the *hadiths* (accounts of Muhammad's life and teachings) demonstrate that Muhammad and his followers required nothing short of death for anyone who would defect from Islam.

Muhammad commanded his followers, "[i]f [a Muslim]

---

[208]RELIANCE OF THE TRAVELLER, *supra* note 10, at 596–98. There is also some indication that at least during the time of Muhammad, even failure to attend certain prayers was tantamount to apostasy, thus warranting death. *See* SAHIH BUKHARI, *supra* note 69, at Vol. 1, Bk. 11, No. 626 ("The Prophet said, 'No prayer is harder for the hypocrites than the Fajr and the 'Isha' prayers and if they knew the reward for these prayers at their respective times, they would certainly present themselves (in the mosques) even if they had to crawl.' The Prophet added, 'Certainly I decided to order the Mu'adh-dhin (call-maker) to pronounce Iqama and order a man to lead the prayer *and then take a fire flame to burn all those who had not left their houses so far for the prayer* along with their houses.'" (emphasis added)).

[209]QUR'AN, *supra* note 11, at 257 n.738 (holding apostates culpable of "the double crime of treason against the State, combined with treason against Allah").

[210]*Id.* at *Surah* 5:33.

discards his religion, kill him."[211] The statements and conduct of Muhammad's contemporary followers affirmed the harshness of Muhammad's words. In one instance, one of Muhammad's followers approached another follower and asked him who the chained man beside him was. The follower explained that the chained man "was a Jew [who] became a Muslim and then reverted back to Judaism."[212] Knowing Allah's decrees, the follower responded: "I will not sit down till he has been killed. This is the judgment of Allah and His Apostle [Muhammad] (for such cases) and repeated it thrice."[213] The convert was immediately ordered to be killed.[214] In another instance, a follower declared:

> During the last days there will appear some young foolish people who will say the best words but their faith will not go beyond their throats (i.e., they will have no faith) and will go out from (leave) their religion as an arrow goes out of the game. So, wherever you find them, kill them, for *whoever kills them shall have reward* on the Day of Resurrection.[215]

In yet another instance, Muhammad "ordered to cut [apostates'] hands and feet (and it was done), and their eyes were branded with heated pieces of iron[.] They were put in [the desert,] and when they asked for water, no water was given to them."[216] Accordingly, the *Shafi'i* school of Islamic jurisprudence maintains that there is no consequence for apostates other than death: "When a person who has reached puberty and is sane voluntarily apostatizes from Islam, he deserves to be killed."[217]

---

[211]SAHIH BUKHARI, *supra* note 69, at Vol. 4, Bk. 52, No. 260 (internal quotation marks omitted).
[212]*Id.* at Vol. 9, Bk. 84, No. 58. *Cf. id.* at Vol. 5, Bk. 59, No. 632.
[213]*Id.*
[214]*Id.*
[215]*Id.* at Vol. 9, Bk. 84, No. 64–65 (emphasis added).
[216]*See id.* at Vol. 1, Bk. 4, No. 234.
[217]RELIANCE OF THE TRAVELLER, *supra* note 10, at viii, 595. Muslims are also instructed to make their children pray and to beat them if they do not pray. SAHIH MUSLIM *supra* note 46, at Bk. 002, No. 0495 ("The Apostle of Allah (peace_be_upon_him) said: Command your children to pray when they become seven years old, and beat them for it (prayer) when they become ten years old . . . .").

Imposing the death sentence on apostates is not a relic of classical *Shariah*. Both the Cairo Declaration, adopted in 1990, and the OIC Charter, adopted in 1974, indirectly affirm the *Shariah* punishments for apostates. Article 2 of the Cairo Declaration specifically declares that all human beings have a right to life *except* for those whose lives may be taken "for a shari ´ah prescribed reason."[218] As the above sections demonstrate, apostasy is one such "shari ´ah prescribed reason."[219] Similarly, section (d) of the same article proclaims, "[s]afety from bodily harm is a guaranteed right" that may not be breached *except* for a "shari ´ah prescribed reason."[220] The OIC Charter likewise declares that Member States' participation in international treaties is subject to *Shariah*. Specifically, it declares that its own Human Rights Commission—and not that of the overarching United Nations (U.N.)—"shall promote the civil . . . rights enshrined in the [OIC's] covenants and declarations and in universally agreed human rights instruments, *in conformity with Islamic values*."[221]

Additionally, OIC Member States that have implemented *Shariah* have made apostasy a *criminal* offense, carrying sentences as severe as the death penalty in their domestic legal systems. For example, in Saudi Arabia, where there is no codified criminal law, courts are given broad authority to punish apostasy with death.[222]

---

[218]CAIRO DECLARATION, *supra* note 42, art. 2(a).

[219]*See* discussion *supra* notes 208–217 and accompanying text.

[220]CAIRO DECLARATION, *supra* note 42, art. 2(d).

[221]Organisation of the Islamic Conference Charter art. 15 (emphasis added) ("The Independent Permanent Commission on Human Rights shall promote the civil, political, social and economic rights enshrined in the organisation's covenants and declarations and in universally agreed human rights instruments, in conformity with Islamic values."); *see also Status of Treaties*, UNITED NATIONS TREATY SERIES (Feb. 4, 2011), http://treaties.un.org/Pages/ViewDetails.aspx?src=TREATY&mtdsg_no=IV-4&chapter=4&lang=en#EndDec (Islamic countries' reservations to conform with Islamic *Shariah*).

[222]*Saudi Arabia: Criminal Justice Strengthened*, HUMAN RIGHTS WATCH NEWS (Jan. 14, 2010), http://www.hrw.org/en/news/2010/01/14/saudi-arabia-criminal-justice-strengthened ("Saudi Arabia has no penal code, and judges can issue death sentences in three types of cases: offenses against God (*hudud*), including apostasy, offenses against persons, such as murder and rape, both of which are defined under Shari'a, or Islamic law, or on a 'discretionary basis' for any act that a judge considers merits the death penalty, even where those acts are not defined as criminal offenses.").

Iran similarly punishes apostasy. Although the Iranian Constitution calls for respect for human rights, such respect *"only* applies to all who refrain from *engaging in conspiracy or activity against Islam* and the Islamic Republic of Iran."[223] As discussed above, apostasy is equivalent to treason against both the state and Islam.[224]

The Iranian Penal Code mandates execution for anyone whose "insults [to] the Islamic sanctities" rise to the level of "speaking disparagingly of Prophet Muhammad."[225] The Press Code also requires that a person whose "insults [to] Islam and its sanctities through the press" amount to apostasy must be "sentenced as an apostate."[226] Under this law, virtually any insult to Islam amounts to apostasy, thus rendering conversion from Islam—without more— inherently disparaging of Muhammad and deserving of death. These laws thus create an atmosphere of active government hostility toward those who change their religious faith from Islam.

Like Iran, Afghanistan treats apostasy as a criminal offense punishable by death. In a 2010 case, Said Musa, a Christian convert, was arrested in Afghanistan for changing his religious belief.[227] Musa and twenty-five other Christian converts were taken into police custody on May 25, 2010, after a news station broadcasted a video of the group conducting a Christian worship service.[228] A war veteran and father of eight young children, Musa was placed on trial

---

[223]QANUNI ASSASSI JUMHURII ISLAMAI IRAN [THE CONSTITUTION OF THE ISLAMIC REPUBLIC OF IRAN] 1980, art. 14 (emphases added).

[224]*See supra* notes 209–210 and accompanying text; *see also* SAEED & SAEED, *supra* note 207, at 90; Barnabas Aid, *Iranian Parliament Provisionally Approves Death Penalty for Leaving Islam* (Oct. 2, 2008), http://www.barnabasfund.org/?m=7%23227&a=608 (Apostasy from Islam is "viewed by most Muslims as equivalent to treason," i.e., "activity against Islam.").

[225]PENAL CODE [C. PEN.] art. 513 (Iran), *available at* www.iranhrdc.org/httpdocs/english/pdfs/Codes/ ThePenalCode.pdf ("Anyone who insults the Islamic sanctities or any of the *imams* or her excellency *Sadigheh Tahereh* should be executed if his insult equals to speaking disparagingly of Prophet Muhammad. Otherwise, [he] should be imprisoned from one to five years.").

[226]PRESS CODE [C. PR.] art. 26 (Iran), *available at* http://www.parstimes.com/law/press_law.html.

[227]Paul Marshall, *America Quiet on the Execution of Afghan Christian Said Musa*, NAT'L REVIEW ONLINE (Feb. 18, 2011), http://www.nationalreview.com/corner/260050/america-quiet-execution-afghan-christian-said-musa-paul-marshall.

[228]*Id.*

for apostasy without any legal representation or knowledge of the charges brought against him.[229] Although the Afghani government received considerable criticism from the international community, government officials remained completely unapologetic for his prosecution: "The sentence for a convert is death and there is no exception . . . . They must be sentenced to death to serve as a lesson for others."[230] While international pressure prompted Afghani officials to release Musa, some of his fellow congregants and others still remain in prison where they await possible execution.[231]

Numerous recent incidents demonstrate the real consequences that befall apostates even in contemporary Western societies. Recently, in the Netherlands (a nation renowned for its commitments to liberty and tolerance), Ehsan Jami, who was born into a Muslim family but now rejects Islam as an adult, has begun a campaign with the express purpose of "mak[ing] it easier to renounce Islam."[232] Not surprisingly, his announcement was met with death threats, forcing him into hiding.[233] In both the Netherlands and in Germany, the leaders of the national chapters of the Council of Ex-Muslims are under constant police protection.[234] In Great Britain, "a significant portion of British Muslims think that [killing apostates] is not merely right, but a religious obligation: a survey by the think-tank Policy Exchange, for instance, revealed that 36 per cent [sic] of young Muslims believe that those who leave Islam should be killed."[235]

---

[229] Id.

[230] Id.

[231] Patrick Goodenough, *Plight of Christian Converts Highlights Absence of Religious Freedom in Afghanistan*, CNSNEWS.COM (Feb. 25, 2011), http://www.cnsnews.com/news/article/plight-apostate-converts-highlights-abse.

[232] David Charter, *Young Muslims Begin Dangerous Fight for the Right to Abandon Faith*, THE TIMES (Sept. 11, 2007), http://www.timesonline.co.uk/tol/news/world/europe/article2426314.ece.

[233] Id.

[234] *Muslim Apostates Threatened over Christianity*, THE TELEGRAPH (Dec. 09, 2007), http://www.telegraph.co.uk/news/uknews/1571970/Muslim-apostates-threatened-over-Christianity.html.

[235] Id.

Sofia Allem testified firsthand about the personal effects of this belief.[236] Sofia was raised in London by Muslim parents, but she in no way classifies them as extremists.[237] They sent her to attend school at a university, respected her choice in rejecting a proposal of arranged marriage, and allowed her to dress how she wanted.[238] But things changed after Sofia's mother discovered a Bible in her bedroom. Her parents initially became distraught, but their despondency soon turned into wrath, threats, and violence.[239] Her mother began to "beat [her] about the head," and soon her parents brought in all of her uncles, who tried to intimidate Sofia out of her conversion (i.e., apostasy).[240] Finding her unmoved by their threats and violence, her parents resorted to kicking her out of the house, but not before both of them had shouted death threats and told her that she deserved to die.[241] "They put their loyalty to Islam above any love for me," Sofia stated.[242]

In the United States, a teenage girl, Rifqa Bary, made national news in 2009 when she ran away from her parents in Ohio after they threatened to kill her for becoming a Christian.[243] When Rifqa's family moved from Sri Lanka to Ohio, Rifqa excelled in school as a straight "A" student, cheerleader, and member of the track and field teams.[244] What her parents did not expect, however, was that Rifqa would one day convert from Islam to Christianity.[245] At age thirteen, Rifqa made the decision to become a Christian; and in 2009, shortly after she was baptized, Rifqa ran away from her

---

[236]The name "Sofia Allem" is an alias. The young woman spoke out on condition of anonymity. *Id.*
[237]*Id.*
[238]*Id.*
[239]*Id.*
[240]*Id.*
[241]*Id.*
[242]*Id.* (internal quotation marks omitted).
[243]Arian Campo Flores, *The Christian Runaway*, NEWSWEEK (Sept. 9, 2009), http://www.newsweek.com/2009/09/09/the-christian-runaway.html.
[244]*Id.*
[245]*Id.*

Muslim parents.[246] In a television interview, Rifqa explained in her own words the impetus for her flight from her parents: "He [Rifqa's father] would kill me or send me back to Sri Lanka."[247]

Regardless of the consequence that *Shariah* mandates for apostates, the mere fact that Islam punishes a person for disbelief *at all* diametrically opposes U.S. law guaranteeing freedom of religion, which is among the most cherished and fundamental rights under U.S. law.[248] Further, *Shariah* not only dictates that apostates deserve death, but it also declares that those who kill apostates deserve *reward*.[249] *Shariah* therefore encourages vigilante-type assassinations of those deemed to be apostates. It is clear that any law utterly forbidding a right as fundamental as freedom of religion and prescribing the slaughter of those who choose to exercise that freedom cannot exist in a just and free society.

B. FREEDOM OF SPEECH

The First Amendment to the U.S. Constitution also protects the right to freedom of speech: "Congress shall make no law . . . abridging the freedom of speech."[250] Outside of the "uninhibited, robust, and wide-open" free speech protection of the First Amendment,[251] only several narrow categories of speech are exempted from constitutional protection, including fighting

---

[246]*Id.*

[247]Tim Padgett, *A Florida Culture-War Circus over Rifqa Bary*, TIME (Aug. 24, 2009), http://www.time.com/time/nation/article/0,8599,1918228,00.html.

[248]*E.g.*, Church of Lukumi Babalu Aye v. City of Hialeah, 508 U.S. 520, 531 (1993) ("'[R]eligious beliefs need not be acceptable, logical, consistent, or comprehensible to others in order to merit First Amendment protection.'" (quoting Thompson v. Review Bd. of Ind. Empl. Sec. Div., 450 U.S. 707, 714 (1981))); *see also* Zorach v. Clauson, 343 U.S. 306, 314 (1952) ("We are a religious people whose institutions presuppose a Supreme Being. We guarantee the freedom to worship as one chooses. We make room for as wide a variety of beliefs and creeds as the spiritual needs of man deem necessary . . . . The government must be neutral when it comes to competition between sects. It may not thrust any sect on any person. It may not make a religious observance compulsory. It may not coerce anyone to attend church, to observe a religious holiday, or to take religious instruction.").

[249]*See* SAHIH BUKHARI, *supra* note 69 and accompanying text.

[250]U.S. CONST. amend. I.

[251]New York Times Co. v. Sullivan, 376 U.S. 254, 270 (1964).

words,[252] defamatory falsehoods,[253] and obscene materials.[254]

The Supreme Court has reasoned that these forms of speech fall outside the scope of the First Amendment because they are "of such slight social value as a step to truth that any benefit that may be derived from them is clearly outweighed by the social interest in order and morality."[255] These narrow categories of regulated speech demonstrate the firm commitment the United States has made to uphold the freedom of speech guaranteed by the Constitution.

Islamic law, on the other hand, prohibits "blasphemy" of Allah and Muhammad.[256] Moreover, some Islamic countries criminalize any speech or act insulting Islam or its prophets or desecrating the *Qur'an* or any of its verses.[257] For Muslims, blasphemy can also constitute the crime of apostasy,[258] which is the "ugliest form of unbelief."[259] Moreover, most schools of Islam do not extend repentance as an option for blasphemy.[260] Consequently,

---

[252]Chaplinsky v. New Hampshire, 315 U.S. 568, 574 (1942).

[253]*Sullivan*, 376 U.S. at 279–80.

[254]Miller v. California, 413 U.S. 15, 23 (1973).

[255]*Chaplinsky*, 315 U.S. at 571–72.

[256]QUR'AN, *supra* note 11, at *Surah* 4:140 ("Already has [Allah] sent you word in the book, that when ye hear the signs of Allah held in defiance and ridicule, ye are not to sit with them unless they turn to a different theme . . . ."); *see also* SAHIH BUKHARI, *supra* note 69, at Vol. 3, Bk. 46, No. 705 ("The Prophet said, 'Allah has accepted my invocation to forgive what whispers in the hearts of my followers, *unless* they put it to action *or utter it.*'" (emphasis added)).

[257]*See, e.g.*, PAK. PENAL CODE, ch. XV (1860), *available at* http://www.pakistani.org/pakistan/legislation/1860/actXLVof1860.html.

[258]RELIANCE OF THE TRAVELLER, *supra* note 10, at 596–97.

> Among the things that entail apostasy from Islam . . . are: to speak words that imply unbelief such as 'Allah is the third of three,' or 'I am Allah'; to revile Allah or His messenger; to be sarcastic about Allah's name; to deny any verse of the Koran or anything which by scholarly consensus belongs to it, or to add a verse that does not belong to it; to mockingly say, "I don't know what faith is"; to describe a Muslim or someone who wants to become a Muslim in terms of *unbelief*; to revile the religion of Islam; to be sarcastic about any ruling of the Sacred Law [Shariah]; or to deny that Allah intended the Prophet's message . . . . to be the religion followed by the entire world.

[259]*Id.* at 596.

[260]RUDOLPH PETERS, CRIME AND PUNISHMENT IN ISLAMIC LAW: THEORY AND PRACTICE FROM THE SIXTEENTH TO THE TWENTY-FIRST CENTURY 65 (2005) ("If the apostasy consisted in insulting the prophet (*sabb al-nabi*), according to most schools the apostate is not given an opportunity for repentance, but is killed immediately after the sentence."); *see also* SAHIH BUKHARI, *supra* note 69, at Vol. 3, Bk. 46, No. 705 ("The Prophet said, 'Allah has accepted my invocation to forgive what whispers in the hearts of my followers, *unless* they put it to action *or utter it.*'" (emphasis added)).

the lot of the blasphemer is death—and the death sentence may be carried out immediately after the blasphemous act.[261]

Some Islamic nations—including Saudi Arabia, Afghanistan, and Pakistan—have strict blasphemy laws that prescribe the death penalty upon conviction.[262] Other countries call for imprisoning such offenders.[263] Of the countries mentioned above, Pakistan has the strictest blasphemy laws. And, although Pakistan is not governed entirely by *Shariah* principles, it is increasingly intolerant of blasphemy, including mere "defamation" of Islam. For example, Pakistan's Penal Code institutes strict criminal liability for blasphemy of Islamic religious figures,[264] desecration

---

[261]PETERS, *supra* note 260, at 65.

[262]BUREAU OF DEMOCRACY, HUMAN RIGHTS, & LABOR, U.S. DEP'T OF STATE, INTERNATIONAL RELIGIOUS FREEDOM REPORT 2010: SAUDI ARABIA (Nov. 17, 2010), *available at* http://www.state.gov/g/drl/rls/irf/2010/148843.htm (In Saudi Arabia,"[b]lasphemy is a crime punishable by long prison terms or, in some cases, death."); BUREAU OF DEMOCRACY, HUMAN RIGHTS, & LABOR, U.S. DEP'T OF STATE INTERNATIONAL RELIGIOUS FREEDOM REPORT 2010: AFGHANISTAN (Nov. 17, 2010), *available at* http://www. state.gov/g/drl/rls/irf/2010/148786.htm ("Blasphemy is a capital crime under some interpretations of Islamic law in [Afghanistan], and according to such interpretations, an Islamic judge could punish blasphemy with death, if committed by a male over age 18 or a female over age 16 of sound mind."); PAK. PENAL CODE, ch. XV, § 295-C (1860) (providing that "[w]hoever . . . defiles the sacred name of the Holy Prophet Muhammad (peace be upon him) shall be punished with death, or imprisonment for life, and shall also be liable to fine").

[263]*E.g.*, PENAL CODE art. 98(f) (Egypt) (as amended in 2006) ("Whoever exploits religion in order to promote extremist ideologies by word of mouth, in writing or any other manner, with a view to stirring up sedition, disparaging or contempt of any divine religion or its adherents, or prejudicing national unity shall be punished with imprisonment between six months and five years or paying a fine of at least 500 Egyptian pounds."); BUREAU OF DEMOCRACY, HUMAN RIGHTS, & LABOR, U.S. DEP'T OF STATE, INTERNATIONAL RELIGIOUS FREEDOM REPORT 2005: JORDAN (2005), *available at* http://www.state.gov/g/drl/rls/hrrpt/2004/41724.htm ("[I]n February 2003, three journalists were charged with blasphemy and slandering the government. They received prison terms ranging from 2 to 6 months and returned to work after their release."); BUREAU OF DEMOCRACY, HUMAN RIGHTS, & LABOR, U.S. DEP'T OF STATE, INTERNATIONAL RELIGIOUS FREEDOM REPORT 2005: KUWAIT (2005), *available at* http://www.state. gov/g/drl/rls/irf/2005/51603.htm ("The 1961 Press and Publications Law specifically prohibits the publication of any material that attacks religions or incites persons to commit crimes, create hatred, or spread dissension among the public. There are laws against blasphemy, apostasy, and proselytizing. These laws sometimes have been used to restrict religious freedom."); BUREAU OF DEMOCRACY, HUMAN RIGHTS, & LABOR, U.S. DEP'T OF STATE, INTERNATIONAL RELIGIOUS FREEDOM REPORT 2010: KUWAIT (Nov. 17, 2010), *available at* http://www.state.gov/g/drl/rls/irf/2010/148828.htm. Indonesia, although not an official Islamic country, has a large Muslim population and punishes blasphemy. PENAL CODE art. 156a (Indonesia) (1952) (last amended in 1999) ("By a maximum imprisonment of five years shall be punished any person who deliberately in public gives expression to feelings or commits an act, which principally have the character of being at enmity with, abusing or staining a religion, adhered to in Indonesia; with the intention to prevent a person to adhere to any religion based on the belief of almighty God.").

[264]PAK. PENAL CODE, ch. XV (1860), § 298-A, *available at* http://www.pakistani.org/pakistan/legislation/1860/actXLVof1860.html.

of the *Qur'an*,[265] and anything that may be interpreted as blasphemy against Muhammad.[266] Additionally, the Pakistani Federal Shariat Court, which is specifically empowered to "examine and decide the question whether or not any law or provision of law is repugnant to the injunctions of Islam, as laid down in the Holy Quran and Sunnah of the Holy Prophet," and to "enhance the sentence" of any criminal punishment,[267] has made blasphemy of Muhammad an offense mandating the death penalty.[268]

Pakistan is rife with examples of the often-deadly effects of blasphemy laws on Muslims as well as non-Muslims.[269] In July 2010, two Christian brothers who had allegedly distributed blasphemous tracts were gunned down outside a Pakistani courthouse where they were being tried.[270] The shooters, allegedly connected with a local mosque, could not wait for the court to adjudicate the matter.[271] Instead, taking the law into their own hands, the gunmen executed the brothers in the street.[272] On November 8, 2010, a trial court in Pakistan sentenced a Christian mother of five to death by hanging for allegedly blaspheming Muhammad.[273] The woman, a farmhand,

---

[265]*Id.* § 295-B.

[266]*Id.* § 295-C ("Whoever by words, either spoken or written, or by visible representation or by any imputation, innuendo, or insinuation, directly or indirectly, defiles the sacred name of the Holy Prophet Muhammad (peace be upon him) shall be punished with death, or imprisonment for life, and shall also be liable to fine.").

[267]CONST. art. 203(D)–(DD) (Pak.).

[268]Qureshi v. Pakistan, PLD 1991 Federal Shariat Court 10 (1990) (holding alternate punishment of life imprisonment, as provided in PAK. PENAL CODE, ch. XV, § 295-C (1860), repugnant to the injunctions of Islam as given in the *Qur'an* and *Sunnah*).

[269]*See E.g.*, HUMAN RIGHTS FIRST, BLASPHEMY LAWS EXPOSED: THE CONSEQUENCES OF CRIMINALIZING "DEFAMATION OF RELIGIONS," *available at* http://www.humanrightsfirst.org/wp-content/uploads/Blasphemy_Cases.pdf ("In the words of Hina Jilani, a lawyer at the Human Rights Commission of Pakistan and former United Nations Special Rapporteur on Human Rights Defenders, the blasphemy laws in Pakistan are being used 'to spread fear and terror.'").

[270]*Two Christians Shot Dead Outside Pak Court*, SIFY NEWS (July 20, 2010), http://sify.com/news/two-christians-shot-dead-outside-pak-court-news-crime-khumAdjfcif.html.

[271]*Id.*

[272]*Id.* Additionally, it is clear that under *Shariah*, the killers would be immune from punishment because the men they killed were non-Muslims. *See infra* note 382.

[273]Rob Crilly & Aoun Sahi, *Christian Woman Sentenced to Death in Pakistan 'for Blasphemy'*, THE TELEGRAPH (Nov. 9, 2010), http://www.telegraph.co.uk/news/newstopics/religion/8120142/Christian-woman-sentenced-to-death-in-Pakistan-for-blasphemy.html; Saroop Ijaz, Opinion, *The Real Blasphemy*, L.A. TIMES (Jan. 5, 2011), http://articles.latimes.com/2011/jan/05/opinion/la-oe-ijaz-

was despised by her Muslim co-workers, who viewed her as unclean because she was not a Muslim.[274] While many in the international community, including Pope Benedict XVI, pleaded for the woman's death sentence to be dropped, a local Muslim cleric offered 500,000 rupees (6,000 USD) to anyone who would kill the Christian woman.[275] In making this offer, the cleric announced: "We will strongly resist any attempt to repeal laws which provide protection to the sanctity of Holy Prophet Mohammad."[276]

Additionally, in January 2011, Salmaan Taseer, Governor of the Punjab and a Muslim himself, was assassinated by one of his own bodyguards, who fired twenty-seven bullets into the governor's back.[277] Taseer had publicly advocated for the Christian woman who had been sentenced to death for blasphemy and, consequently, was himself declared a "blasphemer" by Islamic clerics.[278] Following Taseer's visit to the imprisoned woman, Muslim clerics warned Pakistan's president that he would experience "a countrywide agitation against him" if a presidential pardon was granted to the woman.[279] Intolerance of allegedly "blasphemous" speech in Pakistan is so strong that "[a]s Qadri [(Taseer's assassin)] was escorted into court in Islamabad, a rowdy crowd patted his back and kissed his cheek, as lawyers at the scene threw flowers."[280] Since the governor's murder, the Pakistani government has announced that it has no intention of amending the blasphemy laws.[281]

---

blasphemy-20110105.

[274]*Id.*

[275]*Cleric Offers Reward to Kill Christian Woman*, MSNBC (Dec. 3, 2010), http://www.msnbc.msn.com/id/40490458/ns/world_news-south_and_central_asia/.

[276]*Id.*

[277]*Punjab Governor Martyred*, DAILYTIMES (Jan. 5, 2011), http://dailytimes.com.pk/default.asp?page=2011\01\05\story_5-1-2011_pg1_1.

[278]Amir Mir, *The Controversy That Led to the Murder*, THE NEWS (Pakistan) (Jan. 5, 2011), http://www.thenews.com.pk/TodaysPrintDetail.aspx?ID=24010&Cat=2.

[279]*Id.*

[280]Sebastian Abbot, *Cheers and Tears in Pakistan After Assassination*, SEATTLE TIMES (Jan. 5, 2011), http://seattletimes.nwsource.com/html/nationworld/2013845535_apaspakistan.html?syndication=rss.

[281]*Id. Government Not Amending Blasphemy Laws, Says PM*, DAWN.COM (Jan. 18, 2011), http://www.

On the international level, OIC Member States have repeatedly refused to guarantee freedom of speech, particularly religious speech, to their citizens, with their very Charter declaring the purpose of "combat[ing] defamation of Islam" to be among the OIC's primary objectives.[282] OIC Member States have effectively disregarded religious free speech rights altogether because the OIC Charter limits speech to that which is "in *conformity with Islamic values*,"[283] meaning that blasphemy against Islam is unprotected speech. This limitation on the freedom of speech is also evidenced by some OIC Member States' reservations to the International Covenant on Civil and Political Rights' (ICCPR) free speech provisions.[284] The United States, on the other hand, qualified its acceptance of the ICCPR's speech provisions to guarantee *more* free speech rights than the covenant provided for and remain consistent with the U.S. Constitution.[285] In addition to Islamic countries' reservations to

---

dawn.com/2011/01/18/govt-not-amending-blasphemy-law-says-pm.html.

[282]Organisation of the Islamic Conference Charter art. 1, para. 12.

[283]*Id.* art. 15 ("The Independent Permanent Commission on Human Rights shall promote the civil, political, social and economic rights enshrined in the organisation's covenants and declarations and in universally agreed human rights instruments, in conformity with Islamic values.") (emphasis added); *see also Status of Treaties*, UNITED NATIONS TREATY SERIES (Feb. 4, 2011), http://treaties.un.org/Pages/ViewDetails.aspx?src=TREATY&mtdsg_no=IV-4&chapter=4&lang=en#EndDec.

[284]Article 19 of the ICCPR provides "the right to freedom of expression," which includes the "freedom to seek, receive and impart information and ideas of all kinds, regardless of frontiers, either orally, in writing or in print, in the form of art, or through any other media of his choice." International Covenant on Civil and Political Rights, Dec. 19, 1966, 999 U.N.T.S. 171. While some of the OIC Member States that have ratified the ICCPR have made reservations to Article 19, their other reservations pertaining to articles that apply to all other articles (like Article 3, which requires equal treatment of men and women) or to freedom of religion in general (Article 18) effectively limit Article 19 as well. *E.g.*, *Status of Treaties*, UNITED NATIONS TREATY SERIES: BAHRAIN ("The Government of the Kingdom of Bahrain interprets the Provisions of Article 3, (18) and (23) [marriage and family] as not affecting in any way the prescriptions of the Islamic Shariah."), MAURITANIA ("The Mauritanian Government, while accepting the provisions set out in Article 18 concerning freedom of thought, conscience and religion, declares that their application shall be without prejudice to the Islamic Shariah."), PAKISTAN ("'[The] Islamic Republic of Pakistan declares that the provisions of Articles 3, 6, 7, 18 and 19 shall be so applied to the extent that they are not repugnant to the Provisions of the Constitution of Pakistan and the Sharia laws.'"), (Feb. 4, 2011), http://treaties.un.org/Pages/ViewDetails.aspx?src=TREATY&mtdsg_no=IV-4&chapter=4&lang=en#EndDec.

[285]The United States accepted Article 20 only to the extent that it "does not authorize or require legislation or other action by the United States that would restrict the right of free speech and association protected by the Constitution and laws of the United States." *Status of Treaties*, UNITED NATIONS TREATY SERIES: UNITED STATES (Feb. 4, 2011), http://treaties.un.org/Pages/ViewDetails.aspx?src=TREATY&mtdsg_no=IV-4&chapter=4&lang=en#EndDec.

the ICCPR's speech provisions, the OIC Member States adopted their own version of international human rights standards through the Cairo Declaration.[286] This declaration dramatically reduced free speech rights to speech that "would not be contrary to the principles of the Shari'ah."[287] *Shariah* forbids whatever the authorities deem to be blasphemous and penalizes offenders with capital punishment.[288]

In addition to inward-focused efforts to stifle freedom of speech and expression, Islamic governments have moved their focus outward, repeatedly presenting resolutions to the U.N. Human Rights Council condemning "defamation of religions" worldwide.[289] Many Western nations, including the United States, oppose these resolutions every year because their purpose is to use an international mechanism to prevent people from speaking out against Islam.[290] Moreover, it is "problematic to reconcile the notion of defamation (of religion) with the concept of discrimination."[291] A Canadian representative at the U.N. also protested against extending the notion of defamation beyond its proper scope.[292] He argued that such an extension would "jeopardize the fundamental right to freedom of expression, which includes freedom of expression on religious subjects."[293]

American citizens have already begun to experience the chilling effects of foreign anti-defamation laws. Just last year, Congress passed a bill expressly designed to disregard any foreign defamation judgment that threatens to restrict Americans' freedom

[286]CAIRO DECLARATION, *supra* note 42, art. 22 (emphasis added).
[287]*Id.* art. 22.
[288]*See supra* note 256 and accompanying text.
[289]*See, e.g.*, U.N. Doc. A/C.3/65/L.46/Rev.1 (Nov. 19, 2010), *available at* http://www.eyeontheun.org/assets/attachments/documents/defrev.pdf; *see also* Laura MacInnis, *U.N. Body Adopts Resolution on Religious Defamation*, REUTERS (Mar. 26, 2009), http://www.reuters.com/article/idUSTRE52P60220090326.
[290]MacInnis, *supra* note 289.
[291]*Id.* (comments by the German representative at the resolution hearing) (internal quotation marks omitted).
[292]*Id.*
[293]*Id.*

of speech. In 2010, Congress passed the "Securing the Protection of our Enduring and Established Constitutional Heritage Act" (the "SPEECH Act"), which declares that the United States will only recognize foreign defamation judgments to the extent that "the defamation law applied in the foreign court's adjudication provided at least as much protection for freedom of speech and press in that case as would be provided by the First Amendment to the Constitution of the United States."[294]

In addition, concerns that anti-defamation laws will be used not only to suppress freedom of speech and the press, but also to suppress religious minorities have already been substantiated in Pakistan, where the U.S. Department of State's 2009 Human Rights Report recounts:

> Laws prohibiting blasphemy continued to be used against Christians, Ahmadis, and members of other religious groups, including Muslims. Lower courts often did not require adequate evidence in blasphemy cases, which led to some accused and convicted persons spending years in jail before higher courts eventually overturned their convictions or ordered them freed.
>
> [Additionally, o]riginal trial courts usually denied bail in blasphemy cases, claiming that because *defendants faced the death penalty*, they were likely to flee. Many defendants appealed the denial of bail, but bail often was not granted in advance of the trial. Lower courts frequently delayed decisions, experienced intimidation, and refused bail for fear of reprisal from extremist elements.[295]

As a result of blasphemy laws, persons whose speech

---

[294]Securing the Protection of our Enduring and Established Constitutional Heritage Act, Pub. L. No. 111-223, 124 Stat. 2380 (2010) (to be codified at 28 U.S.C. §§ 4101 et seq.).
[295]BUREAU OF DEMOCRACY, HUMAN RIGHTS, & LABOR, U.S. DEP'T OF STATE, 2009 HUMAN RIGHTS REPORT: PAKISTAN (Mar. 11 2010) (emphasis added), *available at* http://www.state.gov/g/drl/rls/hrrpt/2009/sca/136092.htm.

and conduct are determined to be "blasphemous" against Islam experience threats and acts of retaliation all over the world. Even citizens of nations that do not recognize *Shariah* find their freedom of speech stifled by threats of violence. Such was the experience of the Florida pastor who planned to burn the *Qur'an*. Notwithstanding the lack of wisdom and tactfulness of the proposed gesture, such expressive conduct is permissible speech in the United States. Yet, the plan elicited threats of retaliation and cautions of global unrest from all over the Muslim world, including Lebanon, Saudi Arabia, Indonesia, Syria, and Iran.[296] Similarly, Comedy Central, the U.S. television network that airs the irreverent adult cartoon "South Park"—a series that has mocked Protestants, Catholics, Mormons, Scientologists, Jews, and countless individuals and ideologies—censored an entire episode that satirically criticized Islam and Muhammad, citing death threats from Muslims to the show's creators.[297] The Danes received threats from Muslims in Pakistan and the Gaza Strip when, in a demonstration of support for the Danish cartoonist who had produced derogatory images of Muhammad, Denmark's leading newspapers reproduced one of his "blasphemous" cartoons in response to the discovery of a plot to kill the cartoonist.[298] Dutch politician Geert Wilders has been engaged in ongoing legal battles over his unfiltered criticism of political Islam and the dangers of *Shariah* because Holland, his homeland, has bowed to international and domestic pressure by Muslims seeking to silence Wilders' so-called blasphemy.[299] Finally, Salman Rushdie, who in 1988 authored the highly incendiary book, "The Satanic

---

[296]Black, *supra* note 138.

[297]Ed Pilkington, *South Park Censored After Fatwa Over Muhammad Episode*, THE GUARDIAN (Apr. 22, 2010), http://www.guardian.co.uk/tv-and-radio/2010/apr/22/south-park-censored-fatwa-muhammad.

[298]Associated Press, *Muslims Protest Danish Muhammad Cartoons*, MSNBC (Feb. 15, 2008), http://www.msnbc.msn.com/id/23186467/ns/world_news-europe.

[299]*See* Ayaan Hirsi Ali, *Free Speech on Trial in the Netherlands*, WALL ST. J. (Oct. 11, 2010), http://online.wsj.com/article/SB10001424052748704657304575539872944767984.html.

Verses," which portrayed Muhammad as a prophet misled by the devil, has received countless death threats from Muslims all over the world ever since. The threats were revived in 2007 after the Queen of England knighted him for his literary achievements in celebration of his sixtieth birthday.[300] Notably, worldwide protests over his knighthood included burning Rushdie and the Queen in effigy, offering bounties, and declaring religious and legal justification for any Muslim who would assassinate Rushdie by "strapping bombs to his body to protect the honour of the Prophet."[301]

While Islamic blasphemy laws are harmful enough in nation-states that have willfully opened their legal systems to *Shariah*, attempts to impose similar laws at the international level indicate that Islamic governments aspire to impose Islamic *Shariah* on the West, where speech that offends Muslims, Christians, or Jews—or any other faith, for that matter—is currently permissible.[302]

C. HOMOSEXUAL ACTS

Although most U.S. states do not recognize same-sex marriages or treat homosexual relations the same as heterosexual relationships,[303] United States law no longer punishes homosexual acts between consenting adults.[304]

Shariah, on the other hand, prescribes the death penalty for homosexual conduct. Muhammad said: "If you find anyone [engaging in homosexuality], kill the one who does it, and the one to whom it is done."[305] Homosexual sodomy is thus generally considered

---

[300]Ben Hoyle, *Muslim World Inflamed by Rushdie Knighthood*, THE TIMES (June 19, 2007), http://www.timesonline.co.uk/tol/comment/faith/article1951462.ece.

[301]*Id.* (internal quotation marks omitted).

[302]*See, e.g.*, Floyd Abrams, *UN-acceptable Censorship: The United Nations Tries to Outlaw Criticism of Islam*, DAILY NEWS (Jan. 14, 2009), http://www.nydailynews.com/opinions/2009/01/14/2009-01-14_unacceptable_censorship_the_united_natio.html.

[303]*See Issues by State*, DOMAWATCH.ORG, http://www.domawatch.org/stateissues/index.html (last visited Mar. 21, 2011).

[304]*See* Lawrence v. Texas, 539 U.S. 558, 583–85 (2003) (interpreting the Fourteenth Amendment's Due Process Clause to provide a right to engage in homosexual activity).

[305]ABU DAWUD, *supra* note 187, at Bk. 38, No. 4447 ("[Muhammad] said: If you find anyone doing as Lot's people did (i.e., committing homosexual sodomy), kill the one who does it, and the one to whom

a *hadd* offense (one requiring severe prescribed penalties) and is "equated to unlawful heterosexual intercourse by most [Islamic schools of jurisprudence]," but with heightened punishments:

> The Malikites, the Shiites and some Shafi'ites and Hanbalites are of the opinion that the penalty is death, either by stoning (Malikites), the sword (some Shafi'ites and Hanbalites) or, at the discretion of the court, by killing the culprit in the usual manner with a sword, stoning him, throwing him from a (high) wall or burning him (Shiites). Among the Shafi'ites and Hanbalites there are also scholars who hold that the death penalty by stoning applies only to the active partner . . . and that otherwise the punishment is flogging in combination with banishment.[306]

Based on the prohibition of homosexuality in *Shariah*, Islamic cultures continue to this day to punish homosexual behavior with harsh penalties, even up to death of the parties. For example, Articles 108 to 134 of the Islamic Penal Code of Iran are all dedicated to proscribing homosexual and lesbian acts.[307] In Iran, sexual intercourse between members of the same sex is a crime punishable by death for men[308] and by lashing for women.[309] Extreme punishment of homosexual acts is not isolated to Iran. In April 2005, Saudi Arabian officials sentenced more than 100 men to flogging and imprisonment for alleged homosexual conduct.[310] More recently, in March 2009, a Muslim cleric in Great Britain announced at a press conference that he believed, under *Shariah*, all

it is done."); *see also* RELIANCE OF THE TRAVELLER, *supra* note 10, at 665 (recounting Muhammad's statement that Muslims should kill "the one who sodomizes and the one who lets it be done to him"); MUHAMMAD SUBHI BIN HASAN HALLAQ, 2 FIQH ACCORDING TO THE QUR'AN & SUNNAH 442 (Sameh Strauch trans., Darussalam Books 2008) [hereinafter FIQH]. "*Fiqh*" means "the science of religious law, jurisprudence in Islam." WEHR, *supra* note 52, at 847.

[306] PETERS, *supra* note 260, at 61.

[307] MAJMUAHI QAVANINI JAZAI [CODE OF CRIMINAL LAWS] Tehran arts. 108–134 [1991] (Iran), *available at* http://mehr.org/Islamic_Penal_Code_of_Iran.pdf.

[308] *Id.* art. 110.

[309] *Id.* art. 129.

[310] *Saudi Arabia: Men 'Behaving Like Women' Face Flogging*, HUMAN RIGHTS WATCH (Apr. 6, 2005), http://www.hrw.org/en/news/2005/04/06/saudi-arabia-men-behaving-women-face-flogging.

homosexuals should face stoning to death.[311] The same cleric is also widely known for his belief that *Shariah* should be the law of the land in Great Britain and the United States.[312]

D. ALCOHOL CONSUMPTION

In 1933, the United States repealed the Eighteenth Amendment,[313] which banned alcoholic beverages.[314] Alcohol consumption has since become a matter governed by individual states, and none prohibits consumption by persons at least twenty-one years of age.[315] Punishments for violating alcohol consumption laws involve fines and, in some cases, short periods of confinement, but no state punishes violations of consumption laws with corporal punishment.[316]

Shariah, however, forbids consuming alcoholic beverages in any amount and at any age.[317] Moreover, drinking alcohol—from table wine to hard liquor—is classified as a *hadd* offense, which,

---

[311]Sam Greenhill, *All Homosexuals Should Be Stoned to Death, Says Muslim Preacher of Hate*, MAIL ONLINE (Mar. 21, 2009), http://www.dailymail.co.uk/news/article-1163510/All-homosexuals-stoned-death-says-Muslim-preacherhate.html#ixzz1DOjUWZK9.

[312]*Id.*; *supra* note 8.

[313]U.S. CONST. amend. XVIII (repealed 1933).

[314]U.S. CONST. amend. XXI (repealing the Eighteenth Amendment).

[315]*E.g.*, *Alcohol and DUI Laws*, ALCOHOLLAWS.ORG, http://www.alcohollaws.org/index.html (last visited Feb. 9, 2011); *see also, e.g.*, 18 PA. CONS. STAT. § 6308(a) (establishing the minimum age for consuming alcohol at twenty-one); South Dakota v. Dole, 483 U.S. 203, 211–12 (1987) (holding that Congress has authority under the Spending Clause to make receipt of federal funds conditional on whether a state's minimum drinking age is twenty-one).

[316]*E.g.*, ALASKA STAT. §§ 04.16.060, 04.16.180 (2010) (making it unlawful for anyone under the age of twenty-one years to purchase alcoholic beverages or to solicit another to purchase on his or her behalf, and penalizing such a violation with a class A misdemeanor); FLA. STAT. §§ 562.111, 775.082 (2003) (declaring it "unlawful for any person under the age of 21 years . . . to have in her or his possession alcoholic beverages" and penalizing violations with imprisonment of not more than sixty days); MASS. GEN. LAWS ch. 138, § 34A (2010) (punishing the purchase or solicitation for purchase of alcohol by anyone under the age of twenty-one years with a $300 fine); *see also generally LexisNexis 50 State Comparative Legislation/Regulation*, LEXISNEXIS (Apr. 2009).

[317]QUR'AN, *supra* note 11, at *Surah* 5:90–91 ("O ye who believe! Intoxicants and gambling . . . are an abomination—of Satan's handiwork; eschew such (abomination), that ye may prosper. Satan's plan is (but) to excite enmity and hatred between you, with intoxicants . . . , and hinder you from prayer: will ye not then abstain?"); *see also* SAHIH BUKHARI, *supra* note 69, at Vol. 8, Bk. 81, No. 763 ("Allah's Apostle said, 'When an adulterer commits illegal sexual intercourse, then he is not a believer at the time he is doing it; and when somebody drinks an alcoholic drink, then he is not believer at the time of drinking[;] and when a thief steals, he is not a believer at the time when he is stealing; and when a robber robs and the people look at him, then he is not a believer at the time of doing it.'"); *id.* at Vol. 9, Bk. 89, No. 284 (responding to mention of a regional alcoholic beverage, "[Muhammad] said, 'Every intoxicant is prohibited'").

according to *hadiths*, is punishable by a flogging of forty strokes.[318]

E. OFFERING ASYLUM TO VICTIMS OF HUMAN RIGHTS VIOLATIONS

United States law, consistent with international law on the status of refugees, offers asylum to "refugees."[319] Both U.S. and international law broadly define a "refugee" as one who is outside his country of nationality and who is "unable or unwilling to return to . . . that country because of persecution or a well-founded fear of persecution on account of [his] race, religion, nationality, membership in a particular social group, or political opinion."[320]

Countries governed by *Shariah* do not share this definition. The Cairo Declaration on Human Rights, which has been adopted by Islamic states, limits asylum to "[e]very man . . . *within the framework of the Shari'ah*."[321] This means that persons may seek asylum and be considered refugees only so long as their persecution is *not* on the basis of "an act regarded by the Shari'ah as a crime."[322] This limitation effectively bars all refugee claims in which the applicants are alleged blasphemers or apostates because both blasphemy and apostasy are crimes under *Shariah*.[323] Thus, while the United States offers asylum to individuals who experience persecution for exercising freedom of religion or speech, the *Shariah*-governed nations from which such individuals flee demand that the individuals be *denied* asylum on the ground that they committed a crime under *Shariah*. These two views are incompatible.[324]

---

[318]SAHIH BUKHARI, *supra* note 69, at Vol. 8, Bk. 81, No. 764 ("The Prophet beat a drunk with palm-leaf stalks and shoes. And Abu Bakr gave (such a sinner) forty lashes."); *see also* RELIANCE OF THE TRAVELLER, *supra* note 10, at 617 (prescribing a scourging of forty stripes but permitting as many as eighty stripes for voluntary alcohol consumption by post-pubescent individuals); PETERS, *supra* note 260, at 64.

[319]*See* Immigration and Nationality Act, 8 U.S.C. §§ 1101(a)(42), 1157, 1159; *The Refugee Convention of 1951 and Protocol of 1967*, art. 1 (1951), *available at* http://www.unhcr.org/3b66c2aa10.html.

[320]8 U.S.C. § 1101(a)(42).

[321]CAIRO DECLARATION, *supra* note 42, art. 12 (emphasis added).

[322]*Id.*

[323]*See supra* Chapter 3.A, B.

[324]This is not to say that Islamic countries would not accept as refugees Muslims who face persecution based on their religion; the point is simply that Islamic governments will not accept refugees whose basis of persecution is a crime under *Shariah*.

CHAPTER FOUR

ISLAMIC CRIMINAL LAW

Legal systems generally reflect prevalent societal values. Societies criminalize or otherwise penalize conduct of which they disapprove and, conversely, reward behavior of which they approve. Consequently, a wide-ranging spectrum of punishments and rewards based on the corresponding degree of societal approval or disapproval becomes the legal system.[325] Therefore, conduct a society condemns the most strongly is conduct that it punishes the most severely. *Shariah* is no exception.[326] The Islamic principles that underlie criminal *Shariah* serve to classify offenses and to dictate corresponding consequences; the punishments that follow depend upon the significance of the religious values breached by the offense.[327] Accordingly, to understand criminal *Shariah* and its many applications, it is crucial to recognize the unique Islamic values that give rise to particular offenses.

Crucially, the objectives of *Shariah* punishments cannot be compared to Western penal systems' objectives.[328] While *Shariah* punishments do recognize some Western objectives, such as deterrence (general and specific), retribution, and rehabilitation, *Shariah* is unlike Western legal systems in at least one very significant respect: Islamic criminal *Shariah* intertwines significant religious rules with commonly held societal objectives.[329] Among

---

[325]PETERS, *supra* note 260, at 1 ("Criminal laws . . . give an insight into what a society and its rulers regard as its core values.").
[326]See the discussion of *Shariah* offenses in Section A.
[327]*See* PETERS, *supra* note 260, at 1.
[328]Islamic criminal law has been recognized by the West as "repugnant to natural justice." *Id*. at 109.
[329]*See* RELIANCE OF THE TRAVELLER, *supra* note 10, at 674 ("[I]n the hadith of the adulteress who purified herself by voluntarily being stoned to death, [Muhammad's] remark [was], 'She has made a repentance so sincere that if even a tax taker repented with the like of it, he would be forgiven.'"); *see also* PETERS, *supra* note 260, at 30.

these societal objectives are two religion-based goals: 1) satisfying claims that Allah holds against perpetrators (*hadd* offenses); and 2) modeling, in this life, rewards and punishments that Allah has promised for the afterlife.[330] This reward-punishment paradigm influences all aspects of Islamic criminal justice. Accordingly, *Shariah* emphasizes deterrence, *even if it leads to an injustice to the accused*, to elicit "moral" behavior in the present life that will reap spiritual reward in the afterlife.[331] This required union of the sacred and the secular reveals the "deep divide between [American] and Muslim cultural assumptions and notions of justice."[332] Thus, rendering a side-by-side comparison between the two systems is exceedingly difficult.

A. CLASSIFICATION OF *SHARIAH* OFFENSES

Islamic criminal *Shariah* is not a "single, unified branch of the law" but rather a conglomeration of personal, societal, and religious offenses, all of which are punishable by the state and some of which are either avenged or pardoned by individual victims (or their families), without any intervention by the state.[333] Islamic criminal law can be divided into three subcategories: (1) offenses against persons, (2) offenses against Allah, and (3) offenses against society.[334] Offenses against persons include acts such as homicide and personal injury. These offenses are generally punished with

---

[330]*See* QUR'AN, *supra* note 11, at *Surah* 4:31 (promising paradise to those who avoid "the most heinous of the things which ye are forbidden to do"); RELIANCE OF THE TRAVELLER, *supra* note 10, at 652 (Because of the verse that promises admittance to paradise upon avoidance of the most heinous things, Muslims "are obliged to learn what [the heinous things] are, that the Muslim may avoid them."); *see also* PETERS, *supra* note 260, at 30–31.

[331]QUR'AN, *supra* note 11, at *Surah* 5:38 ("As to the thief, male or female, cut off his or her hands: a punishment *by way of example*, from Allah, for their crime . . . ." (emphasis added)); *id.* at *Surah* 79:25 ("But Allah did punish him (and made an) *example of him—in the hereafter, as in this life.*" (emphasis added)); PETERS, *supra* note 260, at 30 ("Deterrence (*zajr*) is the underlying principle of all fields of Islamic criminal law."); *see also* QUR'AN, *supra* note 11, at *Surah* 24:2 ("The woman and the man guilty of adultery or fornication—flog each of them with a hundred stripes . . . and *let a party of believers witness their punishment.*" (emphasis added)).

[332]PETERS, *supra* note 260, at 106.

[333]*Id.* at 7.

[334]*Id.*

"eye for an eye" retaliation (*qisas*)[335] or by financial penalties (*diya*).[336] Offenses against Allah and offenses against society differ dramatically from typical Western penal systems and therefore require a more careful analysis when evaluating the compatibility of *Shariah* with U.S. law.

1. Offenses with Fixed, Mandatory Punishments (*Hadd* Offenses)

Offenses against Allah (*hadd* offenses) are those that are mentioned in the *Qur'an* and that specifically violate a "claim of [Allah]."[337] *Hadd* offenses include theft, banditry, unlawful sexual intercourse, slander of a woman's chastity, alcohol consumption, and apostasy.[338] These crimes have severe prescribed penalties that must be carried out in public and often involve loss of life or limb.[339]

2. Offenses with Discretionary Punishments (*Tazir* Offenses)

Offenses against society (*tazir*) involve conduct that is sinful, forbidden, or harmful to public order or peace.[340] This catch-all category arms states with plenary power, as states may utilize offenses against society to punish those who they suspect have committed *hadd* offenses (those with severe prescribed penalties) that could not be proven, as well as to "punish at their discretion *all other* forms of sinful or socially and politically undesirable

---

[335]*See, e.g.*, Qur'an, *supra* note 11, at *Surah* 2:178 ("O ye who believe! The law of equality is prescribed to you in cases of murder: the free for the free, the slave for the slave, the woman for the woman."); Reliance of the Traveller, *supra* note 10, at 585 ("Retaliation is obligatory in return for injuries (A: part for commensurate part . . . ."). See Section E on Remedies for a detailed discussion of *qisas* and *diya* laws.

[336]Reliance of the Traveller, *supra* note 10, at 588 ("Indemnity (*diya*) is obligatory . . . in cases of death . . . .").

[337]Peters, *supra* note 260, at 7.

[338]*See id.*; Law in the Middle East, *supra* note 54, at 227; Fiqh, *supra* note 305, at 429–71. Apostasy (changing one's religion), is considered a civil liberty in the United States. *See supra* Chapter 3.A.

[339]Peters, *supra* note 260, at 7, 30, 55–65; *see also* Fiqh, *supra* note 305, at 429.

[340]*See* Reliance of the Traveller, *supra* note 10, at 619 ("Someone who commits an act of disobedience to Allah . . . that entails neither a prescribed legal penalty nor expiation, such as bearing false witness, is disciplined to the extent the caliph deems appropriate.") (internal citations omitted); Peters, *supra* note 260, at 7.

behaviour."[341] Moreover, for *tazir* offenses, "[t]he punitive powers of the authorities are hardly restricted by law and, as a consequence, the doctrine offers little protection to the accused."[342] *Tazir* offenses thus include "illegal sexual acts not amounting to intercourse; misappropriation not amounting to theft, such as embezzlement; and defamation on other grounds than forbidden sexual intercourse."[343] They also encompass failures to observe certain religious duties, such as praying or fasting.[344]

B. PROCEDURAL AND EVIDENTIARY REQUIREMENTS

In the United States, criminal conviction requires proof beyond a reasonable doubt for every element of an offense.[345] To meet its burden, the prosecution may submit both documentary and testimonial evidence—and the defendant may use documentary and testimonial evidence to rebut evidence submitted by the prosecution—so long as it is relevant.[346] Additionally, the testimonies of men and women and of religious and non-religious persons are of equal weight in U.S. courts.[347]

Under *Shariah*, the prosecution must generally prove its case by either testimony of witnesses or admissions from the defendant.[348] Generally, witnesses' testimony is only admitted if it comes from two male witnesses or one male and two female

---

[341]PETERS, *supra* note 260, at 7 (emphasis added).

[342]*Id.*

[343]*Id.* at 66.

[344]*Id.*

[345]*E.g.*, Patterson v. New York, 432 U.S. 197, 210 (1977) ("[T]he Due Process Clause requires the prosecution to prove beyond a reasonable doubt all of the elements included in the definition of the offense of which the defendant is charged.").

[346]FED. R. EVID. 402.

[347]*See* FED. R. EVID. 601 ("Every person is competent to be a witness except as otherwise provided in these rules."); FED. R. EVID. 610 ("Evidence of the beliefs or opinions of a witness on matters of religion is not admissible for the purpose of showing that by reason of their nature the witness' credibility is impaired or enhanced."). Moreover, the Constitution requires that men and women be treated equally. U.S. CONST. amend. XIV, § I ("No state shall . . . deny to any person within its jurisdiction the equal protection of the laws."). Any attempt to ascribe different weights to the testimony of men and women would violate the Fourteenth Amendment. *Id.*

[348]FIQH, *supra* note 305, at 514–16; PETERS, *supra* note 260, at 12.

witnesses.[349] *Hadiths* explain that the testimony of a woman is equal to half that of a man because of a supposed "deficiency of a woman's mind."[350] However, for crimes of unlawful sexual intercourse (such as rape), *Shariah* requires four male eyewitnesses to substantiate the woman's claim.[351]

Under *Shariah*, a defendant on trial for a fixed-punishment crime may face a discretionary penalty imposed by a *Shariah* court judge (*qadi*) despite a lack of evidence to support punishment for an otherwise fixed-punishment crime.[352] For example, if it is otherwise plausible that a man enters a prostitute's house and stays with her for some time, he may be beaten or imprisoned at the discretion of the *qadi*.[353]

C. THE WIDE-RANGING SPECTRUM OF CRIMINAL *SHARIAH* PUNISHMENTS

Consequences for committing criminal acts under *Shariah* range from punishments as lenient as verbal reprimands and payment of "blood money" to punishments as severe as public flogging, amputations, and even death by stoning.

1. Reprimand and Public Ridicule

Reprimand, typically applied to members of the elite, is the "lightest form of discretionary punishment" and consists of public disapproval of the offender's conduct.[354] Essentially, a reprimand can be thought of as a sort of "slap on the wrist." Similar to reprimand is public exposure to scorn (*tashhir*), except that instead of offenders

---

[349]QUR'AN, *supra* note 11, at *Surah* 2:282 ("And get two witnesses, out of your own men, and if there are not two men, then a man and two women, such as ye choose, for witnesses, so that if one of them errs, the other can remind her."); RELIANCE OF THE TRAVELLER, *supra* note 10, at 637 (maintaining that the testimony of two women is necessary to equal the testimony of one man).

[350]*See* SAHIH BUKHARI, *supra* note 69, at Vol. 3, Bk. 48, No. 826 ("The Prophet said 'Isn't the witness of a woman equal to half of that of a man?' The woman said, 'yes.' He said, 'This is because of the deficiency of a woman's mind.'").

[351]RELIANCE OF THE TRAVELLER, *supra* note 10, at 638; *see also infra* Chapter 5.B & Chapter 4.E.3.

[352]PETERS, *supra* note 260, at 16.

[353]*Id.*

[354]*Id.* at 33.

being chastised merely by authorities, they are made the objects of public ridicule,[355] which may be accomplished by blackening the face of the offenders and parading them through the area on the back of a donkey.[356]

2. Flogging

Flogging (*jald*) is a common penalty under *Shariah* for offenses ranging from alcohol consumption to unlawful sexual intercourse.[357] Flogging is typically administered with a leather whip, and the force to be used in lashing the offender varies depending upon the severity of the crime.[358] Based on the *Qur'an*'s instruction, flogging is even more commendable when the punishment is carried out before public witnesses.[359]

3. Amputation

Theft and rebellion are notoriously met with severe punishment under *Shariah*. Thieves are punished by amputating their right hand.[360] The left foot is also commonly removed from repeat offenders and other rebels who have previously lost their right hand as a punishment.[361] The act of cutting off the right hand

---

[355]*Id.* at 34 (providing examples from the Ottoman period of the use of public humiliation and explaining that offenders were "parad[ed] . . . through the streets" with a "town-crier announcing the culprit's offences").

[356]*E.g.*, *Historic Death Sentence for Christian Woman for Blasphemy in Pakistan*, CROSS RHYTHMS (Nov. 8, 2010), http://www.crossrhythms.co.uk/articles/life/Historic_Death_Sentence_For_Christian _Woman_For_Blasphemy_In_Pakistan/42088/p1/. Aasia, a young Pakistani Christian woman, served as a farm worker for a Muslim landlord. One day while working in the fields, her fellow workers pressured her to renounce Christ and accept Islam. Aasia responded by telling them that "Christ had died on the cross for their sins and then asked them what Mohammed had done for them." *Id.* The Muslim women then beat her, and men locked her in a room. After announcing what she had done over a PA system of a local mosque, leaders informed the village of plans to "parad[e] her through the village on a donkey" with "her face blackened." *Id.* Aasia's children were also beaten. She was sentenced to death for blasphemy. *Id.*

[357]QUR'AN, *supra* note 11, at *Surah* 24:2; SAHIH BUKHARI, *supra* note 69, at Vol. 8, Bk. 82, Nos. 772, 823.

[358]PETERS, *supra* note 260, at 35.

[359]QUR'AN, *supra* note 11, at *Surah* 24:2 ("The woman and the man guilty of adultery or fornication— flog each one of them with a hundred stripes: Let not compassion move you in their case . . . and let a party of believers witness their punishment.").

[360]*Id.* at *Surah* 5:38; RELIANCE OF THE TRAVELLER, *supra* note 10, at 613–14; *see also infra* Chapter 4.E.1.

[361]RELIANCE OF THE TRAVELLER, *supra* note 10, at 614.

and left foot is known as "cross-amputation" (*al-qat' min-khilāf*).[362]

4. Stoning

The most severe punishment under *Shariah* is death by stoning. Unlike U.S. and international law, which prohibit "cruel and unusual punishment" by the state,[363] *Shariah* imposes the death penalty by stoning for offenses seldom, if ever, punished in the West, such as homosexual intercourse[364] and adultery.[365]

D. REMEDIES

1. Retaliation (*Qisas*)—Equality in Punishment

Another distinctive feature of Islamic criminal *Shariah* is retaliation (*qisas*).[366] In cases of bodily harm or homicide, the *Qur'an* mandates retaliation (essentially, punishment in kind), declaring, "O ye who believe! The law of equality (retaliation) is prescribed to you in cases of murder: the free for the free, the slave for the slave, the woman for the woman."[367] Elsewhere the *Qur'an* states, "We [have ordained] for them: 'Life for life, eye for eye, nose for nose, ear for ear, tooth for tooth, and wounds equal for equal.'"[368]

Additionally, numerous *hadiths* provide examples in which Muhammad either broadly allowed for or applied to a particular instance "eye for an eye" retaliation. In one case, a Jew who allegedly

---

[362]PETERS, *supra* note 260, at 36.

[363]*See, e.g.*, U.S. CONST. amend. VIII ("Excessive bail shall not be required, nor excessive fines imposed, nor cruel and unusual punishments inflicted."); UDHR, *supra* note 178, art. 5 ("No one shall be subjected to torture or to cruel, inhuman or degrading treatment or punishment."); European Convention on Human Rights, art. 3, Council of Europe (Sept. 3, 1953) ("No one shall be subjected to . . . inhuman or degrading treatment or punishment.").

[364]RELIANCE OF THE TRAVELLER, *supra* note 10, at 610–11 (mandating stoning for homosexuals "with the capacity to remain chaste" and scourging with 100 stripes for those lacking "the capacity to remain chaste"); *see also supra* Chapter 3.C.

[365]*See, e.g.*, SAHIH BUKHARI, *supra* note 69, at Vol. 6, Bk. 60, No. 79.

[366]*E.g.*, RELIANCE OF THE TRAVELLER, *supra* note 10, at 585 (treating the word "*qisas*" as synonymous with "retaliation for bodily injury or death").

[367]QUR'AN, *supra* note 11, at *Surah* 2:178 (After prescribing retaliation, the passage goes on to state, "But if any remission is made by the brother of the slain, then grant any reasonable demand, and compensate him with handsome gratitude (blood money) . . . ."); *see also* RELIANCE OF THE TRAVELLER, *supra* note 10, at 585 ("Retaliation is obligatory . . . when there is a[n] intentional injury against life or limb.").

[368]QUR'AN, *supra* note 11, at *Surah* 5:45.

crushed a girl's head between stones was brought to Muhammad for justice; Muhammad required that the Jew's head also be crushed between stones.[369] In another instance, Muhammad himself carried out his right to retaliation when he forced his companions to drink medicine after they, misunderstanding his commands when he was ill, gave him medicine after he refused to take any more.[370] Muhammad also approved retaliation for homicide when he stated that it was permissible to kill a Muslim in only three instances, one of which was retaliation for murder.[371]

Under *Shariah*, the prosecutor in homicide cases is not always the state, but often the victim's next of kin.[372] This is because *Shariah* views homicide not as an offense against the state, but as an offense against a person.[373] Consequently, the victim's next of kin may decide to initiate prosecution, reach a financial settlement,[374] or pardon the criminal defendant.[375] If a person who is entitled to retaliation forgoes his right to retaliate and instead pardons the offender, then "retaliation is no longer called for, and the deserving person is entitled to the indemnity."[376] Under retaliation rules, then, if an individual victim (in bodily injury cases) or his next of kin (in homicide cases) pardons an assailant or murderer in exchange

---

[369]SAHIH BUKHARI, *supra* note 69, at Vol. 9, Bk. 83, No. 15 ("A Jew crushed the head of a girl between two stones . . . [and] was brought to the Prophet and the Prophet kept on questioning him till he confessed, whereupon his head was crushed with stones.").

[370]*Id.* at Vol. 9, Bk. 83, No. 25 (Aisha narrated, "We poured medicine into the mouth of the Prophet during his ailment. He said, 'Don't pour medicine into my mouth.' (We thought he said that) out of the aversion a patient usually has for medicines. When he improved and felt better he said, 'There is none of you but will be forced to drink medicine, except Al-'Abbas, for he did not witness your deed.'").

[371]*Id.* at Vol. 9, Bk. 83, No. 17 ("The blood of a Muslim . . . cannot be shed except in three cases: In *Qisas* (retaliation) for murder, a married person who commits illegal sexual intercourse and the one who reverts from Islam (apostate) and leaves the Muslims.").

[372]PETERS, *supra* note 260, at 39 (stating that for the Islamic law of homicide prosecution is conducted by the victim's next of kin).

[373]*See id.* (discussing the underlying principles of the Islamic law of homicide, which include private prosecution by the victim or his next of kin and redress through retaliation or financial compensation).

[374]FIQH, *supra* note 305, at 476 (citing Bukhari (1/205, no. 112) and Muslim (2/988, no. 447/1335)).

[375]*Id.* at 485–86 (citing Ibn Majah (2/884, no. 2647), Abdu Dawwod (4/691-694, no. 4564), An-Nasa'i (8/42-43, no. 4801)).

[376] RELIANCE OF THE TRAVELLER, *supra* note 10, at 586–87; *see also* QUR'AN, *supra* note 11, at *Surah* 5:45 ("But if anyone remits the retaliation by way of charity, it is an act of atonement for himself.").

for a fee, the offender could go free, suffering no more punishment than payment of a sum demanded by the victim or his family.[377] Supporting this practice, Muhammad announced that, "if somebody is killed, his closest relative has the right to choose one of two things, i.e., either the blood money or retaliation by having the killer killed."[378]

Not only does *qisas* preclude justice between an offender and the society he has wronged, but it may also be applied inequitably. Specifically, most schools of Islamic jurisprudence allow *qisas* remedies for homicide or bodily harm but *only if* the victim's blood price is the same as or higher than the offender's blood price.[379] Under this system of social hierarchy enforced by *Shariah*, a free man cannot be executed for killing a slave;[380] no one may be sentenced to death for killing an apostate;[381] and a Muslim may not be killed for killing a non-Muslim.[382] However, Christians and Jews who live in Muslim countries are generally protected if they pay *jizyah* (poll tax).[383]

Further conflicts between U.S. law and *Shariah* arise in the area of parental rights. Under *qisas* (retaliation) rules, a parent may not be put to death for killing his child. "[N]or is retaliation permissible to a descendent [child] for . . . killing someone whose death would otherwise entitle the descendant to retaliate, such as

---

[377]*See id.*

[378]SAHIH BUKHARI, *supra* note 69, at Vol. 9, Bk. 83, No. 19.

[379]PETERS, *supra* note 260, at 47.

[380]QUR'AN, *supra* note 11, at *Surah* 2:178; FIQH, *supra* note 305, at 482–83.

[381]SAHIH BUKHARI, *supra* note 69, at Vol. 9, Bk. 89, No. 271; RELIANCE OF THE TRAVELLER, *supra* note 10, at 584; *see also* discussion *supra* Chapter 3.A.

[382]RELIANCE OF THE TRAVELLER, *supra* note 10, at 584; SAHIH BUKHARI, *supra* note 69, at Vol. 9, Bk. 83, No. 50; SAHIH BUKHARI, *supra* note 69, at Vol. 4, Bk. 52, No. 283 (stating that "no Muslim should be killed for killing an infidel"); *see also* FIQH, *supra* note 305, at 483.

[383]Christians and Jews who live in the territory of Islam are protected if they pay *jizyah*. QUR'AN, *supra* note 11, at *Surah* 9:29 ("Fight those who believe not in Allah nor the last day, nor hold that forbidden which hath been forbidden by Allah and his messenger, nor acknowledge the religion of truth, from among the people of the book, until they pay the *Jizyah*.").

when his father kills his mother."[384] Essentially, if the offender and the victim have the same heirs, the heirs may not retaliate against the offender.

2. Financial Penalties and "Blood Money" (*Diya*)— Indemnity

An alleged offender may be subject to financial penalties for his criminal act either in the form of fines, which are paid to the state, or "blood money" (*diya*), which is compensation paid directly to the offender's victim or the victim's heirs.[385] *Diya* is referred to in the *Qur'an* and practiced by Muhammad himself. One *hadith* recounts how Muhammad believed it was so important to preserve the blood money of the deceased that he paid 100 camels out of the camels of the *zakat* (obligatory charitable fund) when he feared that the blood money would be satisfied no other way.[386] Further, interpreting the *Qur'anic* principle of *diya* in case of intentional murder, Muhammad explained that the demand for *diya* should be reasonable and be compensated with handsome gratitude.[387]

Payment of the blood price thus essentially allows those who are guilty of homicide merely to pay the victim's next of kin a fee in exchange for pardon by the victim's family and avoiding imprisonment or the death penalty.[388] The value of the blood price can vary with the victim's sex, religion, and legal status. For example,

---

[384]RELIANCE OF THE TRAVELLER, *supra* note 10, at 584; *see also* FIQH, *supra* note 305, at 484 (citing Ibn Al-Jarood in '*Al-Muntaqa*' (no. 788), Ad-Daraqutni (3/140, no. 179), Al-Baihaqi in '*As-Sunan Al-Kubra*' (8/38)); PETERS, *supra* note 260, at 48.

[385]QUR'AN, *supra* note 11, at *Surah* 4:92.

[386]SAHIH BUKHARI, *supra* note 69, at Vol. 9, Bk. 83, No. 36.

[387]*Id.* at Vol. 9, Bk. 83, No. 20 (citing QUR'AN, *supra* note 11, at *Surah* 2:178 ("O ye who believe! The law of equality is prescribed to you in cases of murder: the free for the free, the slave for the slave, the woman for the woman. But if any remission is made by the brother of the slain, then grant any reasonable demand, and compensate him with handsome gratitude. This is a concession and a mercy from your lord.")).

[388]*See* QUR'AN, *supra* note 11, at *Surah* 4:92 (explaining that if a believer kills a fellow believer by mistake, he must pay the blood price); RELIANCE OF THE TRAVELLER, *supra* note 10, at 588 (providing the option of payment of the blood price in exchange for pardon even in cases of "purely intentional homicide").

the blood price for a Christian or Jewish man who lives in an Islamic country is only half of the price for a Muslim.[389] Similarly, the blood price of a woman is half that of a man.[390]

The practice of *diya* still thrives in nations where *Shariah* is dominant. For instance, in February 2011, eight Indian nationals who were on trial in Dubai in the United Arab Emirates (U.A.E.) for murdering a Pakistani man were officially pardoned by the victim's father after they paid the blood price.[391] This was on the heels of the U.A.E. Supreme Court's ruling that "[j]udges in capital murder cases must follow Sharia law without exception," which means that the victim's relatives may either prosecute the offender under *Shariah*'s retaliation law or accept the blood money for the victim, exonerating the murderer from the charge.[392] Additionally, in 2004, the "Presidency of *Shari'a* Courts"[393] in Qatar indicated that Qatar has no intention of abolishing *diya* when it announced that the blood price for killing a person was being *raised*.[394] Yemen is yet another *Shariah*-compliant nation that endorses blood money. In fact, its government came under fire two years ago for enforcing the death penalty against offenders whose offenses had been pardoned in exchange for blood money.[395] Criticizing the imposition of the

---

[389]Fiqh, *supra* note 305, at 494–95 (citing Abu Dawood (4/707, no. 4583), Ibn Majah (2/883, no. 2644), At-Tirmizi (4/25, no. 1413)) ("The blood-wit for a (Christian or Jewish) man who makes a covenant is half of the blood-wit for a free man.").

[390]*Id.* at 495 (citing Ibn Abi Shaibah (11/28/2), Al-Baihaqi (8/95-96)).

[391]I.P. Singh, *Indians on Death Row Pay Blood Money*, Times of India (Feb. 2, 2011), http://timesofindia.indiatimes.com/india/Indians-on-death-row-pay-blood-money/articleshow/7408241.cms. The payment of the blood money, however, did not completely absolve the Indian youth of government penalties, which their lawyer said could range from anywhere to 3 to 7 years' imprisonment, notwithstanding the degree of criminal homicide. *Id.*

[392]Hassan Hassan, *Murder Trials Must Follow Sharia Law, Supreme Court Rules*, The Nat'l (Jul. 16, 2010), http://www.thenational.ae/news/uae-news/courts/murder-trials-must-follow-sharia-law-supreme-court-rules.

[393]The Presidency of *Shari'a* Courts is composed of the 1st and 2nd stage *Shari'a* appeal courts, the Preliminary *Shari'a* Court, and various other offices. *The Judiciary*, Welcome to Qatar, http://www.qatarembassy.net/judiciary.asp (last visited Apr. 19, 2011).

[394]*Blood Money Raised to QR150~000*, Peninsula News Paper (Feb. 23, 2004), http://archive.thepeninsulaqatar.com/component/content/article/349-qatar-newsarchive/38376.html.

[395]Muadh Al-Maqtari, *315 Death Penalties Legislated by Four Yemeni Laws—Al-Lewa Faces Execution After Being Pardoned for Blood Money*, Yemen Times (Feb. 23, 2009), http://www.

death penalty in such cases, the Secretary General of the Social Democratic Forum in Yemen declared, "Yemeni laws are limited to . . . what is stipulated by the Islamic Sharia law."[396]

E. COMPARATIVE ANALYSIS BETWEEN SPECIFIC U.S. AND ISLAMIC CRIMINAL LAWS

When comparing the constitutional safeguards inherent in the American penal system to the punishments prescribed under Islamic criminal law, one can easily observe that the two systems are facially incompatible, giving the United States a compelling reason to bar within its boundaries any application of a contrary legal system like *Shariah*.

For example, the United States safeguards against cruel and unusual punishment. Although the Supreme Court of the United States has upheld the death penalty as constitutional in certain circumstances,[397] the Constitution prohibits cruel and unusual modes of execution.[398] In *Louisiana ex rel. Francis v. Resweber*, the Supreme Court interpreted the Eighth Amendment's Cruel and Unusual Punishment Clause to mean that, under the "traditional humanity of modern Anglo-American law," no punishment may inflict "unnecessary pain."[399] The Court in that case protected the state's imposition of death by electrocution, specifically noting that "[t]he cruelty against which the Constitution protects a convicted man is cruelty inherent in the method of punishment, not the

---

yementimes.com/DefaultDET.aspx?i=1236&p=local&a=1; Nasser Arrabyee, *Blood Money for Killing Yemeni Jew*, YEMEN OBSERVER (Mar. 3, 2009), http://www.yobserver.com/front-page/10015885.html (a Yemeni court ruled that payment of $27,500 in blood money be made for the murder of a Jewish man).
[396]*Id.* (internal quotation marks omitted).
[397]Roper v. Simmons, 543 U.S. 551, 568–69 (2005) (noting that "[b]ecause the death penalty is the most severe punishment, the Eighth Amendment applies to it with special force" and that "the death penalty is reserved for a narrow category of crimes and offenders"); *see also Roper*, 543 U.S. at 575 (holding that a death sentence for children under 18 is disproportionate and thus violates the Eighth Amendment); Atkins v. Virginia, 536 U.S. 304, 321 (2002) (holding that executing mentally retarded offenders violates the Eighth Amendment).
[398]U.S. CONST. amend. VIII ("Excessive bail shall not be required, nor excessive fines imposed, nor cruel and unusual punishments inflicted.").
[399]Louisiana *ex rel.* Francis v. Resweber, 329 U.S. 459, 463 (1947).

necessary suffering involved in any method employed to extinguish human life humanely." [400]

In determining which sentence to impose, the Federal Sentencing Act contains several guidelines which emphasize principles of proportionality and describe the practical implications of the Eighth Amendment.[401] A sentence must be "sufficient, but not greater than necessary," among other requirements, "to reflect the seriousness of the offense, to promote respect for the law, . . . to provide [a] just punishment for the offense; [and] to afford adequate deterrence to criminal conduct."[402] To achieve these goals, courts may consider the nature and circumstances of the offense, the "history and characteristics of the defendant," the "kinds of sentences available," and the sentencing ranges applicable to the specific category of offense.[403]

Shariah, however, follows no such standards in sentencing for crimes.[404] As explained above, there is no similar ban on punishments that demean human dignity or subject criminals to cruel and unusual punishments, especially for *hadd* offenses for which the penalties are harsh and immutable.[405]

1. Theft Crimes

The American Law Institute's Model Penal Code (MPC) classifies ordinary theft as a misdemeanor offense.[406] Under the MPC, theft constitutes a more serious third-degree felony offense

---

[400]*Id.* at 464.

[401]18 U.S.C. § 3553(a) (2006).

[402]18 U.S.C. § 3553 (a)(1)–(2)(A), (B) (2006).

[403]18 U.S.C. § 3553 (a)(1), (3)–(4) (2006); *see also* 28 U.S.C. § 994 (2006) (requiring the Sentencing Commission to provide sentencing guidelines to courts of law).

[404]*See* PETERS, *supra* note 260, at 16.

[405]*See id.* at 53–55; *see also* discussion *infra* Chapter 4.A.1.

[406]MODEL PENAL CODE § 223.1(2)(b) (last updated 1981); *see also* CAL. PEN. CODE §§ 489, 490 (2011) (specifying that punishment for larceny (theft without force or threat of force) should be fine or imprisonment, depending on the severity of the larceny); CAL. PEN. CODE §§ 211–213 (2011) (punishing robbery (theft by means of force or fear) by varying terms of imprisonment, depending on the severity of the robbery).

only under specific circumstances.[407] Even then, both a third-degree felony theft conviction and a misdemeanor theft conviction are punished with relatively minor monetary fines (less than $5,000 for conviction of a third-degree felony and less than $500 for a misdemeanor).[408] Even if a theft is elevated to a robbery offense, the highest monetary fine one could incur for robbery would be $10,000.[409]

Shariah's penalty for theft would violate the Eighth Amendment of the U.S. Constitution. *Shariah* punishes theft by amputating the thief's hands. The punishment is derived from explicit language in the *Qur'an*, which states, "[a]s to the thief, male or female, cut off his or her hands: A punishment by way of example, from Allah, for their crime . . . ."[410] A *hadith* explains that "[a] woman committed theft in the Ghazwa [(battle)] of the Conquest (of Mecca) and she was taken to the Prophet [Muhammad] who ordered her hand to be cut off."[411] In another instance, Muhammad cut off a thief's hand for stealing a shield.[412]

Amputations for thievery have been reported in both Iran and Saudi Arabia (both *Shariah*-compliant nations) as recently as 2010.[413] Amputation consists of severing the right hand from the wrist, although some Islamic sects cut off the four fingers and leave the thumb.[414] If the offender has already had his right hand amputated for a previous offense, or if his right hand is paralyzed, his left foot is amputated instead.[415] In fact, a repeat offender may

---

[407]MODEL PENAL CODE § 223.1(2)(a).

[408]*Id.* § 6.03(2), (4).

[409]*Id.* § 6.03(1).

[410]QUR'AN, *supra* note 11, at *Surah* 5:38; *see also* FIQH, *supra* note 305, at 445–52.

[411]*See* SAHIH BUKHARI, *supra* note 69, at Vol. 3, Bk. 48, No. 816.

[412]*Id.* at Vol. 8, Bk. 81, No. 788.

[413]Romulo Tangbawan, *Iran Orders Hand Amputation of Confessed Thief*, ARAB NEWS (Oct. 16, 2010), http://arabnews.com/middleeast/article162623.ece; *Thief's Hand Amputated as Punishment in Saudi Arabia*, EARTH TIMES (Aug. 15, 2010), http://www.earthtimes.org/articles/news/339474,amputated-punishment-saudi-arabia.html.

[414]PETERS, *supra* note 260, at 36.

[415]*Id.; see also* RELIANCE OF THE TRAVELLER, *supra* note 10, at 614 (explaining the amputation procedure

have his right hand amputated, followed by his left foot, then his left hand, and then his right foot.[416] Following an amputation, the amputee's newly-exposed tissue on the affected limb is burned with oil to stop the bleeding, and the cost for doing so is charged to him.[417]

The amputation procedure is primarily used to punish theft of a particular kind, which Muslim jurists generally agree requires surreptitiously taking movable property from a place either locked or guarded.[418] Because Islamic law places a high premium on the deterrence component of punishment,[419] amputation is often executed publicly.[420] Moreover, the punishment continues to serve as a deterrent whenever the criminal, or any other member of society, subsequently takes notice of his missing limb.

Although many Islamic scholars today argue that amputation is applied very sparingly, recent examples demonstrate otherwise. In 2009, a *Shariah* court in Somalia gained international attention after publicly amputating the hands and feet from four men who were convicted of stealing phones and guns.[421] According to one witness's account of the amputation, "[t]he men were bleeding and crying when the man cut their hands and feet off with a long knife . . . ."[422] News of the public amputation brought to the forefront the gruesomeness of *Shariah* punishments that will become the norm in Somalia if the Islamic terrorist group, *al-Shabab*, successfully

---

for repeat offenders).

[416]RELIANCE OF THE TRAVELLER, *supra* note 10, at 614.

[417]*Id.*; *see also* PETERS, *supra* note 260, at 36.

[418]PETERS, *supra* note 260, at 56; *see also* RELIANCE OF THE TRAVELLER, *supra* note 10, at 614 (requiring normal security for safeguarding similar articles in that place and time).

[419]*See, e.g.*, QUR'AN, *supra* note 11, at *Surah* 5:38 ("[a] punishment by way of example from Allah . . . ."); *see also* PETERS, *supra* note 260, at 30.

[420]*E.g.*, *Saudi Arabia Executions Disproportionately Target Foreign Nationals*, AMNESTY INT'L (Oct. 14, 2008), http://www.amnesty.org/en/news-and-updates/report/saudi-arabia-executions-target-foreign-nationals-20081014 (describing Saudi Arabia's implementation of the death penalty, "usually by beheading, generally in public," and "[i]n some cases, crucifixion follows execution.").

[421]Associated Press, *Somali Islamists Cut off Hands, Feet of Thieves*, MSNBC (June 25, 2009), http://www.msnbc.msn.com/id/31492608/ns/world_newsafrica/.

[422]*Id.*

overthrows Somalia's U.N.-backed government; *al-Shabab* would replace it with a strict Islamic government based on *Shariah*.[423]

In July 2010, Iranian government officials amputated the hands of five Iranian thieves following reported repeat offenses.[424] Even as recently as October 2010, Iranian authorities amputated the hand of a man convicted of two thefts in the Iranian city of Mashhad; and a judge sentenced an alleged "chocolate thief," who was found to have $900 and "a large amount of chocolate in his car," to amputation followed by a year of prison.[425]

Like Iran, reports of punishments carried out in Saudi Arabia, in accordance with Islamic *Shariah*, show cause for concern. According to a report by Neil Mackay, a journalist at the *Sunday Herald*, "[i]n 2000, there were 34 amputations—seven of which were 'cross amputations' where a prisoner's left hand and right foot are cut off. Under Sharia law, Saudi [judges have] also ordered prisoners to have their eyes removed."[426] Even after the United Nations Committee Against Torture (CAT) condemned Saudi Arabia in 2002 for its "imposition of corporal punishments, which are in breach of the [Convention against Torture and Other Cruel, Inhuman or Degrading Treatment or Punishment],"[427] and recommended that Saudi Arabia re-examine and alter its laws to "guarantee that no person is thereby subjected to torture or cruel,

---

[423]*Id.*

[424]The press has noted that amputations have lately been on the rise in Iran. *Five Amputated for Theft in Iran*, Now Lebanon (July 22, 2010), http://www.nowlebanon.com/NewsArchiveDetails. aspx?ID=188120.

[425]*Iranian Chocolate Thief Faces Hand Amputation*, BBC News (Oct. 16, 2010), http://www.bbc. co.uk/news/world-middle-east-11559750.

[426]Neil Mackay, *Saudi Justice Leaves Little Room for Sentiment; Lashings, Amputations*, Sunday Herald (Feb. 11, 2001), http://findarticles.com/p/articles/mi_qn4156/is_20010211/ai_ n13957022/?tag=content. This article reported that for cross-amputation, a prisoner's left hand and right foot are amputated. However, see Chapter 4.E.1 for a full discussion of amputation in theft crimes.

[427]U.N. Comm. Against Torture (CAT), UN Committee Against Torture: Conclusions and Recommendations: Saudi Arabia para. 8(b) (2002), *available at* http://www.unhcr.org/cgi-bin/texis/ vtx/refworld/rwmain?page=publisher&docid=3de279334&skip=0&publisher=CAT& amp;querysi=saudi&searchin=title&display=10&sort=date.

inhuman or degrading treatment or punishment," instances of such punishments have occurred through 2010.[428]

2. Violence Against Women

a. Domestic Violence

United States law condemns violence against women. Generally, in the United States, women are not only encouraged to leave violent relationships and are given safe harbor, both legally and institutionally,[429] but there is even a federal law banning such violence and imposing harsh sentences on offenders.[430] Additionally, in states with "fault" divorce grounds, domestic violence is uniformly considered a ground for divorce.[431] *Shariah*, on the other hand, permits men to use physical force to compel their wives to obey. *Qur'an, Surah* 4:34 states:

> (Husbands) are the protectors and maintainers of their (wives) because Allah has given the one more (strength) than the other, and because they support them from their means. Therefore the righteous women are devoutly obedient. . . . As to those women on whose part ye fear disloyalty and ill-conduct,

---

[428]*Id.* para. 8(d); *see also, e.g., Thief's Hand Amputated As Punishment in Saudi Arabia,* EARTH TIMES (Aug. 15, 2010), http://www.earthtimes.org/articles/news/339474,amputated-punishment-saudi-arabia.html. "A man has had his hand amputated as punishment for robbing a shop, Saudi Arabian officials said Sunday in a statement. . . . In Saudi Arabia, which follows strict Islamic law, corporal punishment is common, and convicted thieves often have a hand amputated." *Id.*

[429]Family courts throughout the United States treat domestic violence as grounds for divorce and consider domestic violence in determinations of awards for spousal support. Additionally, there are non-profit shelters throughout the United States that provide a home, basic necessities, and psychological and spiritual counseling for abused women and children. Moreover, women who are abused, or even threatened, may obtain permanent or temporary relief from abusive husbands or partners. *See, e.g., United States v. Young,* 2000 U.S. App. LEXIS 2443 (6th Cir. 2000) (affirming an abusive husband's conviction for violating the protective order issued in favor of his wife); *see also* Corrado v. Hedrick, 841 N.E.2d 723 (Mass. 2006) (affirming a protective order against a woman's fiancé (and his son) when they threatened her with physical violence).

[430]The Violence Against Women Act (VAWA) is a federal statute making interstate travel for the purpose of harassing, injuring, intimidating, or intending to kill a person's spouse or even dating partner a federal crime punishable with imprisonment ranging from one to twenty years. 18 U.S.C. § 2261 (2006); *see also* 18 U.S.C. §§ 2261A–2266 (2006). Moreover, the United States Department of Justice has established the Office on Violence Against Women to "reduce violence against women through the implementation of the [VAWA]." OVERVIEW, OFFICE ON VIOLENCE AGAINST WOMEN, U.S. DEP'T OF JUSTICE, http://www.ovw.usdoj.gov/overview.htm (last visited Apr. 1, 2011).

[431]*See* H. D. Warren, Annotation, *Single Act as Basis of Divorce or Separation on Ground of Cruelty,* 7 A.L.R.3d 761 (2010).

> admonish them (first), (next,) refuse to share their
> beds, (and last) beat them (lightly) . . . .[432]

Each parenthetical in the above *Qur'anic* text, which collectively aim to soften the harshness of the text, was inserted by the editors' own initiative and is not in the original Arabic version of the *Qur'an*.[433] Even so, there is not much that editors can do to mitigate what the text actually says—husbands may, and even should, beat their rebellious wives.

Although Muhammad is said to have personally disapproved of wife-beating, he instructed his followers to obey Allah's commands after Allah revealed to him the verse "authorizing the beating of a refractory (disobedient) wife."[434] Muhammad said, "I wanted one thing, but God has willed another—and what God has willed must be best."[435] On this basis, Muhammad declared to married men that "it is your right upon [your wives] that they do not allow any man whom you dislike to sit on your mattress; and if they do so, beat them, but not violently . . . ."[436] Muhammad also proclaimed in his "Farewell Pilgrimage, shortly before his death, that beating should be resorted to only if the wife 'has become guilty, in an obvious manner, of immoral conduct,' and that it should be done 'in such a way as not to cause pain . . . .'"[437] Thus, some interpreters of the *Qur'an* hold that beating, if done at all, should be done "with a

---

[432]QUR'AN, *supra* note 11, at *Surah* 4:34; *see also* MUHAMMAD ASAD, THE MESSAGE OF THE QUR'AN 126–27 (5th ed. 2003) ("Men shall take full care of women with the bounties which God has bestowed more abundantly on the former than on the latter, and with what they may spend out of their possessions. And the righteous women are the truly devout ones, who guard the intimacy which God has [ordained to be] guarded. And as for those women whose ill-will you have reason to fear, admonish them [first]; then leave them alone in bed; then beat them . . . .").

[433]*See* Int'l Inst. of Islamic Thought, *Preface to the New Edition, in* QUR'AN, *supra* note 11, at ix–x (explaining the editors' liberties in updating the text to meet "the ever-changing needs and demands of countless readers [of the *Qur'an*]" and their "desire to improve upon" the original text).

[434]ASAD, *supra* note 432, at 127 n.45.

[435]*Id.* (citing *Manār* V, 74) (internal quotation marks omitted).

[436]FIQH, *supra* note 305, at 156 (citing *hadiths* narrated by Al-Hakim (2/189–190), Al-Baihaqi (7/293), and At-Tabarani).

[437]ASAD, *supra* note 432, at 127 n.45.

toothbrush, or some such thing . . . ."[438]

The *Sunni* schools, however, agree that permissible wife-beating is not quite so benign. Generally, *Sunni Shariah* considers a "rebellious" wife deserving of physical correction; it accordingly sets forth the proper procedure for wife-beating. First, a husband must detect "signs of rebelliousness" in his wife (or wives). This is evident,

> whether in words, as when she answers him coldly when she used to do so politely, or he asks her to come to bed and she refuses, contrary to her usual habit; or whether in acts, as when he finds her averse to him when she was previously kind and cheerful . . . .[439]

Upon recognizing these "signs of rebelliousness" in his wife, a Muslim man should "warn[] her in words."[440] If she persists in her so-called rebellious attitude and "*commits* rebelliousness," he is then instructed to deny her sexual relations "and may *hit* her."[441]

To place some limitations on a husband's use of corporal punishment against his wife, some *Shariah* commentators would limit the striking to blows that will not "break bones, wound her, or cause blood to flow,"[442] and some would limit a husband's right to hit his wife (or wives) to repeated instances of rebellion. *Sunni Shariah* flatly rejects this view as weak: "[A husband] may hit [his wife or wives] whether she is rebellious only once or whether more than once, though a *weaker* opinion holds that he may not hit her

---

[438]*Id.* (citing *Tabari* and *Rāzi*) (internal citations and quotation marks omitted). A traditional Arab toothbrush is called a *miswak* or *siwak* and comes from the branch of an Arak tree. *Forget About your Toothbrush! Try Miswak*, DENTALHEALTHCITE.COM (Oct. 5, 2008), http://www.dentalhealthsite.com/what-is-miswak/. It is a *Sunnah* for Muslims to brush their teeth with a *miswak* as it was a practice and command of Muhammad. SAHIH BUKHARI, *supra* note 69, at Vol. 2, Bk. 13, No. 13 ("[Muhammad] . . . said, 'I have told you repeatedly to (use) the Siwak [or miswak]. (The Prophet put emphasis on the use of the Siwak.)'").

[439]RELIANCE OF THE TRAVELLER, *supra* note 10, at 540–41.

[440]*Id.*

[441]*Id.* at 541 (emphasis added).

[442]*Id.*

unless there is repeated rebelliousness."[443]

Some incorrectly suggest that domestic violence in Islamic countries is not religiously motivated because other nations also face this problem. Horrific displays of domestic violence by Muslims from all over the world, including many Western countries, prove just the opposite. For example, in the United Kingdom—a non-Islamic state, which is religiously and culturally distinct from most Islamic nations—domestic violence in Muslim families has even included honor killings. This wave of violence has prompted the British-based Centre for Social Cohesion to publish a study on the phenomenon.[444] Researchers emphasize that this is not a fleeting problem resulting from cultural clashes, but rather such customs are deeply rooted in Muslim societies (and hence not likely to improve through adjudication in *Shariah* courts):

> [H]onour killings, domestic violence, forced marriage and FGM [(female genital mutilation)] are not isolated practices but are instead part of a self-sustaining social system built on ideas of honour and cultural, ethnic and religious superiority. As a result of these ideas, every day around the UK women are being threatened with physical violence, rape, death, mutilation, abduction, drugging, false imprisonment, withdrawal from education and forced marriage by their own families. This is not a one-time problem of first-generation immigrants bringing practices from "back home" to the UK. Instead honour violence is now, to all intents and purposes, an indigenous and self-perpetuating phenomenon which is carried out by third and fourth generation immigrants who have been raised and educated in the UK.[445]

---

[443]*Id.* (emphasis added).
[444]CTR. FOR SOCIAL COHESION, CRIMES OF THE COMMUNITY: HONOUR-BASED VIOLENCE IN THE UK 1 (2d ed. 2010) [hereinafter HONOUR-BASED VIOLENCE IN THE UK], *available at* http://www.socialcohesion.co.uk/files/1229624550_1.pdf.
[445]*Id.*

This study provides harrowing anecdotes of the role Islamic teachings on female chastity have played in cultures that have traditionally embraced *Shariah*. As a result, Muslim women who live in the West, go to school in the West, and perhaps even work in the West still find themselves victims of domestic violence.

In Great Britain, for instance, Shahien Taj, director of a women's group in Cardiff, says that members of the city's Muslim community

> have distributed circulars that "name and shame" women who are seen acting too "western." Some of these detailed newsletters have . . . been sent to almost 1,250 Muslim homes with the aim of publicising the "immoral" behaviour of certain individuals—mainly women—and calling on the community to take action against them.[446]

What "action" the community should take is left open for interpretation. Statistics indicate that at least one method of dealing with women whose Western ways and alleged imprudence bring shame to their Muslim families is to attempt to subdue them by violent means, perhaps even by killing them.[447] For example, in 2005, Samaira Nazir, a twenty-five-year-old woman of Pakistani origin living in the UK, was a university graduate and businesswoman whose father, brother, and cousin "stabbed her 17 times and slashed her throat."[448] Nazir had refused an arranged marriage, instead choosing to continue a relationship with her boyfriend, and consequently suffered the ultimate punishment—death.[449]

Additionally, even if a woman were to successfully prosecute a man for domestic violence, the punishments dealt to men charged

---

[446]*Id*. at 32 (quotations in original).
[447]Tellingly, "[m]ost victims of honour killings reported in the UK are Muslim women from South Asia who are below the age of thirty." *Id*. at 41.
[448]*Id*. at 41–42.
[449]*Id*.

with domestic violence in *Shariah* courts tend to be heavily skewed in favor of men.[450] In Britain, where *Shariah* court judgments have been given the full force of law since 2008, those courts—rather than punishing abusive husbands or issuing protective orders for the victims—only ordered the abusive husbands to take anger management classes.[451] Doubtlessly feeling helpless after such mild rulings, in most cases, the abused women subsequently withdrew their complaints at local police departments and put an end to further investigations.[452]

In neighboring France, in April 2010, a French minister announced that a polygamous Muslim butcher living in France would be prosecuted for allegations of "beating at least one of his female companions and keeping his children 'locked away.'"[453] In a press conference, the accused Muslim remained completely unapologetic about his lifestyle and conduct, which he argued *were not forbidden under Islam*.[454] These examples from the United Kingdom and France refute the false assertion by some that instances of domestic abuse are limited to Islamic cultures instead of being permitted under *Shariah*, wherever practiced.

Domestic violence within Islam is primarily used as an instrument for maintaining family honor and female chastity. In keeping with the text and underlying principle of the *Qur'an*, *Surah* 4:34,[455] men (usually from within women's immediate household,

---

[450]*See generally* Sanjiv Buttoo, *Some Imams 'Biased Against Women'*, BBC NEWS (Dec. 15, 2008), http://news.bbc.co.uk/2/hi/7783627.stm.

[451]Abul Taher, *Revealed: UK's First Official Sharia Courts*, SUNDAY TIMES (Sept. 14, 2008), http://www.timesonline.co.uk/tol/comment/faith/article4749183.ece (recounting that in the six documented domestic violence cases adjudicated in Britain's *Shariah* courts as of September 2008, the *Shariah* judge in each case "ordered the husbands to take anger management classes and [obtain] mentoring from community elders"—without levying any other punishments).

[452]*See id.*

[453]*Suspected Polygamist Accused of Domestic Violence*, FRANCE24 (Apr. 29, 2010), http://www.france24.com/en/20100428-france-islam-suspected-polygamist-accused-domestic-violence-veil-niqab-burqa.

[454]*Id.*

[455]*See supra* note 432 and accompanying text.

but sometimes in concert with members of the extended family) use domestic violence to force women to comply with *Shariah* (e.g., forcing women, by abuse or threats of abuse, to wear traditional Islamic clothing such as the burqa).[456] Some social activists in Arab communities in the West estimate that domestic violence is an issue in as many as sixty percent of Arab families, a figure which they attribute in part to an Islamic hierarchy of values that disadvantages women.[457] Exalting a husband's honor and family cohesiveness over and against a woman's right to be free from abuse appears to have directly descended from Islamic *Shariah*.

Many women from Islamic countries seek refuge in Western countries where the laws protect their rights equally. For instance, in *In re S-A-*, a young Moroccan woman with "liberal Muslim beliefs" sought asylum in the United States on grounds that her father beat and abused her to enforce Islamic beliefs that women should not receive an education, should be covered all the time, and should not talk to men.[458] The woman's aunt testified that the young woman's father wanted her "'to . . . wear . . . the long robe to cover her face with the veil and when she . . . doesn't listen to him, . . . he abuse [*sic*] her, he beat her up . . . .'"[459] The aunt also testified that reporting the abuse to local police was futile because "under Muslim law . . . a father's power over his daughter is unfettered."[460] The young woman suffered terrible abuse. Her father punched and kicked her and even burned her legs to discourage her from showing her legs in public.[461] The Board of Immigration Appeals awarded her asylum.[462]

---

[456]*See infra* notes 458–474 and accompanying text.

[457]HONOUR-BASED VIOLENCE IN THE UK, *supra* note 444, at 28 ("Domestic violence is a huge problem. I'd say 60 [percent] of Arab families suffer from domestic violence." (quoting Mohammed Baleela, a project worker at the Domestic Violence Intervention Project in West London)).

[458]*In re* S-A-, 22 I. & N. Dec. 1328 (BIA 2000).

[459]*Id.* at 1330.

[460]*Id.*

[461]*Id.* at 1329.

[462]*Id.* at 1337. In *Limani v. Mukasey*, 538 F.3d 25 (1st Cir. 2008), an Algerian family sought asylum based in part on a threat made by a man in Algeria to the wife that "if he saw her again without a hijab

In *Yaylacicegi v. Gonzales*, a young Turkish woman applied for asylum in the United States, seeking to escape violent attacks from her brothers who beat her in order to make her more chaste.[463] Her brothers wanted her to wear "the traditional concealing clothing, such as a scarf covering her head," and to not leave the house, not talk on the phone, not seek employment, and not vote according to her conscience.[464] In one instance, the woman went to visit her family, and because she was not wearing either the head covering or the "head-to-toe clothing" required by her family, her brothers "beat and kicked her."[465] After the attack, she was diagnosed with a herniated disk in her spine.[466]

In 2010 in Somalia, a seventeen-year-old girl who allegedly left the Islamic faith was reported to have been shackled to a tree during the day and locked in a small dark room at night for more than a month by her parents. As reported, her father, in response to her resolve not to renounce her newfound faith, was quoted as saying that she was "very sick."[467]

As previously illustrated, *Shariah*-sanctioned domestic violence is not limited only to traditional Islamic cultures. Rather, migrating Muslims have carried their violent cultures into Western countries such as the United States, Great Britain, Germany, and France. In the United States, a 2010 New Jersey state case illustrates the implications of *Shariah*'s endorsement of violence

---

. . . he would kill her." *Id.* at 29. And in *Malak v. Ashcroft*, 110 Fed. App'x 217 (3d Cir. 2004), asylum petitioner Malak claimed that his neighbor told his wife that she must cover her head when leaving the apartment building and that the neighbor had "attacked and beaten" his wife. *Id.*

[463]Yaylacicegi v. Gonzales, 175 Fed. App'x 33, 34 (7th Cir. 2006).

[464]*Id.* at 33.

[465]*Id.* at 34.

[466]*Id.* Similarly, in *Zaza v. Ashcroft*, a Jordanian woman sought asylum in the United States based on threats made by the Muslim Brotherhood for not wearing the *hijab* (veil) that she "'should pay a price' and 'should be taught a lesson'—in a context where some women who did not wear the *hijab* had acid thrown on them or were cut with blades . . . ." Zaza v. Ashcroft, 106 Fed. App'x 640, 642 (9th Cir. 2004).

[467]*Family of 17-Year-Old Girl Abuses Her for Leaving Islam*, COMPASS DIRECT NEWS (June 15, 2010), http://www.compassdirect.org/english/country/somalia/21600/.

against women, which undoubtedly conflicts with U.S. law. In *S.D. v. M.J.R.*,[468] a New Jersey appellate court rightly refused to accommodate the sincerely held religious beliefs of a Muslim man who physically, verbally, and sexually abused his wife in accordance with *Shariah*.[469] The pattern of domestic abuse that led to the woman's lawsuit included threats of violence and bruises all over the woman's body, undressing her against her will, repeatedly slapping her in the face, and sexually assaulting and raping her on multiple occasions.[470] Despite the evidence of bruising, swelling, and bleeding caused by the abuse,[471] a local *imam* (Islamic spiritual leader) advised the woman that she should reconcile with her husband.[472] Unfortunately, this "reconciliation" only led to further violence and abuse.[473] The husband's justification for his actions was that his wife did not know how to cook, entertain guests, or perform other household functions to his standards.[474] The Muslim man told his wife, "This is according to our religion. You are my wife, I c[an] do anything to you. The woman, she should submit and do anything I ask her to do."[475] The court determined that the defendant did not have the criminal intent to sexually assault his wife because he was "operating under the belief" that "his desire to have sex when and whether he wanted to [] was something that was consistent with his [Islamic] practices and . . . was not prohibited."[476] As the New Jersey Court of Appeals recognized, *Shariah* applicable in domestic disputes cannot be assimilated into American law.

The following sections discuss how the seeds of domestic

---

[468]S.D. v. M.J.R., 2 A.3d 412 (N.J. Super. Ct. App. Div. 2010).
[469]*Id.* at 418–19, 43.
[470]*Id.* at 414–16.
[471]*Id.* at 414–15.
[472]*Id.* at 416.
[473]*Id.*
[474]*Id.* at 414–15.
[475]*Id.* at 416.
[476]*Id.* at 428.

violence under *Shariah* can often lead to intolerable criminal acts: female genital mutilation and honor killings.

b. Female Genital Mutilation

In the name of protecting female chastity, strict adherence to *Shariah* also requires the horrific practice of female genital mutilation (FGM). United States federal law describes FGM as "circumcis[ing], excis[ing], or infibulat[ing] the whole or any part of the labia majora or labia minora or clitoris" and makes it a federal offense to inflict female genital mutilation upon minors.[477] Although the *Qur'an* does not refer to FGM directly, *Sunni* schools generally hold that "circumcision is obligatory," even for women.[478] Oftentimes, proponents of the practice defend it on the ground that it promotes chastity by controlling women's sexual desires.[479] In the event that a woman is not chaste, or engages in extramarital sexual relations, however, *Shariah* allows for punishments including "lashing, imprisonment or stoning to death . . . ."[480]

c. Honor Killings

Under *Shariah*, certain killings are justified. For example, killing a non-Muslim, killing an apostate, or killing one's own offspring are all considered offenses that are "not subject to retaliation."[481] *Shariah's* justification of killing in these circumstances has partially led to so-called "honor killings." Honor killings are often carried out against women in situations when the killing is not justified under *Shariah* but carried out nonetheless. These so-called "honor killings," in which "women and girls are shot, stoned, burned, buried alive, strangled, smothered and knifed to death," are

---

[477]18 U.S.C. § 116(a) ("[W]hoever knowingly circumcises, excises, or infibulates the whole or any part of the labia majora or labia minora or clitoris of another person who has not attained the age of 18 years shall be fined under this title or imprisoned not more than 5 years, or both.").

[478]RELIANCE OF THE TRAVELLER, *supra* note 10, at 59 ("Circumcision is obligatory . . . . [F]or women, [it] consists of] removing the prepuce of the clitoris . . . .").

[479]*See, e.g.*, HONOUR-BASED VIOLENCE IN THE UK, *supra* note 444, at 69.

[480]*Id.* at 7.

[481]RELIANCE OF THE TRAVELLER, *supra* note 10, at 583–84.

too often practiced "[i]n the name of preserving family 'honour.'"[482] The reasons for these killings, U.N. High Commissioner for Human Rights Navi Pillay noted, range from a woman's supposed sexual licentiousness or refusal to comply with a forced marriage to attempts to divorce an abusive husband or even divulge that she has been raped.[483]

In Turkey, for example, a sixteen-year-old girl was buried alive by her father and grandfather for "befriending boys."[484] She was found dead under the family's chicken coop forty days later.[485] In Iran in 2003, a government official stated that in a *two-month* period alone, forty-five young women (under the age of twenty) had been killed because of alleged promiscuity, which was demonstrated by their refusal of arranged marriages, rebellion against Islamic dress codes, or contacts with men outside the family.[486]

In Pakistan, a young woman was murdered for her alleged sexual promiscuity.[487] Her body was found badly decomposed in a drainage ditch with two other tiny corpses; she had been hacked to death, piece by piece, with an ax.[488] As for the two bodies found with her, one belonged to her first-born infant child and the other to a newborn, to whom she appeared to have been giving birth as she was murdered.[489] The local Muslim cleric refused to say prayers for the three as they were interred because she was a "cursed" woman and her children were "illegitimate."[490] In the city of Dyabakir, Turkey, a man admitted to having killed his younger sister, who had

---

[482]U.N. High Comm'r for Human Rights, Statement by Navi Pillay on International Women's Day (March 8, 2010), *available at* http://www.un.org/en/events/women/iwd/2010/documents/HCHR_womenday_2010_statement.pdf.

[483]*Id.*

[484]Robert Fisk, *The Crimewave That Shames the World*, THE INDEPENDENT (Sept. 7, 2010), http://www.independent.co.uk/opinion/commentators/fisk/the-crimewave-that-shames-the-world-2072201.html.

[485]*Id.*

[486]*Id.*

[487]*Id.*

[488]*Id.*

[489]*Id.* The newborn was half-delivered, with only its head emerging from the woman's body. *Id.*

[490]*Id.*

previously eloped with her boyfriend.[491] While he was mustering up the courage to kill her, the local *imam* told him that he would be disobeying the word of Allah if he did not go through with it.[492] In another instance, a young girl named Ghazala was set on fire by her brother after her family suspected her of having an illicit relationship with her neighbor.[493] After she was burned to death, Ghazala's naked body lay in the street for over two hours.[494]

On New Year's Day in 2008, in the town of Irving, Texas, the bodies of two high school sisters were discovered in a taxicab found in a hotel parking lot.[495] The girls, ages seventeen and eighteen, were brutally shot to death, multiple times.[496] They, along with their mother, had fled the area before the Christmas holiday, fearing for their lives. The girls had only returned after their mother, who claimed to have gotten a guilty conscience for leaving her abusive husband, tricked them into coming home.[497] The primary suspect in the double homicide is the girls' own father, who had a history of domestic violence, most of which was undocumented due to the tremendous fear he instilled in both his wife and children.[498] The father, an Egyptian-born, naturalized U.S. citizen, had often chided his daughters for their Western ways and threatened their lives for consorting with boys at school and having non-Muslim boyfriends.[499] One of the girls' friends recalled that on at least one occasion, the father had told his daughter that "he would take her back to Egypt

---

[491] *Id.*

[492] *Id.*

[493] AMNESTY INT'L, PAKISTAN: HONOUR KILLINGS OF WOMEN AND GIRLS 3 (1999), *available at* http://www.amnesty.org/en/library/asset/ASA33/018/1999/en/9fe83c27e0f111ddbe392d4003be4450/asa330181999en.pdf.

[494] *Id.*

[495] Tanya Eiserer et. al., *Lewisville Cab Driver Had Been Investigated for Previous Abuse*, DENTON RECORD-CHRONICLE (Jan. 9, 2008) http://www.dentonrc.com/sharedcontent/dws/dn/latestnews/stories/011008dnmetteenskilled.7ba7cc6.html.

[496] *Id.*

[497] *Id.*

[498] *Id.*

[499] *Id.*

and have her killed . . . [because] it's OK to do that over there if you dishonor your family."[500]

Generally, Islamic states do initiate prosecutions against those guilty of honor killings. These prosecutions often do not move forward, however, because of the *qisas* (retaliation) and *diya* (indemnity or blood money) laws—which give the victim's heirs the power to pardon a murderer.[501] Because honor killings are carried out with the family's consent and generally by a family member, murderers are often pardoned. Once the pardon is given, the state cannot prosecute. For example, in Pakistan in June 2002, Zakir Hussain Shah of Bara Kau murdered his eighteen-year-old daughter, Sabiha, by slitting her throat because he believed that she had become pregnant.[502] Although the father was formally charged, the prosecution was halted after his wife and son, as legal heirs of the deceased, pardoned him under the *qisas* law.[503] Similarly, in Mardan, Pakistan, a man was pardoned by his mother after he killed his four sisters because they were seeking a share of his inheritance.[504] In another instance, in Sarghoda, Pakistan, a man shot multiple members of his family, killing two of his daughters; his wife and surviving daughters pardoned him.[505]

3. Rape

The United States provides rape victims with significant

---

[500]*Id.*

[501]*See supra* Chapter 4.E; QUR'AN, *supra* note 11, at *Surah* 2:178 ("O ye who believe! The law of equality is prescribed to you in cases of murder: The free for the free, the slave for the slave, the woman for the woman. But if any remission is made by the brother [heir] of the slain, then grant any reasonable demand, and compensate him with handsome gratitude. This is a concession and a mercy from your lord. After this, whoever exceeds the limits shall be in grave penalty.").

[502]Rafaqat Ali, *Heirs Pardon Killer Father Under Qisas Law*, DAILY DAWN (July 27, 2002), http://www.hvk.org/articles/0802/32.html; *see also* Fisk, *supra* note 484.

[503]*Id.; see also* THE MAJOR ACTS 178 (36th ed. 2011) (Comments on PAK. PENAL CODE, ch. XVI, § 299(k) (1860) ("Qisas is a right like property inheritable and is excusable by the legal heirs." (citing 200 P.Cr.L.J. 1688))).

[504]*Id.*

[505]*Id.*

protections.[506] Consequently, under the Model Penal Code, rape is considered a felony in the first or second degree.[507] If a rapist inflicts serious bodily injury on a woman while raping her, he is guilty in the first degree.[508] Moreover, many states hold a man liable for rape or another form of sexual assault even if the victim is the man's wife.[509]

In stark contrast, Islamic *Shariah* imposes procedural hurdles that are nearly insurmountable for female rape victims. For a woman to bring a successful claim under *Shariah* against her rapist, she must produce four male eyewitnesses to the crime.[510] Otherwise, she will be prosecuted for *zina* (unlawful sexual intercourse), because under *Shariah*, a woman's accusation of rape (without four eyewitnesses) is treated as an *admission of having unlawful sexual intercourse*.[511]

---

[506]One indication of this is the federal evidentiary requirement that excludes evidence about a victim's sexual disposition or behavior to protect victims from "invasion of privacy, potential embarrassment and sexual stereotyping that is associated with public disclosure of intimate sexual details" and to encourage victims to report rape. FED. R. EVID. 412 advisory committee's note (explaining that the purpose of the amendment was to "to expand the protection afforded alleged victims of sexual misconduct"). This principle is implemented in Fed. R. Evid. 412(a). FED. R. EVID. 412(a) (excluding, with restrictive exceptions, evidence that is "offered to prove that any alleged victim engaged in other sexual behavior" or "to prove any alleged victim's sexual predisposition" in criminal and civil sexual misconduct cases); *see also* OKLA. ST. tit. 21, § 1111 (2010) (defining rape broadly); MICH. COMP. LAWS §§ 750.520 et seq. (2011) (same); WASH. REV. CODE ANN. §§ 9A.44.040, 9A.44.050 (same as well as classifying certain rape offenses as felonies in the first, not second, degree).

[507]MODEL PENAL CODE § 213.1.

[508]*Id.*

[509]*See infra* note 525.

[510]*See* QUR'AN, 11, at *Surah* 4:15 ("If any of your women are guilty of lewdness, take the evidence of four (reliable) witnesses from amongst you against them; and if they testify, confine them to houses until death do claim them, or Allah ordain for them some (other) way."); *see also* RELIANCE OF THE TRAVELLER, *supra* note 10, at 638 ("If testimony concerns fornication or sodomy, then it requires four male witnesses (O: who testify, in the case of fornication, that they have seen the offender insert the head of his penis into her vagina).").

[511]*See* RELIANCE OF THE TRAVELLER, *supra* note 10, at 638 (demonstrating that a woman must have four eyewitnesses to exculpate herself in a rape case). Additionally, according to one authority, a woman must defend herself, if capable, or she will be "regarded as having consented to intercourse." PETERS, *supra* note 260, at 25. The woman's fight is considered an act of holy war, which suggests that if she perishes in the struggle, she will ascend straight to "paradise" as a martyr. *Id. See also* Seth Mydans, *In Pakistan, Rape Victims Are 'Criminals,'* N.Y. TIMES (May 17, 2002), http://www.nytimes. com/2002/05/17/world/in-pakistan-rape-victims-are-the-criminals.html?scp=1&sq= (describing the imposition of the death sentence by stoning for adultery upon a married female rape victim who bore a child as a consequence of the rape and explaining the court's general failure to follow up on alleged rapists). In Iran, accusations of forcible sodomy require the testimony of "four righteous men"; testimony by women is insufficient. ISLAMIC PENAL CODE OF IRAN arts. 117–19 (1991), *available at* http://mehr.org/Islamic_Penal_Code_of_Iran.pdf ("Sodomy is proved by the testimony of four righteous men who might have observed it. If [fewer] than four righteous men testify, sodomy is not proved and the witnesses shall be condemned to punishment for *Qazf* (malicious accusation).

To worsen the plight of the victim, if she is married, she may be sentenced to death for adultery.[512]

In this way, *Shariah* completely disregards the woman's claim that the intercourse was against her will. Instead, rapists often get off either scot free or merely have to pay a marriage payment to the woman (in the case of raping an unmarried woman).[513]

Before Pakistan's Hudood Ordinance, which incorporated *Shariah* principles regarding *zina* into Pakistan's Penal Code, was amended in 2006, rape victims in Pakistan who attempted to bring charges against their attackers were frequently charged with adultery.[514] According to a 2003 study, at that time as many as eighty-eight percent of women prisoners, many of whom were rape victims, were in prison for *zina*.[515] Even in Pakistan—a fully Muslim country—this severe standard was recognized as too harsh; and in 2006, President Musharraf signed a bill removing the Ordinance's standards for rape.[516] To the chagrin of many, however, on December 22, 2010, Pakistan's Federal Shariat Court declared that numerous sections of the bill violated Pakistan's Constitution and gave the federal government a deadline of June 22, 2011, to bring the law into conformance with *Shariah* "as interpreted by the Court."[517]

Similarly, Saudi Arabian courts allow a female rape victim

Testimony of women alone or together with a man does not prove sodomy.").

[512]*See* RELIANCE OF THE TRAVELLER, *supra* note 10, at 610 (prescribing death by stoning for certain adulterers); *see also* Mydans, *supra* note 513 (A Pakistani *Sharia* judge found the married rape victim, who could not meet the evidentiary requirements demanded of rape victims, guilty of adultery and subsequently sentenced her to death by stoning.).

[513]RELIANCE OF THE TRAVELLER, *supra* note 10, at 535 ("A man is obliged to pay a woman the amount typically received as marriage payment by similar brides . . . when a man forces a woman to fornicate with him," i.e., rapes her.).

[514]U.S. COMM'N ON INT'L RELIGIOUS FREEDOM, ANNUAL REPORT OF THE UNITED STATES COMMISSION ON INTERNATIONAL RELIGIOUS FREEDOM 2008: PAKISTAN (May 1, 2008), *available at* http://www.unhcr.org/refworld/docid/48556999c.html.

[515]*Id.*

[516]*Id.*; *see also* Protection of Women (Criminal Laws Amendment) Act (VI of 2006) (Pak.), *available at* http://www.pakistani.org/pakistan/legislation/2006/wpb.html.

[517]Protection of Women Act, *supra* note 516. Notably, the Constitution of Pakistan explicitly empowers the Federal Shariat Court with the task of bringing "[a]ll existing laws . . . in[to] conformity with the Injunctions of Islam as laid down in the Holy Quran and Sunnah." CONST. art. 227 (Pak.).

to be found guilty of "mixing of genders."[518] In 2006, a nineteen-year-old woman was reported to have been gang-raped by seven men who abducted her from a vehicle where she was talking with an old high school friend.[519] When she reported the crime to authorities, she was charged with violating Saudi Arabia's strict gender laws and was sentenced to ninety lashes—"more lashes than one of her alleged rapists received."[520]

Moreover, *Shariah* allows a man to enjoy "full lawful sexual enjoyment" of his wife's person and obliges her to obey his sexual whims.[521] In fact, it is "obligatory for a woman to let her husband have sex with her *immediately* when: (a) he asks her; (b) at home . . . ; (c) and she can physically endure it."[522] If the woman refuses her husband, she is deemed "rebellious," and he is accordingly authorized to take all proscriptive steps permitted by the *Qur'an*, beginning with verbal admonition and escalating to physical beating.[523] This directly conflicts with American laws, which protect women from domestic violence[524] and, in many states, marital rape.[525]

[518]BUREAU OF DEMOCRACY, HUMAN RIGHTS, & LABOR, U.S. DEP'T OF STATE, 2009 HUMAN RIGHTS REPORT: SAUDI ARABIA (Mar. 11, 2010), *available at* http://www.state.gov/g/drl/rls/hrrpt/2009/nea/136079.htm.
[519]*See* Associated Press, *Rape Case Calls Saudi Legal System into Question*, MSNBC (Nov. 21, 2006), http://www.msnbc.msn.com/id/15836746/ns/world_news-mideast/n_africa/ ("[S]he was sentenced to 90 lashes for being alone in a car with a man to whom she was not married . . . at the time that she was allegedly attacked and raped by a group of other men.").
[520]*Id.*
[521]QUR'AN, *supra* note 11, at *Surah* 2:223 ("Your wives are as a tilth unto you so approach your tilth when or how you will . . . ."); RELIANCE OF THE TRAVELLER, *supra* note 10, at 541.
[522]*Id.* at 525.
[523]*Id.* at 542; *see also* QUR'AN, *supra* note 11, at *Surah* 4:34.
[524]*See, e.g.,* N.J. STAT. ANN. § 2C:25-17 (2011) et. seq. ("Prevention of Domestic Violence Act of 1991"); OKLA. STAT. tit. 22, § 40.3 (2010) (providing victims of domestic violence with protective orders and services even when the court is otherwise closed). Additionally, to protect rape victims in rape cases, the Federal Rules of Evidence, with limited exceptions, prohibit any evidence regarding an alleged victim's sexual behavior or sexual predisposition. FED. R. EVID. 412(a).
[525]*E.g.,* CAL PENAL CODE §§ 262, 264 (West 2011) (punishing rape of a spouse for up to eight years); OKLA. STAT. tit. 22, § 1111(B) (2010) ("Rape is an act of sexual intercourse accomplished with a male or female *who is the spouse of the perpetrator* if force or violence is used or threatened, accompanied by apparent power of execution to the victim or to another person." (emphasis added)); N.H. REV. STAT. ANN. § 632-A:5 (2010) (noting that "[a]n actor commits a crime under [the sexual assault] chapter *even though the victim is the actor's legal spouse*" (emphasis added)); People v. M.D., 595 N.E. 2d 702, 711 (Ill. App. Ct. 1992) ("A marriage license should not be viewed as a license to forcibly sexually assault one's spouse with impunity. A married individual has the same right to control his or her body as does an unmarried person." (internal citations omitted)); People v. Liberta,

In 2010, after a Muslim man in New Jersey forced his wife to have non-consensual sex and physically abused her on numerous occasions (because he believed that the *Qur'an* permitted him to do whatever he wanted to his wife), a New Jersey trial judge held that the man had not sexually assaulted the woman because the man believed his religion gave him the right to demand of his wife sexual intercourse whenever he desired.[526] Describing this case as one in which "religious custom clashed with the law," the trial judge decided to accord more weight to the man's religious custom than he did to the woman's legal protection.[527] He set forth his reasoning as follows:

> This court does not feel that, under the circumstances, . . . this defendant had a criminal . . . intent to sexually assault or to sexually contact the plaintiff when he did. The court believes that he was operating under his belief that it is, as the husband, his desire to have sex when and whether he wanted to, was something that was consistent with his practices and it was something that was not prohibited.[528]

Although the appellate court held that the trial court had abused its discretion and ordered the issuance of a restraining order to protect the woman,[529] the trial court still committed a grave error, as the appellate court noted, by deciding *sua sponte* "to except defendant from the operation of the State's statutes as the result of his religious

---

474 N.E.2d 567, 573 (N.Y. 1984) ("We find that there is no rational basis for distinguishing marital rape and nonmarital rape . . . . We therefore declare the marital exemption in the New York statute to be unconstitutional."); State v. Smith, 426 A.2d 38, 44 (N.J. 1981) ("More importantly, this implied consent rationale, besides being offensive to our valued ideals of personal liberty, is not sound where the marriage itself is not irrevocable. If a wife can exercise a legal right to separate from her husband and eventually terminate the marriage 'contract,' may she not also revoke a 'term' of that contract, namely, consent to intercourse? Just as a husband has no right to imprison his wife because of her marriage vow to him, he has no right to force sexual relations upon her against her will . . . .") (internal citation omitted).

[526]S.D. v. M.J.R., 2 A.3d 412, 417–18 (N.J. Super. Ct. App. Div. 2010).

[527]*Id.* at 418.

[528]*See id.*

[529]*Id.* at 426.

beliefs."[530]

To apply or consider *Shariah* in rape cases in the United States is contrary to the principles upon which this society is built. America punishes rapists and protects rape victims. No state requires women to bring the testimony of four eyewitnesses (male or otherwise) to establish a rape claim. In fact, government officials throughout the country are engaged in making it easier for women to report rape and to receive governmental support throughout the process.[531]

4. Polygamy

In the United States, marriages must be monogamous, and marital unions entered into while one of the parties remains married to someone else are void as a matter of law.[532] Further, polygamy is expressly condemned and often criminalized.[533] Under *Shariah*,

---

[530]*Id.* at 422.

[531]*E.g.,* Sabrina Garcia & Margaret Henderson, *Options for Reporting Sexual Violence—Developments over the Past Decade,* FBI LAW ENFORCEMENT BULLETIN (May 2010), *available at* http://www.fbi. gov/stats-services/publications/law-enforcement-bulletin/May-2010/options-for-reporting-sexual-violence.

[532]J. W. Northrop, Annotation, *Construction of Statute Making Bigamy or Prior Lawful Subsisting Marriage to Third Person a Ground for Divorce,* 3 A.L.R.3d 1108 (2008); *see also, e.g.,* TEX. PENAL CODE ANN. § 25.01 (West 2010) (criminalizing bigamy); Grabois v. Jones, 89 F.3d 97, 100 (2d Cir. 1996) (holding that New York law "states unambiguously that a second marriage is invalid if either of the parties to that marriage is already married"); Ledvinka v. Ledvinka, 840 A.2d 173, 182 (Md. 2003) (annulling the second marriage of a man who had entered that union while still legally married to another woman); *In re* Estate of Milliman, 415 P.2d 877, 881 (Ariz. 1966) ("The law is well settled that a marriage between persons, one of whom is married to another, is void.").

[533]*See, e.g., Reynolds,* 98 U.S. 145. In *Reynolds,* the Supreme Court of the United States considered the question of whether a criminal charge against a man in a polygamous union would be excused on the basis of the man's Mormon faith. In holding that the criminal conviction would stand, the Court declared:

> Polygamy has always been odious among the northern and western nations of Europe . . . . [I]t is impossible to believe that the constitutional guaranty of religious freedom was intended to prohibit legislation in respect to this most important feature of social life. Marriage, while from its very nature a sacred obligation, is nevertheless, in most civilized nations, a civil contract, and usually regulated by law. Upon it society may be said to be built, and out of its fruits spring social relations and social obligations and duties, with which government is necessarily required to deal. In fact, according as monogamous or polygamous marriages are allowed, do we find the principles on which the government of the people, to a greater or less extent, rests . . . . [A]s a law of the organization of society under the exclusive dominion of the United States, it is provided that plural marriages shall not be allowed. Can a man excuse his practices to the contrary because of his religious belief? *T*[*o*] *permit this would*

however, polygamy is legal.

Islamic *Shariah* expressly permits polygamy, though it only gives *men* this right. *Surah* 4:3 of the *Qur'an* declares unambiguously that Muslim men may take up to four wives: "[M]arry women of your choice, two, or three, or four; but if ye fear that ye shall not be able to deal justly (with them), then only one, or (a captive) that your right hands possess. That will be more suitable, to prevent you from doing injustice."[534] Muhammad himself had multiple wives, and among his wives was a girl, Aisha, to whom he was engaged when she was just six years old and with whom he had sexual intercourse when she was only nine years old.[535]

Reportedly, even in the United States, where polygamy is expressly banned, some Muslim men, operating with full knowledge that polygamy is forbidden here, nevertheless marry multiple wives because they "believe that the US prohibition of polygamy directly violates their freedom of religion and, [] that Islam supersedes secular law."[536] The marriage ceremonies are either performed abroad in jurisdictions where polygamy is legal or domestically by *imams* (Islamic spiritual leaders) who defy U.S. laws to perform such marriages.[537] The first wives, who feel bound by the *Qur'an* to accept their husband's

---

    be to make the professed doctrines of religious belief superior to the law of the land, and in effect to permit every citizen to become a law unto himself. Government could exist only in name under such circumstances.

Id. at 164–67 (emphasis added).

[534]QUR'AN, *supra* note 11, at *Surah* 4:3; *see also* FIQH, *supra* note 305, at 128 ("'I embraced Islam and at that time, I had eight wives; I mentioned this to the Prophet and he said'": "'Choose four of them.'" (citing Abu Dawood (no. 2241) and Ibn Majah (no. 1952))).

[535]SAHIH BUKHARI, *supra* note 69, at Vol. 5, Bk. 58, No. 236 ("[Muhammad] married 'Aisha when she was a girl of six years of age, and he consum[mated] that marriage when she was nine years old.").

[536]Asifa Quraishi & Najeeba Syeed-Miller, *No Altars: A Survey of Islamic Family Law in the United States, in* WOMEN'S RIGHTS & ISLAMIC FAMILY LAW 192 (Lynn Welchman ed., 2004); *see also* Pauline Bartolone, *For These Muslims, Polygamy Is an Option,* S.F. CHRON. (Aug. 5, 2007), http://articles.sfgate.com/2007-08-05/opinion/17257241_1_african-american-muslims-polygamy-black-muslims/2 ("Shiite Muslims even have a temporary marriage, or mutah, where a man may enter into a sexual union with more than one woman. The arrangement need not involve an imam and could last anywhere from one weekend to several years.").

[537]Quraishi & Syeed-Miller, *supra* note 536, at 192–93.

subsequent marriages, often face significant legal ramifications such as domestic abuse, child custody, and spousal support.[538]

Not only do these marriages violate U.S. law, but they further pose significant problems for women who are part of polygamous marriages and for children who are born into them. State courts in the United States have recognized this dissonance. For example, in *In re Estate of Khabbaza*,[539] the respondent argued that he was married to the decedent at the time of her death.[540] Whether he had obtained a valid divorce pursuant to entering a second marriage was disputed, however.[541] On this point, the New York trial court opined that if the respondent had been validly married to the decedent and had not divorced her, "it would be *against public policy* for this court to condone respondent's second marriage, even though it may be permissible under Iranian [*Shariah*] law."[542]

5. Marriages of Convenience and Contracts for Sexual Services

In the United States, one cannot lawfully enter into an agreement to provide a contractual benefit in exchange for the sexual services of another. In *Marvin v. Marvin*, the California Supreme Court held that an agreement for which sex is the sole consideration is unenforceable as a matter of public policy because "such a contract is, in essence, an agreement for prostitution."[543] It is for this reason that the California Supreme Court refuses to recognize putative domestic partnerships that are established solely, or even predominantly, on meretricious sexual services.[544]

---

[538]*See id.* at 193.
[539]*In re* Estate of Khabbaza, 662 N.Y.S.2d 996, 997 (1997).
[540]*Id.* at 997.
[541]*Id.*
[542]*Id.* (emphasis added).
[543]Marvin v. Marvin, 557 P.2d 106, 116 (Cal. 1976).
[544]*Id.* at 113 (holding agreements between non-marital partners are unenforceable when they "rest upon a consideration of meretricious sexual services"). The Massachusetts Supreme Judicial Court has also stated that,
    [t]o the extent we have not previously done so, we adopt the view that unmarried

Marvin illustrates that contracts for sexual services are not only unenforceable under U.S. civil laws, but also under the majority of states' criminal codes because these contracts essentially amount to prostitution.[545] Prostitution is illegal in forty-nine of the fifty states.[546] In fact, many states impose penalties of imprisonment for up to one year and fines of as much as $10,000 for repeat offenses.[547]

Under *Shariah*, however, "*mut'ah*" is a legally permissible form of temporary, contract-based marriage endorsed by *Shia* Islam.[548] The concept of *mut'ah* is derived from Muhammad's early teachings and continues to be a commonly accepted practice by *Shi'ite* Muslims to this day,[549] with justification for the practice found in both the *Qur'an* and *hadiths*. Surah 4:24 of the *Qur'an* declares,

> [Marry women] except those whom your right hands possess; Thus hath Allah ordained (Prohibitions) against you: Except for these, *all others are lawful, provided ye seek (them in marriage) with gifts from*

cohabitants may lawfully contract concerning property, financial, and other matters relevant to their relationship. Such a contract is subject to the rules of contract law and is valid even if expressly made in contemplation of a common living arrangement, except to the extent that sexual services constitute the only, or dominant, consideration for the agreement, or that enforcement should be denied on some other public policy ground.

Wilcox v. Trautz, 693 N.E.2d 141, 146 (Mass. 1998).

[545] *See supra* notes 543 & 544 and accompanying text.

[546] *See U.S. Federal and State Prostitution Laws and Related Punishments*, PROCON.ORG (Mar. 15, 2010) [hereinafter *U.S. Federal and State Prostitution Laws*], http://prostitution.procon.org/view.resource.php?resourceID=000119. Prostitution is legal only in licensed houses of prostitution in Nevada. NEV. REV. STAT. ANN. § 201.354 (2010).

[547] *See U.S. Federal and State Prostitution Laws*, *supra* note 546; *see also* TEX. PENAL CODE ANN. §§ 43.02(c), 12.35(b) (2010) (charging repeat prostitution offenders with a felony punishable by as many as two years in state prison and a fine of up to $10,000).

[548] SHAHLA HAERI, LAW OF DESIRE: TEMPORARY MARRIAGE IN SHI'I IRAN 49–51 (1989) (discussing the historical development of the practice of *mut'ah* marriage, particularly among *Shi'ites*); *see also* FIQH, *supra* note 305, at 120 ("*Mut'ah* marriage is a temporary marriage to a woman, for a period such as two, three days, a month or such like. There is no dispute that *mut'ah* marriage was formerly lawful in Islam."). *But cf. id.* at 120–25 (explaining that all schools of *Sunni* thought claim that Muhammad later abrogated the practice).

[549] *See, e.g.*, Rick Jervis, *'Pleasure Marriages' Regain Popularity in Iraq*, USA TODAY (May 4, 2005), http://www.usatoday.com/news/world/iraq/2005-05-04-pleasure-marriage_x.htm (recounting an admission by an Iraqi lawyer that "[a]ll my friends are doing it" and a comment by a cleric that the practice was "flourishing"). Notably, *Sunni* scholars hold that Muhammad later abrogated the practice. RELIANCE OF THE TRAVELLER, *supra* note 10, at 530; FIQH, *supra* note 305, at 120–25.

> your property—desiring chastity, not lust. *Seeing that*
> *ye derive benefit from them, give them their dowers*
> *(at least) as prescribed . . . .*[550]

The first instances of *mut'ah* marriages are traceable to a military expedition led by Muhammad. According to *hadiths*, during a lengthy expedition, Muhammad's warriors complained that they had gone long without women. Muhammad's response was to create *mut'ah* marriage, by which the men were able to enter into so-called marriages with local women so that their sexual desires would be satiated.[551] The typical contemporary *mut'ah* marriage resembles a short-term contractual relationship whereby a man gives something of value (sometimes $100 for a single encounter or $200 for a whole month) to a woman in exchange for the right to have sex with her for the duration of the contractual relationship.[552]

California dealt with a *mut'ah* "marriage" when a Muslim resident of Iranian descent brought suit for spousal support and equitable division of property upon what she perceived to be dissolution of a valid marriage.[553] Fereshteh Vryonis, a *Shi'ite* Muslim, had dated a college professor, but because she did not feel comfortable dating him without having a commitment from him in accordance with her faith, the two of them performed a secret ceremony, which "conformed to the requirements of a time-

---

[550]*See* QUR'AN, *supra* note 11, at *Surah* 4:24 (emphasis added); HAERI, *supra* note 548, at 49–51.

[551]SAHIH BUKHARI, *supra* note 69, at Vol. 6, Bk. 60, No. 139 ("We used to participate in the holy wars carried on by the Prophet and we had no women (wives) with us. So we said [to Muhammad]. 'Shall we castrate ourselves?' But [Muhammad] forbade us to do that and thenceforth he allowed us to marry a woman (temporarily) by giving her even a garment, and then he recited: 'O you who believe! Do not make unlawful the good things which Allah has made lawful for you.'").

[552]Jervis, *supra* note 549 ("The contracts, lasting anywhere from one hour to 10 years, generally stipulate that the man will pay the woman in exchange for sexual intimacy."); *see also* Camelia E. Fard, *Unveiled Threats*, VILLAGE VOICE (Mar. 27, 2001), http://www.villagevoice.com/2001-03-27/news/unveiled-threats/ (describing the practice of *mut'ah* in Iran, a country governed by *Shi'ite Shariah*, as permitting short-term, usually only hours-long, contractual "marriages" that amount to prostitution).

[553]*In re* Marriage of Vryonis, 248 Cal. Rptr. 807 (Cal. Ct. App. 1988).

specified 'Muta' marriage, authorized by [*Shia* Islam]."[554] The trial court held that Ms. Vryonis was a "putative spouse" and, therefore, entitled to spousal support and property division.[555] The appellate court rejected this holding, however, recognizing that,

> [i]f the trial court based its putative marriage finding on Fereshteh's belief she had celebrated a valid Muta marriage, the ruling was error because the required good faith belief is in the existence of a lawful *California* marriage. If the trial court found Fereshteh had a good faith belief she was validly married under California law, the ruling was error because the requisite good faith belief must have a reasonable basis.[556]

In other words, the appellate court emphasized that for the "good faith belief" component of a putative marriage to be satisfied, the parties must have *objective* good faith to abide by the legal requirements of the *state*, not subjective good faith to adhere to the procedural idiosyncrasies of their religion.[557]

Had the court allowed for the existence of a *mut'ah* marriage, it would have directly contradicted state law and set a precedent that such alleged marital unions were permissible even though they directly contradict state law and violate public policy. Such a precedent would pave the way for *Shi'ite* Muslims to justify contracts solely for sexual services.[558] Further, because the source of this law is religious texts (the *Qur'an* and *hadiths*), *Shi'ite* Muslims might try to justify *mut'ah* marriages or demand recognition of those "marriages" under the right to free exercise of religion. Using a religious justification to legalize prostitution would therefore

---

[554]*Id.* at 809.
[555]*Id.* at 810.
[556]*Id.* at 812 (emphasis added).
[557]*See id.* at 812–815.
[558]*Cf. Marvin*, 557 P.2d at 113 (expressly refusing to uphold contracts based solely on sexual services).

undercut federal and state governments' ability to regulate a practice that they have a compelling interest to proscribe.[559]

---

[559]*See, e.g.*, Déjà Vu of Nashville, Inc. v. Metro. Gov't of Nashville, 274 F.3d 377, 396 (6th Cir. 2001) ("[T]he First Amendment protects the [erotic entertainers' and customers'] right to free expressive association . . . . The right to associate for expressive purposes, however, is not absolute. Infringements on that right may be justified by regulations adopted to serve compelling state interests . . . . In attempting to restrict opportunities to engage in prostitution and to guard against the spread of disease through the public release or exchange of bodily fluids, Metropolitan Nashville has [satisfied a compelling state interest and] gone no farther than necessary . . . .").

CHAPTER FIVE

FAMILY LAW

A. MARRIAGE

In the United States, men and women are on equal footing with regard to entering and dissolving marriage. The Supreme Court has recognized that, as a protected institution, marriage is a right of "fundamental importance"—for men *and* women.[560] In keeping with the protection of marriage's fundamental significance, marriages procured by coercion or duress are voidable.[561] Both parties must consent.[562] Accordingly, minors are not allowed to marry until they have reached the age of legal consent,[563] and minors who do marry before the age of consent may sue to annul the marriage either before or upon reaching the age of consent.[564] Moreover, parents who force their minor children to marry or permit them to marry at an age that is not in their best interests could face criminal charges.[565]

---

[560]*See, e.g.*, Zablocki v. Redhail, 434 U.S. 374, 384 (1978) ("[D]ecisions of this Court confirm that the right to marry is of fundamental importance for all individuals.").

[561]*See, e.g.*, Norvell v. State, 193 S.W.2d 200, 200–01 (Tex. 1946); Newman v. Sigler, 125 So. 666, 666–67 (1930); Fluharty v. Fluharty, 193 A. 838, 839–40 (Del. Super. Ct. 1937); O'Brien v. Eustice, 19 N.E.2d 137, 140 (Ill. App. Ct. 1937).

[562]*See, e.g.*, Tice v. Tice, 672 P.2d 1168, 1171–72 (Okla. 1983); Garrison v. Garrison, 460 A.2d 945, 946 (Conn. 1983); Davis v. Davis, 175 A. 574, 575 (Conn. 1934); Shonfeld v. Shonfeld, 184 N.E. 60, 60–61 (N.Y. 1933); Elkhorn Coal Corp. v. Tackett, 49 S.W.2d 571, 573 (Ky. 1932); Madison v. Robinson, 116 So. 31, 35 (Fla. 1928).

[563]52 AM. JUR. 2D *Marriage* § 16 (2010) (specifying that the age of consent varies under state law). For an example, see TEXAS FAM. CODE § 6.205 (2010) (proscribing marriage if either party is under sixteen years of age and a court order has not been obtained); marriages can also be proscribed based on the relationship of the parties. *E.g.*, N.Y. DOM. REL. LAW § 5 (2011) (proscribing marriage between certain relatives); TEXAS FAM. CODE § 6.206 (2010) (proscribing marriage "if a party is a current or former stepchild or stepparent of the other party").

[564]Hood v. Hood, 178 S.W.2d 670, 672–73 (Ark. 1944) (citing Kibler v. Kibler, 24 S.W.2d 867, 869 (Ark. 1930)).

[565]In *New York v. Benu*, for example, the New York criminal court held the defendant criminally liable for actively participating in a marriage ceremony between his thirteen-year-old daughter and a seventeen-year-old, whom she indicated that she liked. 385 N.Y.S.2d 222, 228 (N.Y. Crim. Ct. 1976). The record indicated that the defendant arranged the elopement because "under the tenets of his faith, matrimony was a desirable alternative to fornication (pre-marital sex)." *Id.* at 225. According to the court, because the defendant knew that marrying off his young daughter was likely to injure her welfare, he violated New York penal laws regarding child endangerment, even though the thirteen-year-old seemed to approve of the idea. *Id.* at 226. Further, because marriage of such a young girl

Additionally, in recognition of religious freedom and the ability of a person to *choose* to marry another, even if the other has different religious beliefs, U.S. law upholds marriages between persons of differing faiths; difference of faith in itself is not a valid ground for divorce.[566]

Contrary to Americans' deeply rooted notions of equality and consent, however, Islamic law operates on the assumption that men are superior to women,[567] with the *Qur'an* itself solidifying this view by teaching that, although women have "rights similar to the rights against them, according to what is equitable," men still "have a degree (of advantage) over them."[568] In the marriage context, this "degree of advantage" encompasses a husband's right to marry without the presence of a guardian,[569] to forbid his wife from leaving the home without his express permission,[570] and to discipline, and

violated public policy, the court declared the marriage to be voidable. *Id*. at 225.

[566]"It is *not* a ground for a divorce or separation that the spouses entertain different views on religion or that they are members of different sects or denominations." M. L. Cross, Annotation, *Racial, Religious, or Political Differences as Ground for Divorce, Separation, or Annulment*, 25 A.L.R.2d 928 (2008) (emphasis added). Grounds for divorce include, but are not limited to, adultery, conviction of a crime, duress, fraud, gross neglect of duty, and nonsupport of a spouse. *See* 27A C.J.S. *Divorce* §§ 88–96.

[567]Although authors like John Esposito take great pains to demonstrate that Islam ascribed to women greater social esteem and legal status than surrounding pre-Islamic Arabic societies ascribed to their women, that is of little relevance in evaluating *Shariah* in a modern context. *Shariah* is in many regards inflexible; and, although at the religion's inception, Islamic treatment of women may arguably have been better than that of its secular or pagan counterparts, the inequities between the sexes were still great. With such disparate views of sexual differences embedded in *Shariah*, *Shariah* cannot be applied equitably to women today unless courts expressly disavow fundamental *Shariah* principles. *See* discussion *supra* Chapter 4.E.2.

[568]QUR'AN, *supra* note 11, at *Surah* 2:228. Muhammad additionally declared that women would constitute the majority of those in hell:

> 'I was shown the Hell-fire and that the majority of its dwellers were women who were ungrateful.' It was asked, 'Do they disbelieve in Allah?' (or are they ungrateful to Allah?) He replied, They are ungrateful to their husbands and are ungrateful for the favors and the good (charitable deeds) done to them. If you have always been good (benevolent) to one of them and then she sees something in you (not of her liking), she will say, 'I have never received any good from you.'

SAHIH BUKHARI, *supra* note 69, at Vol. 1, Bk. 2, No. 29.

[569]*See* RELIANCE OF THE TRAVELLER, *supra* note 10, at 518 (The third element of a lawful marriage is the presence of the bride's male guardian because the Prophet said, "Let no woman marry a woman to another or marry herself to another.").

[570]*Id*. at 538 (Based on *Sunnah*, "[a] husband *may permit* his wife to leave the house for a lesson in Sacred Law, for invocation of Allah (*dhikr*), to see her female friends, or to go to any place in the town. A woman may not leave the city without her husband or a [guardian] accompanying her, unless the

even beat, a wife who does not see things his way.[571]

Under *Shariah*, marriage is viewed as a legal transaction with components mirroring "those of [a] valid sale."[572] These mandatory components include a spoken offer and acceptance, two witnesses to the marriage, and presence of the bride's guardian, the bride, and the groom.[573] While at first glance these components may seem similar enough to various U.S. state requirements for marriage, a closer examination dispels any initial resemblance. First, the spoken form merely requires an oral statement.[574] The requisite statements are tantamount to a standard contractual offer and acceptance.[575] Notably, however, the one who presents the marriage offer is *not* the bride, but her male *guardian*.[576] The *guardian* should say to the potential groom, "I marry you ([] i.e. to her)," to which the prospective groom must respond, "I marry her," or "I accept her marriage."[577] Second, the two required witnesses to the marriage must be male, must be Muslim, and must be "upright."[578]

Third, the bride must be accompanied by her male guardian, and it is he who must make the offer on her behalf, for Muhammad himself commanded, "Let no woman marry a woman to another or

---

journey is obligatory, like the *hajj* (the annual pilgrimage to Mecca). It is unlawful for her to travel otherwise, and unlawful *for her husband to allow her to*." (emphasis added)); *id.* at 541 ("It is not lawful for a wife to leave the house except by the permission of her husband . . . .").

[571] QUR'AN, *supra* note 11, at *Surah* 4:34 ("As to those women on whose part ye fear disloyalty and ill-conduct, admonish them (first), (next), refuse to share their beds, (and last) beat them (lightly)."); RELIANCE OF THE TRAVELLER, *supra* note 10, at 542 ("If the wife . . . is termed 'rebellious,' [then] the husband takes the following steps to correct matters: . . . if [verbally chastising her and not sleeping with her are] ineffectual, it is permissible for him to hit her . . . .").

[572] RELIANCE OF THE TRAVELLER, *supra* note 10, at 517.

[573] *Id.*

[574] *See id.*

[575] *Id.*

[576] *Id.* (The statement that effects the offer is "a statement (N: from the guardian)" on behalf of the bride, but the acceptance is made directly by the groom on his own behalf.).

[577] *Id.* (internal quotations marks omitted).

[578] *Id.* at 518. Consequently, in all *Sunni* schools but the *Hanafi* school, a marriage witnessed by two Muslim women but only one man would be invalid. *Id.* Additionally, a marriage witnessed by more than two non-Muslims would not satisfy the witness requirement, and the marriage would be invalid. *See id.*

marry herself to another."[579] Muhammad thereby expressly forbade women, either the bride herself or any woman she brings to offer marriage on her behalf, from serving as the bride's legal guardian.[580] Rather, the bride's guardian must be a Muslim male who is "upright" in character and "of sound judgment" and one who is "legally responsible" for her.[581] Legal guardians include the bride's father and paternal grandfather (both of whom may compel the marriage whether she consents or not),[582] brother, nephew (brother's son), uncle (father's brother), or male cousin (father's brother's son).[583] Notably, of a woman's potential legal guardians, "none . . . may marry her to someone when a family member higher on the list exists."[584] This means that if a woman's father or paternal grandfather is still living, only he may serve as her guardian in a marriage contract, and either of these has the power to compel her to marry "[w]hen the father or father's father [determines] that the best advantage is to be served by marrying a young boy (or girl) to someone."[585] Finally, the bride's groom—but not the bride, because Muslim men may marry Christian and Jewish women as well[586]—must be a Muslim,[587] for

---

[579]See supra note 569 and accompanying parenthetical text (internal quotation marks omitted); see also SAHIH BUKHARI, supra note 69, at Vol. 7, Bk. 62, No. 70 ("[I[f somebody says to the guardian (of a woman), 'Marry me to so-and-so,' and the guardian remained silent or said to him, 'What have you got (to offer in exchange)?' And the other said, 'I have so much and so much (Mahr),' or kept quiet, and then the guardian said, 'I have married her to you,' then the marriage is valid (legal)."); see also PARTIAL TRANSLATION OF SUNAN ABU-DAWUD (Ahmad Hasan trans.), available at http://www.usc.edu/schools/college/crcc/engagement/resources/texts/muslim/hadith/abudawud/, Bk. 11, No. 2080 ("The Prophet . . . said: There is no marriage without the permission of a guardian.").

[580]RELIANCE OF THE TRAVELLER, supra note 10, at 519.

[581]Id. at 518–19 (setting forth the criteria for a valid guardian in a marriage contract).

[582]Id. at 522 ("Guardians are of two types, those who may compel their female charges to marry someone, and those who may not. (a) The only guardians who may compel their charge to marry are a virgin bride's father or father's father, compel meaning to marry her to a suitable match without her consent.").

[583]Id. at 520.

[584]Id.

[585]Id. at 524.

[586]QUR'AN, supra note 11, at Surah 5:5 ("(Lawful unto you in marriage) are (not only) chaste women who are believers [i.e., Muslim women], but chaste women among the People of the Book . . . ."); see also RELIANCE OF THE TRAVELLER, supra note 10, at 529 (Muslim men may marry women that are "Muslim, Christian, or Jew.").

[587]RELIANCE OF THE TRAVELLER, supra note 10, at 529 ("(N: It is not lawful or valid for a Muslim man to be married to any woman who is not either a Muslim, Christian, or Jew; nor is it lawful or valid for a

the purpose of a guardian marrying his female ward to a man is to "intend[] some form of obedience to Allah, such as [keeping the woman] chaste or having . . . pious son[s]."[588]

As noted earlier, the *Qur'an* also instructs husbands to admonish their disobedient wives, deny sexual relations with them, and if both methods for securing submission are ineffective, husbands may even use physical force to bring them in line.[589] *Shariah* also grants a man the exclusive right to marry up to four wives.[590] Any attempt by the bride to formulate a marriage agreement that limits her husband to a monogamous relationship is deemed to be an "extraneous condition[]" that is not binding but is "meaningless."[591] The following discussion of Islamic marriage and divorce laws further reveal that *Shariah* must not be applied in the United States or given the force of law.

1. The Role of Consent in Marriage

In the United States, marriages procured by coercion or duress are null and void.[592] Valid marriages require both parties' consent.[593] In fact, consent is so fundamental to marriages in the United States that Nevada, a state notorious for impetuous marriages, sets forth a specific provision declaring that marriages without the requisite assent may be annulled.[594]

Muslim woman to be married to anyone besides a Muslim.)" (emphasis added)).

[588]*Id.* at 511 (recommending guardians to marry their marriageable female charges to righteous Muslim men).

[589]*Id.* at 542; *see also supra* note 432 and accompanying text.

[590]QUR'AN, *supra* note 11, at *Surah* 4:3 ("If ye fear that ye shall not be able to deal justly with the orphans, marry women of your choice, two, or three, or four . . . .").

[591]RELIANCE OF THE TRAVELLER, *supra* note 10, at 517 ("Extraneous conditions added to the marriage contract, such as that the husband observe monogamy or the like, are not binding, being meaningless, though they do not invalidate the marriage agreement, which remains effective.").

[592]*See, e.g.*, Norvell v. State, 193 S.W.2d 200, 200–01 (Tex. 1946); Newman v. Sigler, 125 So. 666, 666–67 (1930); Fluharty v. Fluharty, 193 A. 838, 839–40 (Del. Super. Ct. 1937); O'Brien v. Eustice, 19 N.E.2d 137, 140 (Ill. App. Ct. 1937).

[593]*See, e.g.*, Tice v. Tice, 672 P.2d 1168, 1171–72 (Okla. 1983); Garrison v. Garrison, 460 A.2d 945, 946 (Conn. 1983); Davis v. Davis, 175 A. 574, 575 (Conn. 1934); Shonfeld v. Shonfeld, 184 N.E. 60, 60–61 (N.Y. 1933); Elkhorn Coal Corp. v. Tackett, 49 S.W.2d 571, 573 (Ky. 1932); Madison v. Robinson, 116 So. 31, 35 (Fla. 1928).

[594]NEV. REV. STAT. § 125.330 (2009) ("When either of the parties to a marriage for want of understanding

To the contrary, "[a] distinguishing feature of [*Shariah*] is the power (*jabr*) that it bestows upon the father or [paternal] grandfather, who can contract a valid marriage for minors which cannot be annulled at puberty."[595] Under *Shariah*, the age of consent for marriage is shockingly young. *Shariah* permits adults to marry minors who have reached "puberty."[596] And puberty is traditionally twelve years for boys and only nine years for girls.[597] As a consequence, *Shariah* empowers fathers and grandfathers to arrange legally enforceable marriages of their daughters and granddaughters—with adult men—without consent[598]—when the girls are as young as nine years old.[599] This practice was reinforced by Muhammad's own arranged marriage to a six-year-old girl (Aisha), with whom he consummated the marriage when she was nine years old and he was fifty-three.[600] In fact, *hadiths* recount that when Muhammad took Aisha to his house as a bride, she brought her dolls with her.[601]

Because *Shariah* permits such arrangements, minor girls

shall be incapable of assenting thereto, the marriage shall be void from the time its nullity shall be declared by a court of competent authority.").

[595]John L. Esposito, Women in Muslim Family Law 16 (2001); *see also supra* notes 582 & 585 and accompanying text. *But cf.* Sahih Bukhari, *supra* note 69, at Vol. 7, Bk. 62, No. 69 (recounting that Muhammad, upon a woman's request, invalidated her marriage because her father had forced her to marry a man when she was no longer a virgin but was a matron (had been married before)).

[596]Esposito, *supra* note 595, at 15.

[597]*Id.* While it may be true that a younger marrying age was common in pre-Islamic Arab societies and therefore was not exclusive to Islam, modernization has allowed for flexibility in the age of consent in societies not governed by *Shariah*. Conversely, *Shariah* considers authoritative sources that have not allowed for adjustment in the age of consent over time (e.g., the *Qur'an* and *Sunnah*), which provides authority for marriages of minors as young as nine in some *Shariah*-compliant countries even today.

[598]Reliance of the Traveller, *supra* note 10, at 522 ("Guardians are of two types, those who may compel their female charges to marry someone, and those who may not. The only guardians who may compel their charge to marry are a virgin bride's father or father's father, *compel* meaning to marry her to a suitable match [] without her consent.").

[599]Susan W. Tiefenbrun, *The Semiotics of Women's Human Rights in Iran*, 23 Conn. J. Int'l L. 1, 61 (2007).

[600]*See supra* note 535.

[601]Sahih Muslim, *supra* note 46, at Bk. 008, No. 3311 ("[S]he was taken to his house as a bride when she was nine, and her dolls were with her; and when he (the Holy Prophet) died she was eighteen years old."); *see also* Sahih Bukhari, *supra* note 69, at Vol. 8, Bk. 73, No. 151 ("I (A'isha) used to play with the dolls in the presence of the Prophet, and my girl friends also used to play with me. When [Muhammad] used to enter (my dwelling place) they used to hide themselves, but the Prophet would call them to join and play with me.").

who are forced to marry adult men in jurisdictions that integrate *Shariah* find themselves without any recourse in *Shariah* courts, even when those courts are in freedom-loving Western nations. The D.C.-based Center for Islamic Pluralism discovered as much when it interviewed nearly 100 *imams* in England, where Parliament has allowed for a parallel system of *Shariah* courts operating alongside British courts to adjudicate Muslims' legal issues and issuing legally binding judgments.[602] The Center's report highlighted that, under *Shariah*, women often did not receive "fair hearings in forced marriage, arranged marriage and domestic violence matters."[603] For example, a British woman of Pakistani descent told BBC News that, following a forced marriage in Pakistan to a cousin when she was only thirteen, she sought annulment of the marriage from three different *imams* in the UK. Each told her that she was legally married according to *Shariah*, notwithstanding the fact that she was a minor and that she had been forced to proceed with the marriage.[604] The woman lamented, "I went through the proper Islamic way and these men told me to go away."[605]

2. Interfaith Marriage

The United States recognizes a person's ability to *choose* to marry another consenting adult, even if that person has different religious beliefs.[606] Accordingly, U.S. laws permit marriages between persons of differing faiths and do not consider difference of religion a valid ground for divorce.[607]

---

[602]Taher, *supra* note 451.

[603]Sanjiv Buttoo, *Some Imams 'Biased Against Women'*, BBC News (Dec. 15, 2008), http://news.bbc.co.uk/2/hi/uk_news/7783627.stm.

[604]*Id.*

[605]*Id.*

[606]In the landmark anti-miscegenation case, *Loving v. Virginia*, 388 U.S. 1 (1967), the Court held that "[t]he freedom to marry has long been recognized as one of the vital personal rights essential to the orderly pursuit of happiness by free men." *Id.* at 12. Further, "[t]o deny this fundamental freedom on so unsupportable a basis as . . . racial classifications . . . is surely to deprive all the State's citizens of liberty without due process of law." *Id.* Based on the reasoning of this case, any law forbidding interfaith marriages would likely be held unconstitutional in the United States.

[607]"It is *not* a ground for a divorce or separation that the spouses entertain different views on religion

While the *Qur'an* explicitly permits Muslim men to marry "chaste" women "of the Book" (Jews and Christians), Muslim women are forbidden to marry non-Muslims.[608] Contrary to this *Qur'anic* command, there is a trend emerging in the United States in which Muslim women are increasingly marrying non-Muslim men.[609] While the United States courts have, without exception, upheld interfaith marriages, the Muslim community stigmatizes women who marry non-Muslims, and most "respected" *imams* will refuse to perform the ceremonies.[610] Furthermore, Muslim women who choose to marry non-Muslims are persecuted in Islamic countries.

It follows, then, that if the various states in the United States were to allow *Shariah* to govern interfaith marriages of Muslims, all marriages in which Muslim women have married non-Muslim men, no matter the duration of the marriage, would suddenly be rendered void under *Shariah*.[611] Additionally, under *Shariah*, if one spouse leaves Islam or otherwise changes his or her faith, then the marriage is automatically, without any notice or process, legally annulled.[612] In the United States, however, mere differences in faith are not grounds for divorce,[613] let alone an automatic legal annulment of the marital relationship. Moreover, any state laws prohibiting marriage

---

or that they are members of different sects or denominations." Cross, *supra* note 566, at 928 (emphasis added). Fault grounds for divorce include, but are not limited to, adultery, conviction of a crime, duress, fraud, gross neglect of duty, and nonsupport of a spouse. *See* 27A C.J.S. *Divorce* §§ 88–96.

[608]*See* QUR'AN, *supra* note 11, at *Surah* 5:5 ("This day are (all) things good and pure made lawful unto you. The food of the People of the Book is lawful unto you and yours is lawful unto them. (Lawful unto you in marriage) are (not only) chaste women who are believers, but chaste women among the People of the Book, revealed before your time."); *see also* RELIANCE OF THE TRAVELLER, *supra* note 10, at 529 ("It is not lawful or valid for a Muslim man to be married to any woman who is not either a Muslim, Christian, or Jew; nor is it lawful or valid for a Muslim woman to be married to *anyone besides a Muslim*." (emphasis added)).

[609]Quraishi & Syeed-Miller, *supra* note 536, at 194 n.39.

[610]*Id.* at 194.

[611]RELIANCE OF THE TRAVELLER, *supra* note 10, at 529 ("[N]or is it lawful or valid for a Muslim woman to be married to *anyone* besides a Muslim [man]." (emphasis added)).

[612]The waiting period is also imposed upon couples who have had sexual intercourse in order to determine if the woman has since become pregnant. *Id.* at 566–67.

[613]Cross, *supra* note 566.

between persons of different races or religions would be void as against public policy in the United States.

3. Proxy Marriage

In the United States, marriage by proxy, in which a man and woman solemnize a marriage without being present at the same time and place, is allowed only sparingly, and typically only for members of the armed forces who are deployed overseas and consequently unable to solemnize their marriage unions domestically.[614] Marriages by proxy are permitted in only four states: California,[615] Colorado,[616] Montana,[617] and Texas.[618]

Shariah, however, routinely permits marriage by "proxy."[619] Under this arrangement, a third party can agree to the terms of the marriage on behalf of the absent party, and the marriage will still be legally constituted, raising the danger that a proxy could agree to terms that the principal would not have agreed to on his or her own accord. There is also the chance that a proxy could be deceitful in his representations to the parties involved in the marriage.

Moreover, when U.S. courts have granted deference to *Shariah* principles of marriage, the outcome has directly conflicted with American laws. For example, in *Farah v. Farah*, a Virginia trial judge recognized the validity of a Muslim marriage that was conducted through a proxy in England.[620] The trial judge ruled

---

[614]*E.g.*, CAL. FAM. CODE § 420(b) (Deering 2010) ("[A] member of the Armed Forces of the United States who is stationed overseas and serving in a conflict or a war and is unable to appear for the licensure and solemnization of the marriage may enter into that marriage by the appearance of an attorney in fact, commissioned and empowered in writing for that purpose through a power of attorney.").

[615]CAL. FAM. CODE §§ 350–355, 420 (Deering 2010).

[616]COLO. REV. STAT. § 14-2-109 (2010).

[617]MONT. CODE ANN. § 40-1-301 (2009).

[618]TEX. FAM. CODE ANN. § 2.006–2.007 (West 2009).

[619]RELIANCE OF THE TRAVELLER, *supra* note 10, at 521 (Either the male guardian on behalf of the bride or the groom on behalf of himself "may commission someone to accept the marriage agreement on his behalf, provided the person commissioned is someone who would be legally entitled to accept such a marriage for himself.").

[620]Farah v. Farah, 429 S.E.2d 626, 629–30 (Va. Ct. App. 1993).

that the marriage, which was solemnized in England (though no certificate of marriage was issued by any English authority) and its ceremony completed in Pakistan, must be honored in Virginia because "the law of the state of Pakistan sanctions marriages performed under the personal law of the parties which in this case was Moslem law."[621] The Virginia Court of Appeals correctly recognized, however, that Pakistan's recognition of *Shariah* "does not control the issue of the validity of the marriage under Virginia law."[622] Instead, the court applied Virginia law, which only granted comity according to the principles of the location celebrating the marriage, which was England.[623] Applying this standard and finding that English law prohibited marriages by proxy, the court of appeals refused to honor the marriage.[624] Although the court ultimately came to the right decision in that case, if England *had* recognized Islamic marriages affected by proxy, under the analysis in this case, Virginia would likely have recognized a marriage by proxy.[625]

B. PRE- AND EXTRA-MARITAL SEX

The United States does not punish pre-marital sex performed in private by consenting adults.[626] Further, despite such sexual

---

[621]*Id.* at 629 (quoting the opinion of the trial court).

[622]*Id.*

[623]*Id.*

[624]*Id.* at 629–30.

[625]Comity is not without limits, however, for "[n]o state is bound by comity to give effect in its courts to the marriage laws of another state, repugnant to its own laws and policy." Hager v. Hager, 349 S.E.2d 908, 909 (Va. Ct. App. 1986) (citing Toler v. Oakwood Smokeless Coal Corp., 4 S.E.2d 364, 366 (Va. Ct. App. 1939)).

[626]*See* Lawrence v. Texas, 539 U.S. 558, 578 (2003) (quoting Bowers v. Hardwick, 478 U.S. 186, 216 (1986) (Stevens, J., dissenting)) ("[I]ndividual decisions by married persons, concerning the intimacies of their physical relationship, even when not intended to produce offspring, are a form of 'liberty' protected by the Due Process Clause of the Fourteenth Amendment. Moreover, *this protection extends to intimate choices by unmarried as well as married persons*." (emphasis added)). However, many states still consider pre-marital sex a misdemeanor offense, though they do not enforce such laws. WHARTON'S CRIMINAL LAW §§ 210–211 (Charles E. Torcia, ed., 15th ed. 1994); *see also, e.g.*, GA. CODE. ANN. § 16-6-18 ("An unmarried person commits the offense of fornication when he voluntarily has sexual intercourse with another person and, upon conviction thereof, shall be punished as for a misdemeanor."); VA. CODE ANN. § 18.2-344 (2011) ("Any person, not being married, who voluntarily shall have sexual intercourse with any other person, shall be guilty of fornication, punishable as a Class 4 misdemeanor."); Jonathan Turley, *Adultery, in Many States, Is Still a Crime*, USA Today (Apr. 25, 2010), http://www.usatoday.com/news/opinion/forum/2010-04-26-column26_ST_N.htm

conduct's potential harmful effects on families and on society as a whole, in recognition of individual liberties, the act of adultery is not included in the Model Penal Code's categorization of offenses against the family. Although the code does punish a man's fraudulent impersonation of another woman's husband,[627] punishment of even this offense is governed by the principle prohibiting cruel and unusual punishment.

Shariah, however, prescribes severe corporal punishments—ranging from lashing to stoning—for unlawful sexual intercourse. Under *Shariah*, adultery is a *hadd* offense (one with severe prescribed penalties), a criminal act against Allah himself.[628] For instance, *Shariah* declares illegal all sexual intercourse that is not either between a husband and his wife (or wives) or between a man and his slave woman.[629] Unlawful sexual intercourse (*zina*), which includes rape, adultery, and fornication,[630] is not only a sin in Islam, but an offense carrying severe criminal or civil (or both) penalties, depending on the participant's marital status, whether the witness requirement is satisfied,[631] and whether the alleged offender confesses.[632] If a man rapes an unmarried woman and it is treated as a tort, upon proof, the man is liable to pay the "bride price," i.e., the going rate for acquiring a similarly situated woman as a wife.[633] If

---

(explaining that although a number of states have not repealed laws criminalizing adultery, states generally do not enforce the provision any longer).

[627]MODEL PENAL CODE § 213.1 (2)(c).

[628]PETERS, *supra* note 260, at 59.

[629]*Compare* QUR'AN, *supra* note 11, at *Surah* 17:32 (alluding to a category of not only immoral but *unlawful* sexual relationships) *with id.* at *Surah* 24:2 (prescribing the penalty of flogging for *zina* offenders); *see also* RELIANCE OF THE TRAVELLER, *supra* note 10, at 660; SAHIH BUKHARI, *supra* note 69 at Vol. 2, Bk. 23, No. 413; *id.* at Vol. 8, Bk. 82, No. 805; *id.* at Vol. 8, Bk. 82, No. 814; *id.* at Vol. 8, Bk. 82, No. 819.

[630]JAMILA HUSSAIN, ISLAM – ITS LAW AND SOCIETY 145 (2d ed. 2004).

[631]One must produce four eyewitnesses to prove an allegation of *zina*. Although in cases of voluntary unlawful sex, this impractical witness requirement may benefit the couple; in rape cases, the result is that the female victim is punished while the rapist goes unpunished. *See* discussion *supra* Chapter 4.E.3.

[632]PETERS, *supra* note 260, at 59–60.

[633]*Id.*; RELIANCE OF THE TRAVELLER, *supra* note 10, at 535.

an unmarried couple voluntarily fornicates, both participants may be punished with 100 lashes each.[634] But if one of the participants is married, he or she will be stoned to death.[635] In fact, "all the five schools of Islamic jurisprudence—Hanafi, Shafai, Maliki and Hanbali of the Sunnis and the Ja'afri of the Shi'as prescribe [stoning] for adultery. On this point of law, there is complete unanimity of opinion."[636]

Stoning (*rajm*) is a brutal community event, where a large crowd uses stones large enough to kill the offenders, but small enough to avoid killing them too quickly.[637] Just as amputation of one offender is designed to deter unlawful behavior from other potential offenders, so stoning is designed to deter *zina* (unlawful sexual intercourse), both specifically and generally.[638]

Hadiths relate a story about a Bedouin who came to Muhammad to inquire about an adulterous affair the Bedouin's son had committed with a married woman. He relayed the tale and said that in response to his son's indiscretion, he had ransomed him for 100 sheep and a female slave. Muhammad told the Bedouin,

[634]QUR'AN, *supra* note 11, at *Surah* 24:2 ("The woman and the man guilty of adultery or fornication— flog each of them with a hundred stripes: let not compassion move you in their case, in a matter prescribed by Allah . . . ."); RELIANCE OF THE TRAVELLER, *supra* note 10, at 610 ("If the offender is someone with the capacity to remain chaste, then he or she is stoned to death (def: o12.6), *someone with the capacity to remain chaste* meaning anyone who has had sexual intercourse (A: at least once) with their spouse in a valid marriage, and is free, of age, and sane. . . . If the offender is not someone with the capacity to remain chaste, then the penalty consists of being scourged [] one hundred stripes and banished to a distance of at least 81 km./50 mi. for one year.").

[635]The *Sunnah* prescribes stoning for adulterers, whether male or female. SAHIH MUSLIM, *supra* note 46, at Bk. 017, No. 4194 ("Allah's Messenger (may peace be upon him) awarded the punishment of stoning to death (to the married adulterer and adulteress) and, after him, we also awarded the punishment of stoning, I am afraid that with the lapse of time, the people (may forget it) and may say: We do not find the punishment of stoning in the Book of Allah, and thus go astray by abandoning this duty prescribed by Allah. Stoning is a duty laid down in Allah's Book for married men and women who commit adultery when proof is established, or if there is pregnancy, or a confession."); SAHIH BUKHARI, *supra* note 69, at Vol. *3, Bk. 49, Num. 860* ("[G]o to the (adulterous) wife of this (man) and stone her to death"); *id.* at Vol. 7, Bk. 63, Num. 195 (After a married man confessed to the prophet that he had committed adultery, "the Prophet ordered him to be stoned to the death.").

[636]Ishtiaq Ahmed, *View: Stoning to Death*, DAILY TIMES (Pak.) (Sept. 14, 2010), http://www.dailytimes. com.pk/default.asp?page=2010%5C09%5C14%5Cstory_14-9-2010_pg3_2.

[637]PETERS, *supra* note 260, at 37.

[638]*See* QUR'AN, *supra* note 11, at *Surah* 24:2 n.2956 (noting that the punishment should be public "in order to be a deterrent").

By the One Who holds my soul in His hand, I shall certainly pass judgment between you *in accordance with [Allah's] Book.* As for the female slave and the sheep, they must be returned to you. Your son deserves one hundred lashes and banishment for a year. Go . . . [to the adulterous woman,] and if she confesses, stone her to death.[639]

In another instance, Muhammad commanded one of his companions to stone an adulterous woman to death, and the companion did as Muhammad commanded.[640] In yet another instance, after a man from the Bani Aslam tribe told Muhammad that "he had committed illegal sexual intercourse and bore witnesses four times against himself[,] [Muhammad] ordered him to be stoned to death as he was a married person."[641] From this account, the text of the *Qur'an,* and other accounts of Muhammad's treatment of *zina,*[642] the punishments for *zina* are widely considered to be 100 lashes for fornicators and death by stoning for adulterers.[643]

Despite the draconian nature of stoning and lashing, many *Shariah*-compliant nations continue to implement these punishments. For example, in Somalia, a thirteen-year-old girl who had been raped by three men was buried in the ground and then stoned by fifty men—for committing *zina.*[644] Afterwards, as she was

---

[639]PETERS, *supra* note 260, at 60 (quoting 'Asqalani, *Bulugh,* no. 1031) (emphasis added) (internal quotation marks omitted).

[640]*See* SAHIH BUKHARI, *supra* note 69, at Vol. 3, Bk. 49, No. 860.

[641]*Id.* at Vol. 8, Bk. 82, No. 805; *see also id.* at Vol. 4, Bk. 26, No. 859 (Muhammad adjudicated a claim of adultery committed by two Jews and "gave the order that both of them should be stoned to death.").

[642]*Id.* at Vol. 7, Bk. 63, No. 195 (After a man confessed to the Prophet that he had committed adultery, "the Prophet ordered him to be stoned to the death."); *see also* MUSLIM, *supra* note 217, at Bk. 017, No. 4191 ("[I]n case of married male committing adultery with a married female, they shall receive one hundred lashes and be stoned to death.").

[643]PETERS, *supra* note 260, at 55, 60. As a practical matter, a *majority* of stoning accounts today *involve women who have been raped. See, e.g.,* Mydans, *supra* note 513 (A *Shariah* judge declared that the rape victim's claim that her brother-in-law had raped her constituted an admission of guilt of adultery. Since Pakistan adopted *hudood* laws "to ban 'all forms of adultery, whether the offense is committed with or without the consent of [both] parties,'. . .[i]t is almost always the women who are punished, whatever the facts."); *see also* Fisk, *supra* note 484 (Of all the stoning incidents cited, only one was of a man; apparently, the evidentiary requirements of *Shariah* have not been sufficient procedural safeguards to protect rape victims.).

[644]Fisk, *supra* note 484.

being dug out to be buried, she was found to be alive, so she was reburied and stoned for a second time.[645] Also in Somalia, in 2009, a *Shariah* judge entered a stoning sentence against a woman accused of having an affair. Her boyfriend was spared stoning and received a lashing instead.[646] In Iran, authorities punished Sakineh Mohammadi Ashtiani with ninety-nine lashes for allegedly having extramarital sexual relationships *after* her husband had died.[647] Additionally, in July 2010, the authorities planned to stone Ashtiani for adultery, but they were forced to suspend the stoning due to international pressure after Ashtiani's son publicized her plight to international media outlets.[648] Finally, a 2008 independent film recounts the story of Soraya M., a woman who was stoned to death in a rural Iranian village in 1986 after her husband falsely and maliciously accused her of adultery.[649]

Saudi Arabia even punishes people for merely being in the company of persons of the opposite sex without an appropriate guardian. In 2006, a nineteen-year-old woman went to meet a high school friend to retrieve some old pictures.[650] Two men got into their vehicle and drove them to a place where five others were waiting.[651] The seven men then raped the woman and her friend.[652] Following the rapes, both the woman and her male companion were not treated as victims, but were instead prosecuted for the *Shariah* crime of "mixing of the sexes" because *Shariah* prohibits women from being

[645]*Id.*

[646]*Id.*

[647]EUR. PARL. ASS. RES., ON THE HUMAN RIGHTS SITUATION IN IRAN, IN PARTICULAR THE CASES OF SAKINEH MOHAMMADI ASHTIANI AND ZAHRA BAHRAMI (Sept. 8, 2010), *available at* http://www.europarl.europa. eu/sides/getDoc.do?type=TA&reference=P7-TA-2010-0310&language=EN.

[648]*Id.*

[649]Irshad Manji, *The Stoning of Soraya M.—a Must-See Film About Moral Courage*, HUFFINGTON POST (Mar. 8, 2010), http://www.huffingtonpost.com/irshad-manji/emthe-stoning-of-soraya-m_b_489943. html.

[650]Abdullah Shihri, *Saudi King Pardons Rape Victim from Prison, Public Lashing*, SEATTLE TIMES (Dec. 18, 2007), http://seattletimes.nwsource.com/html/nationworld/2004079327_saudi18.html.

[651]*Id.*

[652]*Id.*

alone with an unrelated man.[653] The woman was sentenced to prison and ninety lashes.[654] After her lawyer appealed the decision, the court responded by *increasing* her penalty to six months in prison and *200 lashes*, arguing that she deserved steeper penalties for "her attempt to aggravate and influence the judiciary through the media."[655] Only after the United States publicly condemned the decision did the Saudi king officially pardon the rape victim.[656]

In September 2010, a Dubai-based television network aired gruesome footage of a stoning of a woman in the northwest region of Pakistan.[657] The woman's "offense" was that she had purportedly been seen out with a man.[658] Following the stoning, the U.S. Department of State issued the following statement:

> We condemn in the strongest possible terms the brutal stoning of a woman in Orakzai, Pakistan, allegedly by members of the Pakistani Taliban, which is depicted in a video circulating on the internet.
>
> This vicious attack, carried out as a crowd of onlookers watched, *violates all norms of human decency* and is a chilling example of the *cowardly disregard violent extremists have for human life*. There is no justification for such barbaric and cruel treatment of a fellow human being.[659]

Any system of law that implements punishments that violate "all

---

[653]*Id.* Notably, the woman had met with the man, a friend from high school, to retrieve a picture of both the man and herself out of respect for her husband, whom she had recently married. *See id.*

[654]*Id.*

[655]*Saudi Rape Victim Sentenced to Jail, 200 Lashes*, SEATTLE TIMES (Nov. 16, 2007), http://community. seattletimes.nwsource.com/archive/?date=20071116&slug=saudi16 (internal quotation marks omitted).

[656]Although "Saudi officials . . . bristled at the criticism of what they consider an internal affair," the king succumbed to international pressure because, like other Saudi authorities, he was "wary of hurting [Saudi Arabia's] image in the United States." Shihri, *supra* note 650.

[657]Michael Georgy, *Video Shows Taliban Allegedly Stoning Pakistan Woman*, REUTERS (Sep 27, 2010), http://www.reuters.com/article/idUSTRE68Q2TA20100927.

[658]*Id.*

[659]Press Release, Philip J. Crowley, Assistant Sec'y, Bureau Public Affairs, U.S. Dep't of State, U.S. Strongly Condemns Stoning of Woman in Orakzai, Pakistan (Sept. 28, 2010) (emphasis added), *available at* http://www.state.gov/r/pa/prs/ps/2010/09/148302.htm.

norms of human decency," "shock the conscience,"[660] and indicate "cowardly disregard . . . for human life" should not be tolerated in the United States of America.

C. DIVORCE

The Equal Protection Clause of the U.S. Constitution uniformly places men and women on equal legal terms, including with regard to divorce.[661] In the United States, "[a] divorce proceeding is generally a controversy between a *husband and a wife* to determine who is at fault in causing domestic difficulties," and a divorce is only available as an "extraordinary remedy" for "unavoidable and unendurable" circumstances affecting *either* spouse.[662] Moreover, "[t]he paramount goal of a divorce proceeding is a *just and equitable* resolution of the interests and rights of divorcing spouses."[663] Although many U.S. states require fault for marital partners to divorce, which might include adultery,[664] neglect,[665] abandonment,[666] cruelty,[667] non-support,[668] and felony convictions,[669] "[m]ost states now have statutes which allow for no-fault divorce, or divorce by consent, in which the parties are not required to prove fault or grounds for divorce other than irreconcilable differences or

---

[660]Rochin v. California, 342 U.S. 165, 172 (1952) (establishing the standard that state action that "shocks the conscience" violates due process of law).

[661]U.S. CONST. amend. XIV ("No state shall . . . deny to any person within its jurisdiction the equal protection of the laws.").

[662]27A C.J.S. *Divorce* § 7 (2011) (emphasis added); *see also* 24 AM. JUR. 2D *Divorce & Separation* § 22 (2010) ("[I]n various jurisdictions, divorce or dissolution of marriage is authorized under such 'no-fault' statutes upon a showing that the marriage is 'irretrievably broken,' on a showing of a 'breakdown of the marriage relationship,' on a showing of 'irreconcilable differences, which have caused the irremediable breakdown of the marriage,' or on a similar showing of marital breakdown." (citations omitted)). For examples, see CAL. FAM. CODE § 2310 (2011) (allowing divorce for "irreconcilable differences") and N.Y. DOM. REL. LAW § 170(7) (2011) (allowing divorce if "[t]he relationship between husband and wife has broken down irretrievably for a period of at least six months").

[663]27A C.J.S. *Divorce* § 7 (2011) (emphasis added).

[664]*Id.* § 88.

[665]*Id.* § 92.

[666]*Id.* § 66.

[667]*Id.* § 40.

[668]*Id.* § 93. This is generally only permissible where a state statute expressly includes it as a lawful ground for divorce. *Id.*

[669]*Id.* § 89.

irretrievable breakdown of the marriage."[670]

Under *Shariah*, grounds for divorce are significantly broader for men than they are for women. The five elements of a lawful divorce include "the spoken form," authority to effect divorce, intent, a wife, and the initiator of the divorce (i.e., the husband).[671] Divorces are legally "valid" under *Shariah* when initiated by "*any:* (a) *husband*; (b) who is sane; (c) has reached puberty; (d) and who voluntarily effects it."[672] In fact, a wife's ability to divorce may be contingent upon her husband's desire to be divorced and his oral pronouncement of the same.[673] Finally, according to the *Qur'an*, if a husband divorces his wife and they reconcile after he has made his pronouncement, the two cannot be remarried unless and until the ex-wife marries another man and is divorced by him.[674]

While men generally have the power to divorce at will, women are only permitted to divorce their husbands under limited circumstances. Some *Sunni* schools, in fact, maintain that women do not obtain legal divorces on their own initiative, but merely *dissolve* their marriages and become lawfully separated from their husbands.[675] These dissolutions (*khul*) are limited to very particular grounds; and if women do choose to dissolve the marriage, even when their safety requires it, they forfeit their financial security.[676] This is because both the *Qur'an* and *Sunnah* demonstrate that the

---

[670]4 Am. Jur. 2d *Annulment of Marriage* § 2 (2011).

[671]RELIANCE OF THE TRAVELLER, *supra* note 10, at 557. Noticeably absent from this list are U.S. constitutional due process requirements. *See, e.g.*, Farid v. Farid, No. FA094011049S, 2010 LEXIS 2296, at *7–8 (Conn. Super. Sept. 10, 2010).

[672]RELIANCE OF THE TRAVELLER, *supra* note 10, at 556 (emphasis added).

[673]*See id.* at 557 (If a husband tells his wife, "'Divorce yourself [from me],' [and] then if she immediately says, 'I divorce myself [from you],' she is divorced, but if she delays, she is not divorced unless the husband has said, 'Divorce yourself *whenever you wish.*'" (emphasis added)).

[674]QUR'AN, *supra* note 11, at *Surah* 2:230 ("[I]f a husband divorces his wife (irrevocably), he cannot, after that, remarry her until after she has married another husband and he has divorced her.").

[675]*See* FIQH, *supra* note 305, at 171 (asserting that "*Al-Khul'* is dissolution, not divorce").

[676]*See* QUR'AN, *supra* note 11, at *Surah* 2:229 (providing that in cases where a wife "fear[s] that [she] would be unable to keep the limits ordained by Allah" by remaining in a particular marriage, "there is not blame on either of [the spouses] if she give something for her freedom").

woman's "freedom" costs her something. While the *Qur'an* permits, seemingly broadly, the dissolution so long as the woman gives "something for her freedom,"[677] *hadiths* reveal that Muhammad required a woman seeking such dissolution of her marriage to return the garden that her husband had given her as *mahr* (dower or marriage payment).[678] Therefore, to dissolve her marriage, a woman essentially loses the marriage payment, which would serve as her spousal support following the dissolution.

Further, under *Hanafi* law, which does not consider a husband's inability or refusal to provide for his wife to be legal grounds for women to dissolve their marriages, women may be placed in especially difficult financial circumstances. "For example, a wife, who in traditional society is unable to support herself and her children, is also unable to free herself from a husband who has been imprisoned for a number of years."[679] Even if a *Shariah* court decides to grant dissolution in such circumstances, the woman, under the above-mentioned rule, must forfeit her dower, which would have served as her spousal support.

Additionally, *Shariah* gives men the right to divorce (*talaq*) their wives at will merely by making a pronouncement that the marriage is dissolved.[680] This convenient method of obtaining a divorce merely requires a husband to make three declarations of divorce for a divorce to be legally effective. In fact, "[t]he *sunna* is to make a pronouncement of divorce in an interval between menstruations in which no sexual intercourse with the wife has taken place."[681] The pronouncement of divorce can be made using

---

[677]*Id.*

[678]SAHIH BUKHARI, *supra* note 69, at Vol. 7, Bk. 63, No. 197.

[679]ESPOSITO, *supra* note 595, at 26.

[680]RELIANCE OF THE TRAVELLER, *supra* note 10, at 558; ESPOSITO, *supra* note 595, at 29–30.

[681]RELIANCE OF THE TRAVELLER, *supra* note 10, at 558. The purpose of this is to delay the effectiveness of a divorce until the couple can be sure that the wife is not pregnant to ease paternity determinations.

either "plain" words or "allusive" words.[682] Using "plain words" involves the husband's explicit declaration of divorce: "I divorce you," or "You are divorced."[683] This can be done by "pronouncing one sentence, 'I divorce you thrice,' or three separate sentences, 'I divorce you; I divorce you; I divorce you,' [or '*talaq, talaq, talaq,*'] irrevocably dissolving the marriage."[684] Pronouncements of divorce by "allusive words" are even broader and are legally effective if a husband tells his wife that she is now "alone," "free," or "separated," and even if he tells her nothing but merely denies that he is married to a third party, so long as his intention is for divorce.[685]

Muslims derive this practice from the *Qur'an* in *Surah* 2:227[686] and from the *hadiths*, which permit even a single pronouncement of divorce to constitute a valid divorce:

> If the husband says, "You are divorced," and thereby intends a two[fold] or threefold pronouncement, then whatever number he intends is effected, this rule holding for all words that effect divorce, whether plain or allusive. (O: The proof that a single pronouncement can validly effect a threefold divorce is the hadith classified as rigorously authenticated (sahih) . . . that [Muhammad], when [a man] divorced his wife and then said, "I did not intend it except as one time [[(of the three pronouncements he presumed were required)]]," made him swear an oath to that effect, and then returned her to him. If a single pronouncement could not effect a threefold divorce, there would not have been any point in [Muhammad's] making him swear the oath . . . .).[687]

---

[682]*Id.* at 559–60.

[683]*Id.* at 559.

[684]ESPOSITO, *supra* note 595, at 31.

[685]RELIANCE OF THE TRAVELLER, *supra* note 10, at 559–60; *see also* FIQH, *supra* note 305, at 165 (emphasizing that allusive pronouncements of divorce are effective when they are "accompanied by an intention").

[686]QUR'AN, *supra* note 11, at *Surah* 2:227 ("But if [men's] intention is firm for divorce, Allah heareth and knoweth all things . . . .").

[687]RELIANCE OF THE TRAVELLER, *supra* note 10, at 560; *see also* FIQH, *supra* note 305, at 164 (citing to

Therefore, under Islamic divorce law, a husband may effect a valid divorce by means of a private declaration of divorce that is completely outside of judicial process or other official state recognition.[688]

The extent to which *Shariah* principles have been considered in divorce cases throughout the United States has already shown that

> [c]ivil and religious laws come into more substantial conflict at the point of marriage dissolution . . . [because] divorce disputes involve two individuals with different interests[,] . . . different rights under official and unofficial law [(local religious custom)], different understandings of their religious tradition and practice, and different motivations to seek recourse from the state. In this setting, official law operates to protect a range of individual rights that may stand opposed to religious norms, and unofficial law operates to define and defend the boundaries and membership of those communities.[689]

Even a cursory glance at this issue suggests the total incompatibility of Islamic divorce laws with those of the United States. Closer examination confirms that the two legal systems are wholly incompatible. Furthermore, United States courts have already faced the challenge of whether or not to recognize *Shariah*-compliant divorces in cases before them.

For example, in *Seth v. Seth*, a Texas appellate court was confronted with the issues of whether a polygamous marriage existed; whether there had been a successful divorce; and whether Texas should apply the laws of its own state, the laws of the countries where the alleged marriages and divorces were obtained, or Islamic law.[690] The court found that it was necessary to apply

---

hadiths to support the proposition that "[t]hree pronouncements of divorce at one time count as one divorce").

[688]*See* Quraishi & Syeed-Miller, *supra* note 536, at 208–09.

[689]Ann Laquer Estin, *Unofficial Family Law*, 94 IOWA L. REV. 449, 462 (2009).

[690]Seth v. Seth, 694 S.W.2d 459, 462 (Tex. Ct. App. 1985).

Texas law because the parties, although citizens of India, had taken up residence in Texas and acquired property that must be divided according to Texas property law. Specifically, the court reasoned:

> Our review of the record convinces us that the most critical consideration is . . . the relevant policies of the forum [state of Texas]. Before examining [this] factor . . . , we note that while it is true that the critical events in the case did not occur in Texas, that at the time of the events, the parties themselves had no apparent connection with Texas, and that even today, Husband and Wife Two [(the second wife and the appellant in the case)] are citizens of India and not the U.S., Texas's interest in this suit does not arise simply from the fact that it is the place of the trial. Texas's nexus to this lawsuit lies in the fact that Husband and Wife Two have lived here since 1977 [(for 8 years)], during which time they acquired real property within the State. That connection would enhance the prerogative of the trial court to consider the relevant policies of Texas in deciding the present conflicts of law question.[691]

The court then proceeded to analyze whether the divorce, or *talaq*, would be recognized.[692] The husband, who had left his wife in India and moved to the United States, had pronounced divorce in Kuwait and then married a second wife the following day.[693] In affirming the trial court and rejecting the validity of the divorce and subsequent second marriage, the Texas court held that even though such a divorce may be valid under Islamic law, the state of Texas would not recognize the divorce because "[t]he harshness of such a result to the non-Muslim divorced wife runs *so counter to our notions of good morals and natural justice* that we hold that Islamic

---

[691]*Id.* at 463.
[692]*Id.*
[693]*See id.* at 461. The first wife, still in India, was given no opportunity to be heard. *Id.*

law in this situation need not be applied."[694]

Moreover, *every* situation in which a Muslim man purports to have obtained a valid divorce by pronouncing *talaq* will necessarily conflict with American law since *talaq* fails to satisfy American due process requirements. Specifically, due process requires that the parties to a divorce proceeding be afforded notice and the opportunity to be heard.[695] For instance, in *Farid v. Farid*, the court held,

> [i]t is the settled rule of [Connecticut], if indeed it may not be safely called an established principle of general jurisprudence, that no court will proceed to the adjudication of a matter involving conflicting rights and interests, until all persons directly concerned in the event have been actually or constructively notified of the pendency of the proceeding, and given reasonable opportunity to appear and be heard . . . . It is fundamental in proper judicial administration that no matter shall be decided unless the parties have fair notice that it will be presented in sufficient time to prepare themselves upon the issue . . . . *In cases in which a divorce decree was issued in a foreign court without one party's knowledge or consent, Connecticut courts have refrained from recognizing*

---

[694]*Id.* at 463 (emphasis added).

[695]*In re* Gault, 387 U.S. 1, 33 (1967) ("Notice, to comply with due process requirements, must be given sufficiently in advance of scheduled court proceedings so that reasonable opportunity to prepare will be afforded . . . ."); Moustafa v. Moustafa, 888 A.2d 1230, 1232 (Md. Ct. Spec. App. 2005) ("The Defendant claims that he obtained a divorce from [Mrs. Moustafa] in Egypt on November 4, 2002. Such a divorce is not entitled to comity by this Court which will not proceed to the adjudication of a matter involving conflicting rights and interests until all persons directly concerned in the event have been actually or constructively notified of the pendency of the proceeding and given reasonable opportunity to appear and be heard." (quoting the opinion of the trial court)); Howard v. Howard, No. 89-6-2CV(C), 1990 Del. Fam. Ct. LEXIS 69, at *4–5 (Del. Fam. Ct. Jan. 31, 1990) ("Delaware considers notice to a respondent in a divorce action to be a fundamental concept of due process. In view of the fact that Howard received no notice and no opportunity to be heard, this Court is not under any obligation to recognize the divorce decree issued by the Dominican Republic. Notwithstanding comity, this Court in good conscience cannot recognize or enforce a divorce decree which is inconsistent with established principles of justice in this jurisdiction." (internal citations omitted)); *see also* L. v. L. 305 A.2d 620, 622 (Del. 1973) ("Notice has always been fundamental to the concept of due process, and publication has been the traditional method of supplying legal notice to divorce defendants residing outside the State."); RESTATEMENT (SECOND) OF CONFLICT OF LAWS § 104 (1971) ("A judgment rendered without judicial jurisdiction or without adequate notice or adequate opportunity to be heard will not be recognized or enforced in other states.").

the foreign divorce decree under comity.[696]

It seems to follow that any *Shariah*-appropriate divorce proceeding that does not afford both parties notice and an opportunity to be heard is "not binding" in U.S. courts of law.[697]

D. CHILD CUSTODY

In the United States, child custody disputes are generally determined by the "best interest of the child" standard.[698] As a general rule today, neither father nor mother automatically has a paramount right to custody or legal guardianship of their children; rather, absent parental misconduct of some sort, both parents are deemed to have equal parental rights over their children.[699]

Under *Shariah*, however, the standard for determining custody of children is not the fact-specific "best interests of the child" standard; instead, custody of children is determined by fixed *Shariah* guidelines. First, as a foundational rule, *Shariah* holds that legal guardianship of children, which encompasses the parents' power to enter into agreements on behalf of their children, lies exclusively with fathers or, if a child's father is deceased, paternal grandfathers.[700] In custody disputes, however, custody of children younger than seven or eight years old ("the age of discrimination")[701]

---

[696]*Farid*, 2010 LEXIS 2296, at *7–8 (internal citations and quotation marks omitted) (emphasis added).

[697]*See id.*

[698]*E.g.*, *Ex Parte* Byars, 794 So. 2d 345, 347 (Ala. 2001) ("The controlling consideration in [an initial custody determination] is the best interest of the child."); Montenegro v. Diaz, 27 P.3d 289, 293 (Cal. 2001) ("Under California's statutory scheme governing child custody and visitation determinations, the overarching concern is the best interest of the child."); Martin v. Martin, 74 A.D. 2d 419, 425 (N.Y. App. Div. 1980) ("It is familiar law that in a proceeding involving two natural parents custody is to be determined solely by what is in the best interest of the child . . . ."); *In re* Marriage of Harris, 499 N.W.2d 329, 330 (Iowa Ct. App. 1993) ("In child custody cases, the best interests of the child is the first and governing consideration.").

[699]27C C.J.S. *Divorce* § 994 (2005); *see also Ex Parte* Byars, 794 So. 2d at 347 ("Alabama law gives neither party priority in an initial custody determination."); *In re* Marriage of Harris, 499 N.W.2d at 330 ("Gender is irrelevant, and neither parent should have greater burden than the other in attempting to gain custody in a dissolution proceeding."); In re Custody of Townsend, 427 N.E.2d 1231 (Ill. 1981); *In re* Marriage of Murphy, 592 N.W.2d 681 (Iowa 1999); In Interest of Cooper, 631 P.2d 632 (Kan. 1981); Park v. Park, 610 P.2d 826 (Okla. Ct. App. Div. 2 1980).

[700]RELIANCE OF THE TRAVELLER, *supra* note 10, at 409.

[701]*Id.* at 553.

automatically defaults to the mother based on, *inter alia*, the presumptions that mothers are always "tenderer" toward children and "more steadfast in staying with them."[702] Therefore, rather than focusing on a case-by-case analysis of the children's best interests, legal rights over young children center on a superior legal right of the mother over that of the father in custody determinations and of the father over the mother in legal guardianship.[703] Furthermore, in case of custody disputes, *Shariah* sets forth a comprehensive hierarchy of persons with the "best right to custody of a child," with the rights of maternal grandmothers superseding those of fathers.[704]

The general rule for custody determinations, however, is not absolute. A mother's superior right to custody over her children terminates (or never materializes) if she fails to meet one of three "necessary conditions," two of which are religious: uprightness, sanity, and Islamic faith and practice.[705] "Uprightness" is determined objectively based on *Shariah* standards of religiosity. For instance, *Sunni Shariah* holds that "[i]f the corruptness of a child's mother consists of her not performing the prayer (*salat*), she has *no* right to custody of the child, who might grow up to be like her, ending up in the same vile condition of not praying . . . ."[706] Other indicia of "corruptness" are not as explicit; however, based on the *Qur'an* and *Sunnah*, wives whose husbands classify them as "rebellious" are more likely corrupt than they are upright.[707] Additionally, if a child's father is a Muslim, the mother *must also be a Muslim* to have any

---

[702]*Id.* at 550; *see also* Maria Reiss, *The Materialization of Legal Pluralism in Britain: Why Shari'a Council Decisions Should Be Non-Binding*, 26 ARIZ. J. INT'L & COMP. L. 739, 753 (2009) (citing Kristine Uhlman, *Overview of Shari'a and Prevalent Customs in Islamic Societies-Divorce and Child Custody*, § 8.0 (2004), http://www.expertlaw.com/library/family_law/islamic_custody.html.).

[703]RELIANCE OF THE TRAVELLER, *supra* note 10, at 409, 550.

[704]*Id.* at 550–51; *compare with* Troxel v. Granville, 530 U.S. 57, 66–67 (2000) (acknowledging parents' "fundamental right" to "make decisions concerning the care, custody, and control of their children," and holding that a state statute granting grandparents similar rights "unconstitutionally infringe[d] on that fundamental parental right").

[705]RELIANCE OF THE TRAVELLER, *supra* note 10, at 551–52.

[706]*Id.* at 552 (emphasis added).

[707]*See* discussion *supra* Chapter 4.E.2.

right to custody of the child.[708] Based on the foregoing, mothers who are allegedly "Westernized" or are unbelievers[709] have no right to custody over their children under *Shariah*, no matter how suitable they are as parents. Additionally, mothers lose custody rights over their children if they remarry.[710]

Finally, under *Shariah*, when children are seven or eight years old, they may *choose* which parent may have custody over them because Muhammad is recounted as having given a young boy the choice to live with his father or his mother.[711] This choice is limited, however, to parents who meet the necessary religious requirements.[712] A parent who fails to be "upright" or is a non-Muslim has no right to custody because it is as if he or she is "nonexistent."[713]

Hanafi law is inconsistent with other *Sunni* schools in giving children a choice, however, because it holds that once children reach the appropriate age, custody—as well as legal guardianship, which fathers retain even throughout the mother's custody over the child—automatically diverts to their father.[714] In fact, according to *Hanafi* jurisprudence, even the father's relatives' claims to the children are superior to that of the mother.[715]

To make matters worse for a mother, if she does happen to

---

[708]*See* RELIANCE OF THE TRAVELLER, *supra* note 10, at 552 (holding that "if the child is Muslim, it is a necessary condition that the person with custody be a Muslim (O: because it is a position of authority, and *a non-Muslim has no right to authority and hence no right to raise a Muslim*") (emphasis added); *compare with id.* at 409 (holding that children do not have "full capacity" either to reject or embrace Islam, therefore implying that the Islamic religious status of fathers is imputed to their children).

[709]This is in the event that the father of the child is a Muslim. *See supra* note 708 and accompanying text.

[710]RELIANCE OF THE TRAVELLER, *supra* note 10, at 552 ("[a] woman has no right to custody . . . [if] she remarries"); FIQH, *supra* note 305, at 201 ("The mother has more right to custody of her child, so long as she does not remarry[.]").

[711]RELIANCE OF THE TRAVELLER, *supra* note 10, at 553.

[712]*Id.*

[713]*Id.*; *see also* ESPOSITO, *supra* note 595, at 37.

[714]ESPOSITO, *supra* note 595, at 35; *see also* RELIANCE OF THE TRAVELLER, *supra* note 10, at 553 (noting that although at the age of discrimination a child is given the choice of parent he wants to stay with, if a son chooses his mother, he must be left with his father during the day for teaching and training).

[715]ESPOSITO, *supra* note 595, at 36.

remarry before her children reach the ages of seven and nine (sons and daughters, respectively), her temporary custody terminates prematurely, and the children must return to their father.[716] The differences in these Islamic schools—none of which comports with U.S. child custody laws—further provide insights into the impossible situations into which American courts would be thrust if they were required to interpret and apply *Shariah* instead of U.S. law.

Few published cases have addressed the validity of Islamic child custody determinations in the United States, probably because the issue is primarily handled unofficially.[717] The California case of *Malak v. Malak*,[718] however, does shed some light on the subject. In *Malak*, the court was asked to determine which of two separate child custody determinations, one formulated in a U.A.E. (United Arab Emirates) *Shariah* court and the other in a Lebanese court, was enforceable.[719] The court refused to enforce the U.A.E. custody order on the basis that the wife had no opportunity to be heard in the proceeding.[720] The court determined, however, that the Lebanese order *was* enforceable because even though the Lebanese court had not explicitly applied the "best interests of the child" standard, its decision aligned with California's "best interests of the child" standard.[721]

In *Ali v. Ali*, a New Jersey court found a child custody order obtained in a *Shariah* court in Gaza unenforceable because its custody award comported neither substantively nor procedurally

---

[716]*Id.* This is true of all *Sunni* schools. *See* RELIANCE OF THE TRAVELLER, *supra* note 10, at 552 ("A woman has no right to custody (A: of her child from a previous marriage) when she remarries (O: because married life will occupy her with fulfilling the rights of her husband and prevent her from tending [to] the child. It makes no difference in such cases if the (A: new) husband agrees or not (N: since the child's custody in such a case automatically devolves to the next most eligible on the list . . . ."); *compare with* supra note 704 and accompanying text (discussing the hierarchical list of persons in whom *Shariah* vests custody rights).

[717]*See* Quraishi & Syeed-Miller, *supra* note 536, at 210.

[718]Malak v. Malak, 182 Cal. App. 3d 1018 (Cal. Ct. App. 1986).

[719]*Id.* at 843.

[720]*Id.*

[721]*Id.* at 847 n.1.

with state law.[722] In a well-reasoned holding, the New Jersey court explained the limitations of comity in enforcing the order:

> In *In re the Marriage of Malak*,[723] *Hovav*,[724] *Klont*,[725] and *Custody of a Minor*,[726] as discussed *supra*, the courts recognized the foreign decrees since their decisions were based on an analysis and inquiry *similar to that of the American jurisdiction and thus did not offend public policy*. To the contrary, the defendant seeks to have this court place its imprimatur on a decree that is diametrically opposed to the law of New Jersey and which is repugnant to all case law concerning factors to be considered in making a custody determination.
>
> Thus, for the foregoing reasons, the Sharia Court custody decree cannot be enforced or recognized by New Jersey courts under the doctrine of comity.[727]

Courts that have been confronted with the application of *Shariah* to child custody cases have recognized the irreconcilable discord between American law and Islamic *Shariah*. In fact, as the court in *Ali* candidly acknowledged, custody decisions based on *Shariah* are "repugnant to all case law concerning factors to be considered in making a custody determination."[728] Therefore, while comity generally allows for recognition of custody determinations obtained abroad, it cannot and does not extend to custody awards that do not comport with the "best interests of the child" standard.

---

[722]Ali v. Ali, 652 A.2d 253, 257–59 (N.J. Super. Ct. Ch. Div. 1994).
[723]182 Cal. App. 3d 1018 (Cal. Ct. App. 1986).
[724]Hovav v. Hovav, 458 A.2d 972, 974 (Pa. Super. Ct. 1983).
[725]Klont v. Klont, 342 N.W.2d 549 (Mich. Ct. App. 1983).
[726]Custody of a Minor (No. 3), 468 N.E.2d 251, 252 (Mass. 1984).
[727]*Ali*, 652 A.2d at 260 (emphasis added).
[728]*Id.*

SECTION THREE

JIHAD:

THE MEANS OF IMPLEMENTING SHARIAH WORLDWIDE

Any law, religious or secular, that does not conform to basic human reason and is not compatible with a society's values (values that form the basis of its positive laws) will not be adopted by political and democratic means. Such a law can only be imposed by force. The consistent pattern of forcible implementation of *Shariah* throughout Islamic history demonstrates that the forceful advance of Islam and its law is not a new phenomenon. The current increase in Muslim population and the resultant greater Muslim influence in politics in many Western countries have allowed Muslims to pressure authorities to permit application of *Shariah* in those countries.

Islam's fusion of religion and politics has encouraged Muslims to press for the adoption of *Shariah* by claiming it is their right under religious freedom laws. Because *Shariah* is a religiously-based law (which is also applied to secular matters), it is promoted under the right to free exercise of religion. Yet, political means are only one tool used to impose *Shariah*. When required, Muslims resort to violence to force implementation of *Shariah*.

CHAPTER SIX

THE MEANING OF JIHAD AND ITS THREE FORMS

In Islamic jurisprudence, *jihad* means "to war against non-Muslims."[729] The term *jihad* derives from the word *mujahada*, which means "warfare to establish the religion."[730] Islamic jurists maintain, however, that there are at least three distinct forms of *jihad*.[731] The first form is the "greater *jihad*" of battling against the inner self to attain private holiness and devotion to Allah's path.[732] The second form of *jihad* is *da'wah*, or the invitation addressed to non-Muslims to convert voluntarily to Islam and follow *Shariah*.[733] The third, and most well-known form of *jihad*, is the violent use of the sword in physical conflict with non-Muslims ("unbelievers" or "infidels").[734]

A. SPIRITUAL EXERTION BY INDIVIDUAL MUSLIMS

Spiritual exertion in Allah's path is the first level of *jihad* and is the duty of every Muslim believer. A believer must fulfill his *jihad* duty through exertion within his own heart by attempting to keep the devil out and escape evil.[735] This exertion is the starting point for the Muslim's spiritual journey and is regarded as one of the greater forms of *jihad*.[736] Muhammad "warn[ed] his people against idolatry

---

[729]RELIANCE OF THE TRAVELLER, *supra* note 10, at 599.

[730]*Id.*

[731]*See* WAR AND PEACE IN THE LAW OF ISLAM, *supra* note 48, at 56–57; *see also* RELIANCE OF THE TRAVELLER, *supra* note 10, at 599.

[732]RELIANCE OF THE TRAVELLER, *supra* note 10, at 599.

[733]*See id.* at 3 (maintaining that "a person is not morally obligated by Allah to do or refrain from anything unless the invitation of a prophet and what Allah has legislated have reached him . . . . No one is rewarded for doing something or punished for refraining from or doing something until he knows by means of Allah's messengers what he is obliged to do or obliged to refrain from."); *see also id.* at 602–03; WAR AND PEACE IN THE LAW OF ISLAM, *supra* note 48, at 96 (explaining that "invitation to Islam," i.e., attempts to convert an unbelieving populace to Islam, was a prerequisite to violent *jihad*).

[734]RELIANCE OF THE TRAVELLER, *supra* note 10, at 599–603; *see also* WAR AND PEACE IN THE LAW OF ISLAM, *supra* note 48, at 55–93.

[735]WAR AND PEACE IN THE LAW OF ISLAM, *supra* note 48, at 56–57.

[736]*Id.*

and invit[ed] them to worship Allah,"[737] noting that "if any strive (with might and main), they do so for their own souls."[738]

Since *jihad* requires exertion of oneself in "Allah's path"[739] to ultimately be acceptable in the sight of Allah, this individual exertion forms the foundation for all other forms of *jihad*. As the believer conducts spiritual warfare against his "lower self,"[740] he strengthens himself in Allah's path and prepares himself to conquer unbelievers through other means.

B. DA'WAH

Da'wah literally means "call," "invitation," or "propaganda."[741] Throughout the *Qur'an*, Allah commands believers to call others to join in belief. The *Qur'an*, in *Surah* 16:125, proclaims: "Invite (all) to the way of thy lord with wisdom and beautiful preaching; and argue with them in ways that are best and most gracious . . . ." Elsewhere, the *Qur'an* states, "Let there arise out of you a band of people inviting to all that is good, enjoining what is right, and forbidding what is wrong . . . ."[742] And, in another place, the *Qur'an* designates believers in Allah and Muhammad as "witnesses over the nations . . . , [f]or Allah is to all people most surely full of kindness, most merciful."[743] Believers must participate in this "path" to spread belief in Allah and "mak[e] His word supreme over this world."[744] This invitation, however, serves as a prerequisite to violent *jihad*, for Muslims are commanded to "[f]ight those who believe not in Allah nor the last day . . . nor acknowledge the religion of truth, from among the people of the Book, until they pay the *Jizyah*

---

[737]*Id.* at 56.

[738]QUR'AN, *supra* note 11, at *Surah* 29:6.

[739]WAR AND PEACE IN THE LAW OF ISLAM, *supra* note 48, at 55.

[740]RELIANCE OF THE TRAVELLER, *supra* note 10, at 599.

[741]WEHR, *supra* note 52, at 327.

[742]QUR'AN, *supra* note 11, at *Surah* 3:104.

[743]*Id.* at *Surah* 2:143.

[744]WAR AND PEACE IN THE LAW OF ISLAM, *supra* note 48, at 55; *see also* SAHIH BUKHARI, *supra* note 69, at Vol. 4, Bk. 52, No. 65 ("He who fights that Allah's Word (i.e.[,] Islam) should be superior, fights in Allah's Cause.").

[poll tax] with willing submission, and feel themselves subdued."[745]

Da'wah is a prerequisite to violent *jihad* because the *Qur'an* states that Allah does not punish anyone until one has received the invitation to believe and an introduction to Allah's law (*Shariah*).[746] After the call or invitation to believe is extended, non-Muslims have three choices: convert to Islam; submit to the Islamic ruler and pay *jizyah* (a poll tax) so that their lives are spared (this option is only given to People of the Book—i.e., Christians and Jews); or fight and die.[747] If non-Muslims do not accept Islam after receiving the *da'wah*, Muslims can wage war against them. To transform the *dar al-harb* (territory of war) to *dar al-Islam* (territory under Islam) governed by *Shariah*, Muslims must use every stratagem of war necessary, including lying[748] or making truces and treaties when necessary to advance the cause of Islam.[749] This cause requires believers to use their tongues and hands to "enjoin[] what is right and forbid[] what is wrong," whether the wrong is committed by an individual or, by extension, an entire society.[750] Since the rise of nation-states, Islamic expansion by traditional military means supported by a nation's civil government has become difficult. However, Islam's goals of

---

[745]QUR'AN, *supra* note 11, at *Surah* 9:29. *See* WAR AND PEACE IN THE LAW OF ISLAM, *supra* note 48, at 96 (explaining that "invitation to Islam," i.e., attempting to convert an unbelieving populace to Islam, was a prerequisite to violent *jihad*).

[746]*See* QUR'AN, *supra* note 11, at *Surah* 17:15 ("nor would we make our wrath visit until we had sent a messenger (to give warning)"); *id.* at *Surah* 25:52 ("Therefore listen not to the unbelievers, but strive against them with the utmost strenuousness, with the (Qur'an)."); *see also* RELIANCE OF THE TRAVELLER, *supra* note 10, at 3 (stating that "a person is not morally obligated by Allah to do or refrain from anything unless the *invitation* of a prophet and what Allah has *legislated* have reached him." (emphasis added)).

[747]QUR'AN, *supra* note 11, at *Surah* 9:29; WAR AND PEACE IN THE LAW OF ISLAM, *supra* note 48, at 80 ("Scriptuaries [could] choose one of three propositions: Islam, the poll tax, or the jihad."); HITTI, *supra* note 109, at 161 (recounting the options—"Islam, tribute or the sword"—offered Cyrus upon the conquest of Egypt); RELIANCE OF THE TRAVELLER, *supra* note 10, at 599–602.

[748]RELIANCE OF THE TRAVELLER, *supra* note 10, at 745–46 (explaining the complicated rationale that permits Muslims to lie in numerous instances).

[749]*Id.* at 605.

[750]QUR'AN, *supra* note 11, at *Surah* 3:104 ("Let there arise out of you a band of people inviting to all that is good, enjoining what is right, and forbidding what is wrong . . . ."); *see also* RELIANCE OF THE TRAVELLER, *supra* note 10, at 715 ("People who do not change something wrong when they see it are on the verge of a sweeping punishment from Allah." (internal quotation marks omitted)); *id.* ("The best jihad is speaking the truth to an unjust ruler." (internal quotation marks omitted)).

psychological and political conquest are ongoing. Current political extension of Islam's goal of world domination can be seen in several areas in the United States and abroad.

The Muslim Brotherhood's memorandum, discussed in the Introduction, on the strategic goal of "Civilization Jihad[]" against North America, proposes an Islamic center as "The House of *daw'a*[*h*]" (i.e., center for religious propaganda and invitation to Islam) that would include "place[s] for study, family, battalion, course, seminar, visit, sport, school, social club, women gathering, kindergarten for male and female children, the office of the domestic political resolution, and the center for distributing [their] newspapers, magazines, books and [their] audio and visual tapes."[751] The memorandum further requires that "the center's role should be the same as the mosque's role during the time of [Muhammad]."[752] Interestingly, during Muhammad's time, "[a] mosque was [Islam's] public forum and *military drill ground* as well as its place of common worship."[753] The long list of the so-called Muslim charities and unindicted co-conspirators in the *Holy Land Foundation* cases demonstrates that the Muslim Brotherhood and the entire Muslim *ummah* (Islamic community) have been successful in performing *da'wah* (i.e., propagating Islam) in the United States.[754]

Dr. Tawfik Hamid, a former Islamic extremist from Egypt and current Senior Fellow of the study of Islamic Radicalism at the Potomac Institute for Policy Studies, suggests that the increasing (although inconspicuous) success of political *jihad* in the United States is due largely to Muslims' ability to use Westerners' values of tolerance and political correctness against them. As Dr. Hamid has aptly noted,

---

[751]AKRAM, EXPLANATORY MEMORANDUM, *supra* note 14, at 25.

[752]*Id.* (internal quotation marks omitted).

[753]HITTI, *supra* note 109, at 121 (emphasis added).

[754]Unindicted Co-conspirators, *supra* note 39.

Western academicians and politicians want to appear tolerant at all costs—even to the point of tolerating an illiberal, intolerant ideology—because to appear intolerant is to appear unenlightened, even unintelligent. Peer pressure and political correctness weigh heavily, as do opportunities for promotion or election. Intolerance—at least as deemed so by the multicultural establishment—is an intellectual mark of shame.[755]

Political *jihadists* (those who engage in political holy war against unbelievers) exploit this value system—without ever intending to embrace it for themselves—to establish influence in the United States and to gradually subject to Islamic rule the very people whose tolerance made the *jihadists'* success possible.

Therefore, any so-called religious practice in Islam must not be considered purely religious, as it would be in other religions; for in Islam, it will frequently have political motivations and ramifications. Furthermore, because of Islam's politico-religious nature[756] (i.e., unity of mosque and state), its allegedly peaceful tenets cannot be seen apart from its ultimate aim of universalism, which not only requires physical war but also "*psychological* and *political*" war when strict military campaign is not possible.[757]

1. The Ground Zero Mosque: Symbol of Islamic Political *Jihad*

The *Qur'an* encourages Muslims not only to fight non-Muslims, but also to "seize them, beleaguer them, and lie in wait for them in every stratagem (of war)."[758] The *Qur'an* further commands Muslims to use whatever means (psychological, political, financial, and militaristic) available to wage ongoing *jihad* against the infidels. Not only are many fundamentalist Muslim groups politically active

[755]HAMID, *supra* note 10, at 56.
[756]WAR AND PEACE IN THE LAW OF ISLAM, *supra* note 48, at 63.
[757]*See id.* at 64 (emphasis added).
[758]QUR'AN, *supra* note 11, at *Surah* 9:5.

in the United States, but the push to construct a mosque within three blocks of the former World Trade Center site is in line with the mandate for political exertion,[759] as well as a calculated statement that symbolizes Islam's incremental political expansion within the non-Muslim West.

Symbols of Islamic political *jihad* have traditionally included the systematic destruction and replacement of churches, synagogues, and other establishments representing key cultural institutions with mosques or Islamic symbols that assert Islamic norms, religion, and ideology on the infidels.[760] Throughout Islamic history, the mosque represented transformation of *dar al-harb* (territory of non-Muslims, or territory of war) into *dar al-Islam* (territory under Islam), whether achieved by peace or by force.[761] If a sword was placed on the pulpit, it represented that city or country was taken by force.[762] In contrast, if it was taken by peace, a wooden staff was displayed on the pulpit.[763] If a country voluntarily adopted Islam, however, no sign was placed on the pulpit.[764]

Today, whether or not such symbols are displayed in a particular mosque, replacing a key cultural institution with a mosque is the ultimate representation of Islam's political conquest.[765] Throughout the history of Islamic conquests and expeditions to convert non-Muslims to Islam, a common practice has been to build a mosque on the demolished non-Muslim cultural or religious place of worship. For instance, in A.D. 691, the Caliph Abd-al-Malik built

---

[759]*See* AKRAM, EXPLANATORY MEMORANDUM, *supra* note 14, at 25 (setting forth the "Civilization-Jihadist" purposes of Islamic cultural centers).

[760]*Compare* HITTI, *supra* note 109, at 261–67 (providing descriptions of early mosques, which were often constructed over non-Islamic religious sites and appropriated materials that had been used in the church or temple that the mosque replaced), *with* AKRAM, EXPLANATORY MEMORANDUM, *supra* note 14, at 25 (describing the mosque as a "beehive" of activity advancing the cause of Islam).

[761]WAR AND PEACE IN THE LAW OF ISLAM, *supra* note 48, at 155.

[762]*Id.* at 156.

[763]*Id.*

[764]*Id.*

[765]*See infra* notes 768–783 and accompanying text.

the Dome of the Rock on the site of the Temple of Solomon.[766] He also built the al-Aqsa mosque on the site of St. Mary's Church of Justinian on the Temple Mount in Jerusalem.[767] Al-Walid I turned the Cathedral of St. John into a grand mosque[768] and changed the Cathedral's watch-tower into a minaret.[769]

In Europe, Abd-al-Rahman I built the Mosque of Cordoba, Spain, in A.D. 786 after a Christian church was destroyed on the site.[770] Roughly a century and a half later, Al-Munsur bi-Allah ruled the Cordoba area in Spain. Al-Munsur attacked and conquered the Christians in nearby areas.[771] As a sign of his triumph, Al-Munsur demolished Christian churches and symbols and used their rubble to build his own mosques.[772] For instance, in A.D. 997, he demolished the beautiful church of St. Iago de Compostela, a place where European Christians came on pilgrimage.[773] Then, in A.D. 1099, Muslim leaders had the beautiful Visigoth church of Granada demolished.[774] In the Middle East, Asia Minor, and Eastern Europe, the method remained the same: conquer a significant cultural or religious site and replace it with a mosque to display Islamic cultural dominance.[775] Perhaps the best known example is the Hagia Sophia in Constantinople (today, Istanbul), which Sultan Mehmet converted into a mosque on May 29, 1453, following his capture of the city.[776]

---

[766]HITTI, *supra* note 109, at 264.
[767]*Id.* at 265.
[768]*Id.* at 261, 265.
[769]*Id.* at 262.
[770]*Id.* at 594.
[771]*Id.* at 533.
[772]*Id.*
[773]*Id.*
[774]*Id.* at 544.
[775]*See id.* at 648–65.
[776]HITTI, *supra* note 109, at 709, 712–15; *see also* STEVEN RUNCIMAN, THE FALL OF CONSTANTINOPLE 1453, at 147 (1965); *Hagia Sophia*, HAGIA SOPHIA, http://www.hagiasophia.com/listingview. php?listingID=7 (last visited May 2, 2011); *Hagia Sophia, Istanbul*, SACRED DESTINATIONS, http://www. sacred-destinations.com/turkey/istanbul-hagia-sophia (last visited May 2, 2011).

This pattern has extended beyond Europe and the Middle East and into the present. St. Philippe Cathedral in Algiers was converted into a mosque in 1962 after Muslims regained political control in Algeria.[777] This mosque stands as a significant symbol of Muslim restoration and dominance.[778] Another example is Babar, a Muslim ruler in the sixteenth century A.D., who destroyed several Hindu temples in India and replaced them with mosques.[779] In A.D. 1528, the Babri mosque was built in Ayodhya on the spot that many Hindus believe to be the birthplace of the Hindu god, Rama.[780] Furthermore, Hindus believe that a temple to Rama was destroyed to build the Babri mosque, and that belief has sparked controversy for decades.[781] Muslims and Hindus continue to dispute the ownership of the site and have taken the fight to court.[782] All of these grand and majestic mosques constructed at strategic locations around the world serve the political purpose of sending notice to non-Muslims throughout the world of Islam's dominance and political conquest.[783]

This pattern of political *jihad* is now being continued with the push to build a thirteen-story mosque near Ground Zero.[784] The proposed site of the mosque is part and parcel of the actual Ground Zero site because the landing gear from one of the planes

---

[777]*The Magnificent Ketchaoua Mosque in Algiers*, NORTH AFRICA TIMES, Apr. 6, 2008, at 18, *available at* http://www.alarab.co.uk/previouspages/North%20Africa%20Times/2008/04/06-04/NAT180604. pdf.

[778]*See id.*

[779]GILBERT POLLET, INDIAN EPIC VALUES: RĀMĀYANA AND ITS IMPACT 28 (1995).

[780]Christian H. Brill, *Holy Places in an Unholy World: Will Religious Beliefs Halt India's "Suez of the East"?*, 35 N.C.J. INT'L L. & COM. REG. 447, 464 (2010).

[781]S. P. Udayakumar, *Ayodhya: The "Ram Temple" Drama*, FRONTLINE (July 17, 1998), http://www.hinduonnet.com/fline/fl1514/15141100.htm.

[782]KOENRAAD ELST, AYODHYA: THE CASE AGAINST THE TEMPLE 11.2–11.6 (2002).

[783]Many leaders throughout the West have begun to recognize this fact and have supported legislation aimed at curtailing Islamic construction of political symbols in the form of mosques and minarets. In Switzerland, for example, Martin Baltisser, general secretary of the Swiss People's Party (SVP), told the BBC that the Swiss prohibition on the construction of new minarets was a response to the political message that such minarets were intended to send: "'This was a vote against minarets as symbols of Islamic power.'" *Swiss Voters Back Ban on Minarets*, BBC NEWS (Nov. 29, 2009), http://news.bbc.co.uk/2/hi/8385069.stm.

[784]Margot Adler, *Islamic Center Near Ground Zero Sparks Anger*, NPR (July 15, 2010), http://www.npr.org/templates/story/story.php?storyId=128544392.

went through that building,[785] making it a landmark that should be preserved in remembrance of the thousands of innocent civilians murdered on September 11th.[786] Because a mosque could not be built directly on Ground Zero, the chosen site is equally significant. The political significance of a mosque on this site became even more vivid after the mosque's developer declined then-New York Governor David Patterson's offer to help find an alternate site,[787] demonstrating the political and ideological motivations behind the project.[788] Even some of the wealthiest Islamic contributors to the project have been unsuccessful in convincing the developers to move the proposed mosque to a more neutral location; and *Imam Rauf*, the spiritual leader of the project, and the developers continue to ignore the pleas of Americans, including family members of September 11th victims, to move the project to an alternate site.[789]

Despite the alleged religious purpose for the Ground Zero mosque, history indicates that construction of a mosque on a site of victory of Muslim *jihadists* constitutes a conscious symbol of political conquest. The weight of this symbolism should not be ignored or marginalized in the name of tolerance or political correctness.

Furthermore, Muslim terrorists utilize mosques to conduct terrorist activities. On August 9, 2010, a German spokesman for Hamburg's state interior ministry announced that a mosque and related Muslim "cultural association" that was linked to the September 11th hijackers would be banned by the German government because of their ties to Islamic extremism and

---

[785]*Id.*

[786]*Id.*

[787]*Offer Rejected to Move Mosque Away From Ground Zero to 'State Property'*, Fox News (Aug. 11, 2010), http://www.foxnews.com/politics/2010/08/11/ny-governor-offer-state-property-mosque-built-farther-away-ground-zero/.

[788]Cindy Rodriguez, *Saudi Prince Urges Ground Zero Mosque Be Moved*, ABC News (Oct. 28, 2010), http://abcnews.go.com/US/saudi-prince-urges-ground-mosque-moved/story?id=11997307&page=1.

[789]*Id.*

international terrorism.[790] After a 2009 German intelligence agency report linked the mosque to the September 11th attackers and other Islamic militants, German officials reported, "[w]e have closed the mosque because it was a recruiting and meeting point for Islamic radicals who wanted to participate in so-called jihad or holy war."[791]

In 2007, the Pakistani military raided a fiercely militant mosque in its capital, Islamabad.[792] More than 106 people were killed in the eight-day fight around the Red Mosque.[793] The mosque was being used as "a base to send out radicalized students to enforce [*Shariah*]."[794] Militants within the compound were responding with RPGs, gunfire, and Molotov Cocktails.[795] While the fight was ensuing, the mosque's *imam*, Abdul Rashid Ghazi, was "holed up" in the basement "surrounded by women and children from the women's school."[796] These women and children were used as a protective shield for the *imam*.[797]

In Gaza, Hamas used mosques for military purposes throughout Israeli Operation Cast Lead.[798] The mosque in the Tel al-Hawa area of Gaza City served as a storehouse for armaments and a launching site for terrorist attacks, and the Al-Khulafa mosque in Jabaliya served as a terrorist operations room and a long-range Grad rockets storage arsenal.[799] Such examples demonstrate that Muslims

---

[790]Associated Press, *September 11 Attackers Former Mosque Closed*, THE INDEPENDENT (Aug. 9, 2010), http://www.independent.co.uk/news/world/europe/september-11-attackers-former-mosque-closed-2047530.html.

[791]*Id.*

[792]*See* Associated Press, *Most Red Mosque Deaths Were Militants*, MSNBC (July 11, 2007), http://www.msnbc.msn.com/id/19704888/.

[793]*Id.*

[794]*Id.*

[795]Aryn Baker, *Storming the Red Mosque*, TIME (July 10, 2007), http://www.time.com/time/world/article/0,8599,1641630,00.html.

[796]*Id.*

[797]*Id.*

[798]ISR. MINISTRY OF FOREIGN AFFAIRS, THE OPERATION IN GAZA, 27 DECEMBER 2008–18 JANUARY 2009: FACTUAL AND LEGAL ASPECTS 2, 7, 51–52, 56, 60–61, 68, 70, 86, 88, 132, 144 (2009), *available at* http://www.mfa.gov.il/NR/rdonlyres/E89E699D-A435-491B-B2D0-017675DAFEF7/0/Gaza.

[799]*Id.* at 88.

do not consider mosques to be solely places of worship but also strategic military facilities.

2. Political *Jihad*: Finance and *Zakat*

To achieve the ultimate goal of bringing the world under Islamic law, Muslims must strive to bring all individuals and all institutions—incrementally and unceasingly—into conformity with Islam. As discussed earlier, Islam not only encompasses all aspects of human spiritual life, including philanthropic and charitable works, but it also strictly governs all aspects of secular life, including sales, transactions, and even financial institutions. The recent push to conform financial institutions to *Shariah* can be seen in the OIC's overall goal that its fifty-six Muslim Member States arise, not as a conglomerate of individual sovereign nations, but as the single self-identifying "Islamic world."[800] According to the OIC's Charter, Member States endeavor to participate in "global political, economic and social decision-making processes to secure *their* common interests."[801] One of their main interests is to "strengthen intra-Islamic economic and trade cooperation[] in order to achieve economic integration leading to the *establishment of an Islamic Common Market*[.]"[802] Indeed, "Islamic banking is an instrument for the development of an Islamic economic order,"[803] which serves the ultimate purpose of "defend[ing] the universality of Islamic religion."[804]

a. *Shariah*-Compliant Financing

Islamists around the world are influencing financial institutions to conduct their business according to Islamic religious

---

[800] *See* Organisation of the Islamic Conference Charter arts. 1(2), 7.

[801] *Id.* art. 1(5) (emphasis added).

[802] *Id.* art. 1(9) (emphasis added).

[803] *Islamic Banking: Islamic Economics Order*, INSTITUTE OF ISLAMIC BANKING AND INSURANCE, (last visited Apr. 4, 2011), http://www.islamic-banking.com/islamic_economics_order.aspx (on file with authors).

[804] Organisation of the Islamic Conference Charter pmbl.

law. The general term used to describe conducting business according to Islamic principles is *"Shariʿah*-compliant financing" (SCF).[805] From 2000 to 2008, SCF investing grew from $150 billion to $800 billion globally, growing at an annual rate of ten to fifteen percent per year.[806] With such a rapid growth rate, SCF has begun to have significant influence on the world's financial institutions in favor of conforming their practices to Islamic law, with minimal public awareness or oversight.

SCF is developing as an alternative to Western conventional banking and involves saving, investing, and building wealth according to Islamic religious rules and edicts, especially the teachings of the *Qur'an* and *Sunnah* (Muhammad's teachings).[807]

---

[805]Instead of exchanging money for money—as is the case in traditional, including American, banking systems—Islamic banking, or SCF, operates under a system of asset-backed financing. MUFTI MUHAMMAD TAQI USMANI, AN INTRODUCTION TO ISLAMIC FINANCE 12–13 (2002) [hereinafter ISLAMIC FINANCE], *available at* http://www.muftitaqiusmani.com/images/stories/downloads/pdf/an%20 introduction%20to%20islamic%20finance.pdf. Asset-backed financing requires a bank to purchase an illiquid asset before lending a liquid asset (assuming the risk of the commodity purchased), rather than lending liquid money. *Id.* at 13. As the Islamic Bank of Britain describes, "To make money from money is forbidden—wealth can only be generated through legitimate trade and investment in *assets*." *Sharia Finance*, ISLAMIC BANK OF BRITAIN, http://www.islamic-bank.com/sharia-finance/ (last visited Mar. 29, 2011). Only after a bank purchases assets and creates an inventory may a bank sell an asset to a client for a fixed price. ISLAMIC FINANCE, *supra* note 805, at 12–13. The client (buyer) then has an obligation to repay the fixed price. Payments, however, are due at the debtor's leisure because under *Shariah*, "there is no concept of time due of money," which means that there can be no penalty for late payments. *Id.* at 13. *But cf.* RELIANCE OF THE TRAVELLER, *supra* note 10, at 403 (stating that a debtor is obliged to repay the lender upon the lender's spontaneous demand of payment: "If the lender gives the recipient a loan and later meets him in another town and asks for it back, the recipient must repay it if it was gold or silver and the like, though if the loaned commodity was something troublesome to carry, such as wheat or barley, then the recipient is not obliged to pay it back (A: in kind) but is merely obliged to pay back its value"). Because *Shariah*-compliant banks are prohibited from lending at interest and cannot make profit that way, *Shariah* forces Islamic banks to generate profits in a wholly different manner. Rather than lending at interest, Islamic banks generate profits under, *inter alia*, the principle of *Musharakah*, which literally means "sharing." ISLAMIC FINANCE, *supra* note 805, at 14–15, 17. *Musharakah*, or profit sharing, views a traditional loan as more of a partnership or joint venture rather than a debtor/creditor relationship. *Id.* at 17. Thus, under Islamic banking, when a debtor needs a loan, the lender has two options: lend at no interest or contract with the debtor to share in his profits (*Musharakah*). *Id.* at 17–18. If the lender chooses to contract with the debtor to share in the profits, however, *he also must share in any losses incurred by the debtor. Id.* at 18. Each partner suffers losses according to the amount he invested. *Id.* Thus, as opposed to the free-market model, under Islamic banking/economics, capital and entrepreneur are not separate factors of production. *Id.* at 14–15. Anyone who invests capital—even a lender—assumes the risks incurred by an entrepreneur and therefore shares in both profits and losses.

[806]David Oakley et al., *Islamic Finance Explained*, FINANCIAL TIMES (May 30, 2008), http://www. ft.com/cms/s/0/5067aace-2e67-11dd-ab55-000077b07658.html#axzz1HFFzfGUz.

[807]Tadashi Maeda, *Making Sense of the Fast-Growing Islamic Finance Market, in* CURRENT ISSUES

In particular, SCF is based on the idea of promoting what is *halal* (lawful) and prohibiting what is *haram* (unlawful) under Islamic *Shariah*. Therefore, any action, instrument, or means of trade that Islam prohibits is also unlawful in a *Shariah*-compliant financial market. SCF thus is a spiritually justified way of banking, governed solely by *Islamic* religious principles.

According to Mufti Muhammad Taqi Usmani,[808] one of the foremost Islamic economists and *Shariah* finance experts, "the basic difference between capitalist [or free-market] and Islamic economy is that in secular capitalism, the profit motive or private ownership are [*sic*] given unbridled power to make economic decisions. Their liberty is not controlled by any divine injunctions."[809] A *Shariah*-based financial system, on the other hand, "*has* put certain divine restrictions on the economic activities."[810] Because these restrictions are "imposed by Allah Almighty, Whose knowledge has no limits," they "*cannot be removed by any human*

IN ISLAMIC BANKING AND FINANCE: RESILIENCE AND STABILITY IN THE PRESENT SYSTEM 118 (Angelo M. Venardos ed., 2010).

[808] According to Taqi Usmani's website, Usmani possesses the following credentials:

> He obtained his Takhassus degree (an advanced degree equivalent to Ph.D.) in Islamic education from Darul Uloom Karachi, the largest and most renowned Islamic educational institution in Pakistan. He also obtained a Master's degree in Arabic literature from Punjab University, and a law degree (LLB) from Karachi University.

> He is regarded as an expert in the fields of Hadith (sacred traditions of the Holy Prophet, may Allah's peace and blessings be upon him), Fiqh (Islamic jurisprudence), Economics, and Tasawwuf (Islamic spirituality). He has been teaching these and other branches of Islamic education since 1959.

> He served as Judge of the Shariat Appellate Bench of the Supreme Court of Pakistan from 1982 to May 2002. He is also a permanent member of the International Islamic Fiqh Academy, an organ of OIC based in Jeddah, Saudi Arabia. He has served as the Vice Chairman of the Academy for nine years. He is also the Vice President of Darul Uloom Karachi.

> He is generally known as one of the leading Shariah scholars active in the field of Islamic finance. For more than a decade he has served as chairman or member of Shariah supervisory boards of a dozen Islamic banks and financial institutions in various parts of the world. He presently serves as Chairman of the International Shariah Council for the Accounting and Auditing Organization for Islamic Financial Institutions (AAOIFI) in Bahrain.

Profile, MUFTI MUHAMMAD TAQI USMANI, http://www.muftitaqiusmani.com/index.php?option=com_content&view=article&id=2&Itemid=5 (last visited Apr. 1, 2011).
[809] ISLAMIC FINANCE, *supra* note 805, at 10–11.
[810] *Id.* at 11.

authority."[811] Islam, therefore, rejects capitalism as a secular invention because it has led to all sorts of "evils" that "can never be curbed unless humanity submits to the divine authority and obeys [Allah's] commands by accepting them as absolute truth and obeys [Allah's] super-human injunctions which should be followed at any case and at any price."[812] These divine restrictions include, among other things, "[t]he prohibition of *riba* (usury or lending at interest), . . . dealing in unlawful goods or services,[813] [and avoiding] short sales and speculative transactions . . . ."[814] Instead, SCF is based upon asset-backed financing[815] and profit and loss sharing.[816] And while clients of *Shariah*-compliant financial institutions may be non-Muslim as well as Muslim, all must equally follow the mandates of *Shariah* in the Islamic financial system.

i. *Shariah* Supervisory Boards

To ensure that a financial institution is *Shariah*-compliant, the institution is required to employ a *Shariah* board, which is composed of *Shariah* scholars[817] who are considered experts in Islamic rules of finance.[818] The *Shariah* board is entrusted with the "responsibility of ensuring that all products and services offered by that institution are fully compliant with the principles of shariah

---

[811]*Id.*

[812]*Id.*

[813]This restriction encompasses a wide range of consumer goods and services that are not only permissible in the United States, but are also deeply imbedded in our economic system. Among these are the prohibitions against the sale of alcohol, pork, dogs, cats, blood, unborn animals still in the womb, unripe crops, pictures that depict humans and other living things, selling something not yet in the seller's possession, etc. FIQH, *supra* note 305, at 213–26.

[814]ISLAMIC FINANCE, *supra* note 805, at 11.

[815]*Id.* at 12–13; *see also supra* text accompanying note 805.

[816]*Id.* at 14–18; *see also supra* text accompanying note 805.

[817]"*Shariah* scholar" is translated from the Arabic word "*alim*" and refers to those who serve on *Shariah* boards. Because their position is professional rather than academic, the Islamic Financial Services Board, "an international standard-setting organisation," uses the term "members of the *Shari'ah* board," instead of *Shariah* scholars. ISLAMIC FINANCIAL SERVICES BOARD, GUIDING PRINCIPLES ON *SHARI'AH* GOVERNANCE SYSTEMS FOR INSTITUTIONS OFFERING ISLAMIC FINANCIAL SERVICES 4, (inside cover) (Dec. 2009) [hereinafter ISLAMIC FINANCIAL SERVICES BOARD], http://www.ifsb.org/standard/IFSB-10%20Shariah%20Governance.pdf.

[818]*Id.*

law"[819] and reviewing all potential new product offerings.[820] The Islamic Bank of Britain, for example, retains a "Sharia Supervisory Committee," which is "comprised of experts in the interpretation of Islamic law and its application within modern day Islamic financial institutions."[821] The committee has authority to require that every product and service the bank offers complies with *Shariah*.[822] It thus "review[s] all contracts and agreements" and "certifies every account and service."[823] The Islamic Bank of Britain emphasizes that, "without [the Committee's] approval, we cannot introduce a new product or service."[824]

Consider the approval requirements for purchasing a home through the Islamic Bank of Britain: Before purchasing a home, the customer must receive a "certificate of Shari[ah] Compliance," or a *fatwa* (religious edict), from the "Sharia Supervisory Committee" certifying that the "Home Purchase Plan product is in accordance with the Diminishing Musharakah [(profit sharing)] and Ijarah [(leasing)][825] Principles of Islamic Finance,"[826] or simply, that the product is *Shariah*-compliant. At the top of every certification, the document states:

> All praise is to Allah (swt)[827] and His blessing and peace be upon His beloved Messenger (saw)[828]

[819]*The Role of the Shariah Advisery Board in Islamic Finance*, QFINANCE, http://www.qfinance.com/ capital-markets-checklists/the-role-of-the-shariah-advisery-board-in-islamic-finance (last visited Feb. 23, 2011).

[820]*Id.*

[821]*Role of the Committee*, ISLAMIC BANK OF BRITAIN, http://www.islamic-bank.com/sharia-finance/role-committee/ (last visited Mar. 29, 2011).

[822]*Id.*

[823]*Id.*

[824]*Id.*

[825]*See* discussion *supra* note 805 (explaining the system of profit sharing); *see also* ISLAMIC FINANCE, *supra* note 805, at 109 (discussing *Ijarah*, which means "'to give something on rent,'" and encompasses the employment of a person's services on wages and leases).

[826]Certificate of Sharia'a Compliance for Home Purchase Plan, Islamic Bank of Britain (Oct. 28, 2008), http://www.islamic-bank.com/GetAsset.aspx?id=fAAyADAAMAB8AHwAVAByAHUAZQ B8AHwAMAB8AA2.

[827]SWT is an abbreviation for the Arabic phrase *"subhan wa talla,"* which roughly means "exalted" or "almighty."

[828]SAW is an abbreviation of the Arabic phrase "salla allahu alaihi wa sallam," which has been

[Muhammad] and upon his family and companions;
and upon those who follow [him] with righteousness
till the Day of Judgement.[829]

This certification process must occur with all products and services
offered by the bank, including savings accounts[830] and fixed-term
deposit accounts.[831]

ii. *Shariah*-Financing Scholars

As mentioned, the Muslim scholars who sit on the *Shariah*
boards have enormous power because they essentially govern a
bank's decisions and may veto product and service proposals that
do not conform to *Shariah*. Therefore, it is critical to understand
who these scholars are. Mufti Muhammad Taqi Usmani, cited to
above, currently is the chairman of the Accounting and Auditing
Organization for Islamic Financial Institutions.[832] This organization
seeks to "[a]chiev[e] harmonization and convergence in the
concepts and application among the Shari'a supervisory boards of
Islamic financial institutions to avoid contradiction or inconsistency
between the fatwas [(religious edicts)] and applications by these
institutions . . . ."[833] Usmani has also "served as chairman or member

translated into English as "peace be upon him," sometimes written "PBUH." It is impressed upon
every Muslim to say SAW after saying or writing Muhammad's name. The infusion of religious
terminology and symbolism with *Shariah*-compliant financing documents shows the religious nature
of the financing system that *Shariah* requires.

[829]Certificate of Sharia'a Compliance for Home Purchase Plan, Islamic Bank of Britain (Oct. 28,
2008), http://www.islamic-bank.com/GetAsset.aspx?id=fAAyADAAMAB8AHwAVAByAHUAZQ
B8AHwAMAB8AA2.

[830]*On Demand Savings Account*, ISLAMIC BANK OF BRITAIN, http://www.islamic-bank.com/personal-
banking/savings-products/demand-savings-account/ (last visited Apr. 6, 2011).

[831]*Fixed Term Deposit Accounts*, ISLAMIC BANK OF BRITAIN, http://www.islamic-bank.com/personal-
banking/savings-products/fixed-term-deposit-account/ (last visited Apr. 6, 2011).

[832]*AAOIFI Shari'a Board*, ACCOUNTING AND AUDITING ORGANIZATION FOR ISLAMIC FINANCIAL INSTITUTIONS,
http://www.aaoifi.com/sharia-board.html (last visited Feb. 23, 2011). Formerly, Usmani was the
Shariah Board Chairman for the Dow Jones Islamic Index in New York, the Saudi American Bank in
Jeddah, and the HSBC Amanah Finance in Dubai, among other positions. *Profile*, MUFTI MUHAMMAD
TAQI USMANI, http://www.muftitaqiusmani.com/index.php?option=com_content&view=article&id=2
&Itemid=5 (last visited Apr. 1, 2011).

[833]*AAOIFI Shari'a Board*, ACCOUNTING AND AUDITING ORGANIZATION FOR ISLAMIC FINANCIAL INSTITUTIONS,
http://www.aaoifi.com/sharia-board.html (last visited Feb. 23, 2011). The Board's other objectives are
"[h]elping in the development of Shari'a approved instruments," "[e]xamining any inquiries referred
to the Shari'a Board from Islamic financial institutions or from their Shari'a supervisory boards, either
to give the Shari'a opinion in matter requiring collective ijtihad (reasoning), or to settle divergent

of Shariah supervisory boards of a dozen Islamic banks and financial institutions in various parts of the world."[834]

Notably, in an interview with Usmani, *The Sunday Times* reported that Usmani stated that "Muslims should live peacefully in countries such as Britain, where they have the freedom to practise Islam, *only until they gain enough power to engage in battle*."[835] This statement is not anomalous but rather supports claims made by Usmani in his book, *Islam and Modernism* (translated into English).[836] Usmani devoted an entire chapter of his book to explain his disagreement with a Saudi Arabian Muslim who argued that aggressive *jihad* should not be used against countries that allow preaching Islam:[837]

> [T]he most important purpose of Jihad is to break th[e] grandeur [of the West] so that the resulting psychological subordination should come to an end and the way of acccpting the Truth becomes smooth. As long as this grandeur and domination persists, the hearts of people will remain subdued and will not be fully inclined to accept the religion of Truth. Hence Jihad will continue. . . . [K]illing is to continue until the unbelievers pay Jizyah [(poll tax)] after they are humbled or overpowered. If the purpose of killing was only to acquire permission and freedom of preaching Islam, it would have been said "until they allow for preaching Islam." But the obligation of Jizyah and along with it the mention of their subordination is a clear proof that the purpose

---

points of view, or to act as an arbiter," and "[r]eviewing the standards which AAOIFI issues . . . ." *Id.*

[834]*Profile*, MUFTI TAQI USMANI, http://www.muftitaqiusmani.com/index.php?option=com_content&view=article&id=2&Itemid=5 (last visited Mar. 21, 2011).

[835]Andrew Norfolk, *Our Followers 'Must Live in Peace Until Strong Enough to Wage Jihad'*, SUNDAY TIMES (Sept. 8, 2007) (emphasis added), http://www.timesonline.co.uk/tol/comment/faith/article2409833.ece.

[836]MUFTI MUHAMMAD TAQI USMANI, ISLAM AND MODERNISM (2006) [hereinafter ISLAM AND MODERNISM], *available at* http://www.fahmedeen.org/books/islamandmodernism.pdf; *see also* Norfolk, *supra* note 835 ("Mr. Usmani's justification for aggressive military jihad as a means of establishing global Islamic supremacy is revealed at the climax of his book, Islam and Modernism.").

[837]ISLAM AND MODERNISM, *supra* note 836, at 86.

is to smash their grandeur, so that the veils of their domination should be raised and people get a free chance to think over the blessings of Islam.

. . . .

The other question worthy of notice is: Do we find an example that the Prophet (PBUH) and his companions ever sent any missionary groups in other countries before Jihad and waited for their reaction to allow or disallow the missionary work? Did they go for Jihad only when they were refused to carry out the missionary work for Islam? . . . Obviously it was not so. Thus there can be no other conclusion that only a permit for missionary activities was not the aim. If that would have been the only aim many of the bloody combats could be stopped only on one condition that no obstacle would be placed in the way of the mission of Islam. *But at least in my humble knowledge there has not been a single incident in the entire history of Islam where Muslims had shown their willingness to stop Jihad just for one condition that they will be allowed to preach Islam freely.* On the contrary the aim of Muslims as declared by them in the battle of Qadsi was, "To take out people from the rule of people and put them under the rule of Allah." Similarly, the Qur'an said: "And (you O Believers) fight them until persecution is no more and the Din is all for Allah." (8:39).

. . . .

If the need for Jihad was abandoned just on [securing the right of missionary activities], then we see that Muslims already have this permission in most of the non-Muslim countries of the world . . . [,] which implies that Muslims should never have to lift the sword. As a result disbelievers may establish and hoist flags of grandeur all over the world and their awfulness and supremacy on the people would stay dominating. The policies will be theirs, the commandments will be theirs, ideologies will be theirs, views will be theirs . . . . The question arises how many people would be prepared to listen to the Muslims . . . [in such an atmosphere].

. . . .

[Consequently,] there can be two types of agreement with non-Muslims. 1) Mutual compromise and peace agreements can be made with countries that have no power which could threaten the grandeur and domination of Muslims. This will be enforced as long as they do not become a threat to the Muslims again. 2) *If Muslims do not possess the capability of "Jihad with power" agreement may be made till the power is attained.*[838]

Other SCF scholars include Bassam Osman, Abdalla Idris, and Yusuf al-Qaradawi. Osman is the Chief Executive Officer of Allied Asset Advisors[839] and the portfolio manager of the Iman Fund[840] (symbol: IMANX[841]), which markets itself as the mutual fund for "Muslim Investors, who not only want to have a financially rewarding investment, but a Shariah compatible one as well."[842] Notably, Osman previously served as the director of the Quranic Literacy Institute (QLI), a non-profit organization formerly based in Oak Lawn, Illinois.[843] While Osman was QLI's director, QLI was convicted of financially supporting Hamas.[844] Abdalla Idris, another

---

[838]*Id.* at 86–91 (emphases added).

[839]"The Allied Asset Advisors, Inc. is located at 745 McClintock Drive, Suite 314, Burr Ridge, Illinois 60527. AAA, a Delaware corporation, is a subsidiary of the North American Islamic Trust, Inc. (NAIT) and was formed in 2000 to manage the Fund." *Investment Advisor*, IMAN FUND, http://www.investaaa.com/cgi-bin/client_product.cgi?member=55&product_id=1279 (last visited Apr. 4, 2011).

[840]ALLIED ASSET ADVISORS FUNDS, PROSPECTUS: IMAN FUND 7 (Sept. 30, 2010), http://www.investaaa.com/pdfs/Statutory_Prospectus.pdf. Osman also serves on the NAIT board of trustees. *About: North American Islamic Trust*, NAIT.NET, http://www.nait.net/NAIT_about_%20us.htm (last visited Mar. 21, 2011).

[841]*IMANX*, MSNMONEY.COM, http://investing.money.msn.com/investments/mutual-fundrates/?symbol=imanx&s=qbeb (last visited Mar. 21, 2011).

[842]*Overview*, IMAN FUND, http://www.investaaa.com/ (last visited Nov. 24, 2010).

[843]Alexiev, *infra* note 875; *see also* Boim v. Holy Land Found. for Relief and Dev., 549 F.3d 685, 701 (7th Cir. 2008).

[844]*See infra* notes 909–911.

Iman Fund trustee,[845] was president of the Islamic Society of North America (ISNA) from 1992 to 1997 and is now an ISNA school principal.[846] ISNA was named as an unindicted co-conspirator in the *Holy Land Foundation* cases for being a "member of the U.S. Muslim Brotherhood."[847]

Yusuf al-Qaradawi, "one of Islam's most influential scholars,"[848] is the co-founder and president of the International Union of Muslim Scholars and the European Council for Fatwa and Research,[849] and he was also the chairman of the First Islamic Investment Bank of Bahrain's *Shariah* Supervisory Board.[850] The Investment Bank severed its ties with Qaradawi after Caribou Coffee, a U.S. coffee company owned by the Investment Bank, was harshly criticized for being associated with Qaradawi.[851] Qaradawi aligns himself with the Muslim Brotherhood[852] and publicly advocates for Israel's destruction. For example, in a sermon delivered on January 9, 2009, Qaradawi stated, "Oh Allah, take this oppressive, Jewish, Zionist band of people. . . . [D]o not spare a single one of them. Oh Allah, count their numbers, and kill them, down to the very last one."[853] And at a 2007 conference, he stated,

---

[845]IMAN FUND, MANAGEMENT OF THE FUND, http://www.investaaa.com/pdfs/Boardbios.pdf (last visited Mar. 21, 2011).

[846]*Abdalla Idris Ali, Majlis Member*, ISNA, http://www.isna.net/ISNAHQ/pages/Abdalla-Idris-Ali.aspx (last visited Mar. 21, 2011).

[847]Unindicted Co-conspirator, *supra* note 39, at 8.

[848]Michael Slackman, *Islamic Debate Surrounds Mideast Suicide Bombers*, LA. TIMES. (Mar. 27, 2001), http://articles.latimes.com/2001/may/27/news/mn-3226/2. Qaradawi is described as a "mujtahi of the Modern Age." *Biography: Shaykh Al-Qaradawi*, MUSLIM JUDICIAL COUNCIL, http://www.mjc.org.za/index.php?option=com_content&view=article&id=190:biogr (last visited Apr. 8, 2011).

[849]*Biography: Shaykh Al-Qaradawi*, *supra* note 848; *Sheik Yusuf al-Qaradawi: Theologian of Terror*, ANTI-DEFAMATIONLEAGUE,http://www.adl.org/main_Arab_World/al_Qaradawi_report_20041110.htm?Multi_page_sections=sHeading_4 (last visited May 4, 2011).

[850]John Tevlin, *Caribou Severs Ties with Islamic Adviser*, STAR TRIBUNE (Minneapolis), July 4, 2002, at 1B; *see also* Andrew Schroedter, *Perpetual e-mail Kills North Shore Caribou Coffees*, CHICAGO SUN-TIMES, Oct. 28, 2004, at 60 (labeling al-Qaradawi as a "paid consultant" to the First Islamic Investment Bank of Bahrain).

[851]*Id.*; Daniel Howes, *Caribou CEO Battles False Allegations of Terror Support*, DETROIT NEWS, May 16, 2004, at 1C.

[852]Jonathan Ferziger and Vivian Salama, *Jailbreak Fuels Israel's Post-Mubarak Hamas Fears*, PITTSBURGH POST-GAZETTE, Mar. 13, 2011, at A3.

[853]Shaykh Yusuf al-Qaradawi, Sermon on Al-Jazeera (Jan. 9, 2009), http://www.memritv.org/clip_

"I support the Palestinian cause. I support the resistance and the jihad. I support Hamas, the Islamic Jihad, and Hizbullah. I oppose the peace that Israel and America wish to dictate. This peace is an illusion."[854] Qaradawi also describes Muslim suicide bombings as "heroic martyrdom operations."[855]

Based on such scholars' agendas and Islam's goal of implementing *Shariah* in every aspect of life, any push for SCF must be viewed with skepticism, if not outright alarm. Although financial institutions have the freedom to adopt lawful SCF financial principles, Americans must understand that the goal is not merely to promote an alternative financial system that conforms to Islamic principles, but to "accumulate sources of power," to help strip the "grandeur" held by the West, and to impose Islam—through every possible institution.[856] *Shariah's* acceptance in the financial sector serves the purpose of desensitizing the public to its dangers, thereby paving the way for adoption of other more invasive and incompatible Islamic laws discussed throughout this book. Furthermore, SCF also poses a direct threat to U.S. national security because Islam requires financial institutions to pay *zakat* (obligatory charitable contributions).[857]

b. *Zakat*: One of the Five Pillars of Islam

There are two types of charitable contributions in Islam: obligatory charitable funds (*zakat*) that every Muslim is required to

---

transcript/en/1979.htm (log in information required).

[854]Imam al-Qaradawi, Speech at the Conference A Forum for Students and Friends (July 12-14, 2007), http://www.memri.org/report/en/print2319.htm.

[855]Slackman, *supra* note 848.

[856]*See supra* notes 800–804, 838 and accompanying text. Indeed, many states are taking legislative efforts to prevent this from happening. *E.g.*, Save our State Amendment, H.J.R. 1056, 52d Leg., 2d Sess., (Okla. 2010); S.B. 1028, 107th Leg. (Tenn. 2011); *see also* Bob Smietana, *Tennessee Bill Would Jail Shariah Followers*, USA Today (Feb. 23, 2011), http://www.usatoday.com/news/nation/2011-02-23-tennessee-law-shariah_N.htm (noting that there are about twelve states, in addition to Tennessee, considering "anti-Shariah bills").

[857]*See infra* note 876.

pay for specific Islamic purposes[858] and voluntary charity (*sadqa*).[859] This section will focus on *zakat* and its relation to SCF and Islamic charities.

Paying *zakat* is one of the five fundamental principles of Islamic *Shariah*[860] and its basis is found in *Surah* 9:60: "Zaka[t] is for the poor and the needy, and those employed to administer the (funds); for those whose hearts have been (recently) reconciled (to the truth); for those in bondage and in debt; in the cause of Allah; and for the wayfarer; (thus is it) ordained by Allah, and Allah is full of knowledge and wisdom."[861] *Zakat* literally means "growth, blessings, an increase in good, purification, or praise."[862] *Shariah* mandates that "every free Muslim" pay *zakat* to designated groups for certain purposes.[863] It also provides strict guidelines for the amount of *zakat* to be paid, depending on the type of property on which *zakat* is assessed. One type of property on which *zakat* must be collected is money.[864] A Muslim, or his appointed agent,[865] must pay 2.5% (as *zakat*) of all money saved for more than one year.[866]

Moreover, *zakat* must be distributed among eight categories of recipients.[867] Among these are "the poor,"[868] "those who have debts,"[869] and "*those fighting for Allah*, meaning people engaged

---

[858]RELIANCE OF THE TRAVELLER, *supra* note 10, at 246.

[859]*Id.* at 275.

[860]SAHIH BUKHARI, *supra* note 69, at Vol. 1, Bk. 2, No. 8 ("Islam is based on (the following) five (principles): (1.) To testify that none has the right to be worshipped but Allah and Muhammad is Allah's Apostle[;] (2.) To offer the (compulsory congregational) prayers dutifully and perfectly[;] (3.) To pay Zakat (i.e.[,] obligatory charity)[;] (4.) To perform Hajj (i.e.[,] Pilgrimage to Mecca)[; and] (5.) To observe fast during the month of Ramadan.").

[861]QUR'AN, *supra* note 11, at *Surah* 9:60. Ali notes that those "in the cause of Allah" include "those who are struggling and striving in Allah's cause by teaching or *fighting* or in duties assigned to them by the righteous Imam, who are thus unable to earn their ordinary living." *Id.* at 456 n.1320 (emphasis added).

[862]RELIANCE OF THE TRAVELLER, *supra* note 10, at 246.

[863]*Id.* at 246.

[864]*Id.* at 257.

[865]*Id.* at 265–66. It is "superior" to pay *zakat* to an *imam* and to allow him to distribute it accordingly.

[866]*Id.* at 257.

[867]*Id.* at 266.

[868]*Id.* at 267.

[869]*Id.* at 271.

in Islamic military operations."[870] While *zakat* has social justice elements,[871] it is critical to note that it may never be paid to non-Muslims,[872] and it must be distributed to each of the eight categories *equally*.[873] Therefore, one-eighth of all *zakat* must be given to *those fighting for Allah*—which includes Islamic terrorists. The aforementioned Yusuf al-Qaradawi[874] described it well: "I don't like this word 'donations.' I like to call it *Jihad with money*, because God [(Allah)] has ordered us to fight enemies with our lives and our money."[875]

c. Financial Institutions Paying *Zakat*

To be *Shariah*-compliant, financial institutions must pay *zakat*.[876] According to the *Handbook of Islamic Banking*, "in

---

[870]*Id.* at 272 ("They are given enough to suffice them for the operation, even if affluent; of weapons, mounts, clothing, and expenses.").

[871]*E.g.*, *Islamic Economics Order*, INSTITUTE OF ISLAMIC BANKING AND INSURANCE, http://www.islamic-banking.com/islamic_economics_order.aspx (last visited May 4, 2011) ("While allowing an individual to retain any surplus wealth, Islam seeks to reduce the margin of the surplus for the well-being of the community as a whole, in particular the destitute and deprived sections of society *by participation in the process of Zakat (a tax on wealth that is distributed to the needy).* (emphasis added)); Latifa M. Algaoud & Mervyn K. Lewis, *Islamic Critique of Conventional Financing in* HANDBOOK OF ISLAMIC BANKING 38, 40 (M. Kabir Hassan & Mervyn K. Lewis eds., 2007) [hereinafter HANDBOOK OF ISLAMIC BANKING] ("*Zakat* is the most important instrument for the redistribution of wealth."); Kym Brown, M. Kabir Hassan, & Michael Skully, *Operational Efficiency and Performance of Islamic Banks in* HANDBOOK OF ISLAMIC BANKING, *supra* note 871, at 99 (Islamic banks "pay[] *zakat* on income and inspire[] clients to pay *zakat*, which ensures redistribution of income in favour of the poor"); *id.* at 107 ("the social aspect of Islamic banking such as making *zakat* donations to charities is seen as an important aspect to maintain").

[872]RELIANCE OF THE TRAVELLER, *supra* note 10, at 274.

[873]*Id.* at 273.

[874]*Al-Qaradawi: Freedom Takes Priority over Islamic Law*, MALAYSIA TODAY (Feb. 13, 2011), http://www.malaysia-today.net/mtcolumns/from-around-the-blogs/38093-al-qaradawi-freedom-takes-priority-over-islamic-law.

[875]Alex Alexiev, *Jihad Comes to Wall Street*, NAT'L REVIEW ONLINE (Apr. 3, 2008), http://www.nationalreview.com/articles/223869/jihad-comes-wall-street/alex-alexiev; Press Release, BBC, Panorama: Faith, Hate, and Charity (July 30, 2006), *available at* http://www.bbc.co.uk/pressoffice/pressreleases/stories/2006/07_july/30/panorama.shtml. Sheikh Al-Qaradawi's philosophy is confirmed in the following *Qur'anic* verse: "Allah hath granted a grade higher to those who strive and fight with their goods and persons than those who sit (at home)." QUR'AN, *supra* note 11, at *Surah* 4:95.

[876]Not all *Shariah* scholars, however, overtly promote violent *jihad* or require financial institutions to pay *zakat* (obligatory charitable contribution) to be *Shariah*-compliant. For example, Dr. Hussain Hamed Hassan, a Cairo University professor and chair of several *Shariah* boards, believes that *zakat* is not necessary for *Shariah*-compliance because, in his view, *zakat* is compulsory only for individuals and not for institutions. Babu Das Augustine, *Scholar Against Compulsory Zakat on Islamic Banks*, GULFNEWS.COM (Apr. 18, 2008), http://gulfnews.com/business/banking/scholar-against-compulsory-zakat-on-islamic-banks-1.98342. *But cf. id.* (suggesting that if a *Shariah* board does decide that "zakat is . . . mandatory, it should be made applicable to *all* banks and financial institutions, whether Islamic

countries where zakat is not collected by the state, every Islamic bank or financial institution has to establish a zakat fund for collecting the funds and distributing them exclusively to the poor directly or through other religious institutions."[877] The financial institution's *Shariah* supervisory board is responsible for "advising on *zakat* (charity) and identifying the procedures for its calculation."[878] Islamic financial institutions use their adherence to the *zakat* requirement to show the supposed moral superiority of the Islamic banking system over the non-Islamic conventional system.[879] However, *zakat* may only be distributed to Muslims and one-eighth of it must be distributed to *"those fighting for Allah,"*[880] which often means direct support

or [secular]," in the interest of fairness) (emphasis added).

[877]Latifa M. Algaoud & Mervyn K. Lewis, *Islamic Critique of Conventional Financing in* HANDBOOK OF ISLAMIC BANKING, *supra* note 871, at 41; Latifa M. Algaoud & Mervyn K. Lewis, *Islamic Critique of Conventional Financing in* HANDBOOK OF ISLAMIC BANKING, *supra* note 871, at 38; *see also* M. Kabir Hassan & Mervyn K. Lewis, *Islamic Banking: An Introduction and Overview in* HANDBOOK OF ISLAMIC BANKING, *supra* note 871, at 5 (describing *zakat* as a "responsibility[]" of Islamic banks); *id.* at 10 (describing that the "'cleansing'" of tainted dividends that are not *Shariah*-compliant "cannot be counted as part of *zakat* obligations"); Mervyn K. Lewis, *Comparing Islamic and Christian Attitudes to Usury in* HANDBOOK OF ISLAMIC BANKING, *supra* note 871, at 72 (noting that when a bank determines that a certain transaction has "violated the ban on interest, . . . the earnings are distributed by the *shari'a* board to various *zakat* funds"); Kym Brown, M. Kabir Hassan, & Michael Skully, *Operational Efficiency and Performance of Islamic Banks in* HANDBOOK OF ISLAMIC BANKING, *supra* note 871, at 97 (declaring that banks arranging for the payment of *zakat* or dispersal to charitable organizations is "part of their social responsibility"); The Faisal Islamic Bank of Egypt touts itself as adhering to "Islamic credentials by means of the collection and distribution of *zakat*." M. Kabir Hassan & Mervyn K. Lewis, *Islamic Banking: An Introduction and Overview in* HANDBOOK OF ISLAMIC BANKING, *supra* note 871, at 6.

[878]Said M. Elfakhani, M. Kabir Hassan, & Yusuf M. Sidani, *Islamic Mutual Funds in* HANDBOOK OF ISLAMIC BANKING, *supra* note 871, at 262. Generally, individuals and financial institutions are required to pay 2.5% "on most forms of monetary wealth and earned income." *Id.* at 261. The amount of *zakat* to be paid on investment profits, however, is not settled and is complicated to calculate. *Id.*

[879]*See* Kym Brown, M. Kabir Hassan, & Michael Skully, *Operational Efficiency and Performance of Islamic Banks in* HANDBOOK OF ISLAMIC BANKING, *supra* note 871, at 98–99 (providing a chart that describes conventional banking as unconcerned with the poor and social justice, aiding the rich and hurting the poor, "extend[ing] oppression and exploitation," having "[n]o *zakat* system for the benefit of the poor," etc. and Islamic banking as "ensur[ing] social justice," distributing resources "in favour of the poor," "reduc[ing] the income inequality and wealth disparity," etc.); *The Social Activity*, FAISAL ISLAMIC BANK OF EGYPT, http://www.faisalbank.com.eg/FIB/faisal_en/Egtmayia_1. jsp (last visited Apr. 4, 2011) ("The social services of the bank are represented by the Zakat (alms giving) Fund which is considered one of the main bodies of Faisal Islamic Bank of Egypt and is one of its characteristics as being the first Islamic bank in Egypt that operates in compliance with the rules of Islamic Shari ah [*sic*] which include the payment of the prescribed Zakat on the bank's capital."); *see also Social Responsibility*, Al Rajhi Bank, http://www.alrajhibank.com.sa/AboutUs/ Pages/CorporateSocialResponsibility.aspx (last visited Apr. 8, 2011) ("We are proud of our services to the society through redirecting the funds from the clearance account to serve our community.").

[880]While the Handbook of Islamic Banking notes that those receiving *zakat* "are clearly identified

to Islamic terrorist groups.[881] As such, accepting SCF could mean financially supporting Islamic terrorists.

d. *Zakat* Distributions to Muslim Charitable Organizations

Financial institutions that market and sell SCF products may not distribute *zakat directly* to terrorists; however, financial institutions and individuals may give *zakat* to Islamic charities (because *zakat* can only be distributed to Muslims), some of which are legitimate and some of which are not.[882] This money is then often funneled by Islamic charities to terrorist organizations. The United States government has numerous documented instances of Islamic charities receiving *zakat* and using such funds to support terrorist organizations.[883] Chris Swecker, former Assistant Director of the Criminal Investigative Division of the FBI, testified to the following:

---

in Islamic jurisprudence," only "charities" are specifically mentioned. This is followed by a vague reference to "other bodies identified by the funds' supervisory boards." Said M. Elfakhani ET AL., *Islamic Mutual Funds in* HANDBOOK OF ISLAMIC BANKING, *supra* note 871, at 261. One of the "clearly identified" recipients not mentioned are "those fighting for Allah." RELIANCE OF THE TRAVELLER, *supra* note 10, at 272.

[881]*See* discussion *infra* Chapter 6.B.2.

[882]Indeed, there is a growing trend for a global *zakat* movement:

> The International Zakat Organisation (IZO), a new charitable body of the Organisation of the Islamic Conference (OIC), has announced its selection of BMB Group, the Cayman Islands based global alternative asset management firm, to lead a new charitable initiative, the Global Zakat and Charity Fund. BMB Islamic (BMB Group's subsidiary) is headed by Dr[.] Humayon Dar, a leading figure in Islamic finance. . . . The fund is expected to be $3 billion in size, and its purpose will be to fund charitable causes across the world . . . . *Inevitably, there has been a huge emphasis on Shari'ah compliance in Islamic banking and finance, but the announcement of a Global Zakat and Charity Fund is the beginning of a new Islamic financial trend . . . .*

Rabi Al Thani-Jumada Al Thani, *Global Perspective on Islamic Banking & Insurance*, NEW HORIZON, Apr.–June 2009, at 6 (internal quotation omitted) (emphasis added), *available at* http://www. newhorizon-islamicbanking.com/index.cfm?action=view&id=10760&section=news.

[883]*See* Press Release, U.S. Dep't of the Treasury, Treasury Designates Al-Aqsa International Foundation as Financier of Terror Charity Linked to Funding of the Hamas Terrorist Organization (May 29, 2003), *available at* http://www.treasury.gov/press-center/press-releases/Pages/js439.aspx; *U.S. Internal Revenue Service, Suspensions Pursuant to Code Section 501(p)* (Mar. 17, 2011), http://www.irs.gov/charities/charitable/article/0,,id=141459,00.html; U.S. DEP'T OF THE TREASURY, PROTECTING CHARITABLE GIVING—FREQUENTLY ASKED QUESTIONS 7–8 (2010) [hereinafter PROTECTING CHARITABLE GIVING], *available at* http://www.treasury.gov/resource-center/terrorist-illicit-finance/ Documents/Treasury%20Charity%20FAQs%206-4-2010%20FINAL.pdf.

The FBI and other domestic law enforcement and regulatory agencies have expended considerable effort on the extent to which charities fund terrorist networks. Islamic charitable giving, known as zakat, is one of the five pillars of [the] Islamic faith and results in *billions of dollars raised annually*. In some instances, investigation and intelligence revealed that al Qaeda facilitators corrupted specific foreign branch offices of large, internationally recognized charities. In many cases, lax oversight and the charities' own ineffective financial controls . . . often made it easy for al Qaeda facilitators to divert money from charitable uses.[884]

Jean-Charles Brisard, "an international expert on Terrorism Financing," published similar findings for the President of the United Nations Security Council in a 2002 report, submitting that the largest source of funds for al-Qaeda is *zakat*.[885] In fact, in a videotape seized in 2001, Osama bin Laden praised "those traders and businessmen who give Zakat so that they can help arm th[e] ill-equipped Lashkar [Islamic terrorist organization based in Pakistan]."[886] In a December 1998 ABC news interview, he also encouraged Muslims to give their *zakat* to support the Taliban regime: "Muslims and Muslim merchants, in particular, should give their zakat and their money in support of this state [Taliban regime] which is reminiscent of the state of Medina (Al-Munawwarah), where the followers of Islam

---

[884]Chris Swecker, Ass't Dir. of Criminal Investigative Div., FBI), Statement Before the House Financial Services Subcommittee on Housing and Community Opportunity (Oct. 7, 2004) (emphasis added), http://www.fbi.gov/news/testimony/fbis-efforts-in-combating-mortgage-fraud.

[885]JCB CONSULTING, TERRORISM FINANCING: ROOTS AND TRENDS OF SAUDI TERRORISM FINANCING 2 (Dec. 19, 2002), *available at* http://www.investigativeproject.org/documents/testimony/22.pdf; *id.* at 8 ("Zakat is the most important source of financial support for the al-Qaida network . . . . In several cases, money originating from Islamic banks and charities in the Gulf was moved and laundered through Western and specifically US correspondents, whether banks or charities, before reaching their recipients."); *id.* at 3 ("By mixing religious beliefs, tools and interpretations with financial purposes, without proper regulations and controls, Saudi Arabia opened an avenue for terrorism financing through the traditional Zakat, a legal almsgiving conceived as a way for purification by the Prophet that turned into a financial tool for terrorists.").

[886]JCB CONSULTING, TERRORISM FINANCING: ROOTS AND TRENDS OF SAUDI TERRORISM FINANCING 14 (Dec. 19, 2002) (emphasis added), http://www.investigativeproject.org/documents/testimony/22.pdf.

embraced the Prophet of God [(Allah)] . . . ."[887]

Hamas has likewise capitalized on Islamic charitable organizations' receipt of *zakat* contributions:

> The leaders of Hamas have taken advantage of donations made to NGOs and charities, which may appeal for the need to support orphans and widows, as well as, build schools and hospitals, but are actually "fronts" for Hamas and use a portion of these contributions to support the terrorist organization's military wing. Many donors believe that their charitable contributions were fulfilling one of their tenets of Islam (Zakat), but have unwittingly supported terrorist attacks through payments made to the NGOs and charities, which are actually Hamas "front" companies . . . . These charities are an easy target for fraud, as certain funds, which were originally provided for charitable purposes find their way to supporting Hamas' military wing and ultimately are the source for terrorist attacks.[888]

The Holy Land Foundation, for example, diverted charitable donations to Hamas: "[Holy Land Foundation] routed millions of dollars [to Hamas] through a series of Palestinian charities known as zakat committees."[889] Additionally, in 2006, the U.S. government blocked the assets of KindHearts for Charitable Humanitarian Development, Inc., a non-profit organization operating out of Ohio, based on evidence that the charity was directing financial contributions to Hamas.[890]

The federal government tracks charities such as [Holy Land Foundation] and KindHearts to ensure that they do not finance

---

[887]Interview by John Miller with Osama Bin Laden (Dec. 22, 1998), *available at* http://triceratops. brynmawr.edu/dspace/bitstream/handle/10066/4720/OBL19981222.pdf?sequence=1.

[888]John S. Pistole, Assistant Director, Counterterrorism Division, FBI, Statement Before the House Committee on Financial Service Subcommittee on Oversight and Investigations (Sept. 24, 2003), *available at* http://www2.fbi.gov/congress/congress03/pistole092403.htm.

[889]*HLF Officials Convicted on All Counts*, INVESTIGATIVE PROJECT (Nov. 24, 2008), http://www. investigativeproject.org/865/hlf-officials-convicted-on-all-counts.

[890]PROTECTING CHARITABLE GIVING, *supra* note 883, at 9.

terrorism. Specifically, the U.S. Department of Treasury's Office of Foreign Assets Control (OFAC)[891] is responsible for "designating" U.S.-based charities that are supporting terrorism and subsequently freezing their assets.[892] Of note, six of eight U.S.-based charities that have been designated for supporting terrorism are Islamic: The Holy Land Foundation (as mentioned above),[893] the Global Relief Foundation,[894] Benevolence International Foundation,[895] Al Haramain Islamic Foundation,[896] Islamic African Relief Agency,[897] and the Goodwill Charitable Organization.[898] The Benevolence

---

[891] *About: Office of Foreign Assets Control*, U.S. DEP'T OF THE TREASURY, http://www.treasury.gov/about/organizational-structure/offices/Pages/Office-of-Foreign-Assets-Control.aspx (last visited Feb. 23, 2011); *see also* E.O 13224, Blocking Property and Prohibiting Transactions with Persons Who Commit, Threaten to Commit, or Support Terrorism, 66 Fed. Reg. 49,079 (Sept. 25, 2001).

[892] *See* PROTECTING CHARITABLE GIVING, *supra* note 883, at 1–3; *see also Suspensions Pursuant to Code Section 501(p)*, IRS.GOV, http://www.irs.gov/charities/charitable/article/0,,id=141459,00.html (last visited Feb. 22, 2011).

[893] PROTECTING CHARITABLE GIVING, *supra* note 883, at 8 ("The Holy Land Foundation for Relief and Development (HLF) was designated on December 2, 2001 and May 21, 2002 for providing millions of dollars of material and logistical support to Hamas. HLF, originally known as the Occupied Land Fund, was established in California in 1989 as a tax-exempt charity. HLF supported Hamas activities through direct fund transfers to its offices in the West Bank and Gaza that are affiliated with Hamas and transfers of funds to Islamic charity committees ('zakat committees') and other charitable organizations that are part of Hamas or controlled by Hamas members.").

[894] *Id.* ("The Global Relief Foundation (GRF) was designated on October 18, 2002 for providing support for and assistance to Usama bin Laden (UBL), al-Qaeda, and other known terrorist groups.").

[895] *Id.* ("Benevolence International Foundation (BIF-USA) was designated on November 19, 2002 after its CEO was indicted by the Justice Department for operating BIF-USA as a racketeering enterprise and providing material support to terrorist groups, including al-Qaeda. BIF-USA was incorporated in Illinois in 1992 as a tax-exempt, not-for-profit organization whose stated purpose was to conduct humanitarian relief projects throughout the world.").

[896] *Id.* ("U.S. Branch (AHF) was designated on September 9, 2004 because of AHF's support for al-Qaeda. Individuals associated with the branch tried to conceal the movement of funds intended for Chechnya by omitting them from tax returns and mischaracterizing their use, which they claimed was for the purchase of a prayer house in Springfield, Missouri.").

[897] *Id.* ("Islamic African Relief Agency (IARA) was designated on October 13, 2004 for providing direct financial support for Usama Bin Ladin (UBL) and al-Qaeda's precursor, Maktab Al-Khidamat (MK). IARA, MK and UBL commingled funds and cooperated closely in raising and spending funds. IARA engaged in a joint program with an institute controlled by UBL that was involved in providing assistance to Taliban fighters. IARA was also responsible for moving funds to the Palestinian territories for use in terrorist activities, notably serving as a conduit to Hamas in one Western European country. IARA was headquartered in Khartoum, Sudan and had maintained over 40 offices throughout the world, including one in Columbia, Missouri.").

[898] *Id.* ("The Goodwill Charitable Organization (GCO) was designated on July 24, 2007 for providing financial support to Hizbollah directly and through the Martyrs Foundation in Lebanon. GCO was established as a fundraising office in Dearborn, Michigan by the Martyrs Foundation, which is a Hizbollah front organization that reports directly to the leadership of the Martyrs Foundation in Lebanon. Hizbollah recruited GCO leaders and maintained close contact with GCO representatives in the United States.").

International Foundation, based out of Chicago, "claimed to provide relief to widows and orphans—and it did in fact use some of its funds to provide humanitarian assistance. But the organization was actually a front for al-Qaeda. Its Executive Director pled guilty to racketeering conspiracy and is now serving 11 years in federal prison."[899] Also, the U.S. branch of the Al Haramain Islamic Foundation claimed that its contributions were being used to purchase a domestic house of prayer.[900] In reality, however, Al Haramain was sending the charitable money it received to support al-Qaeda in Chechnya.[901] In 2005, Al Haramain and two of its officers were indicted on charges of conspiring to defraud the U.S. government.[902]

The U.S. government has similarly identified other Islamic charities involved in supporting terrorists. In January 2008, three former officers of the Muslim "charity" Care International, Inc. were convicted of conspiring to defraud the United States for falsely declaring in its Articles of Incorporation that the organization was "exclusively involved in charitable, religious, educational, and scientific purposes," when, in fact, it was also engaged in soliciting and spending funds supporting violent *jihadists* and publishing

---

[899]John S. Pistole, Deputy Director, FBI, Speech at American Bankers Association/American Bar Association Money Laundering Enforcement Conference in Washington, D.C. (Oct. 22, 2007) [hereinafter Pistole], *available at* http://www.fbi.gov/news/speeches/the-fbi-and-the-financial-sector-working-together-to-protect-our-citizens-and-our-economy.

[900]Al Haramain Islamic Foundation is a charity based in Saudi Arabia. Its U.S. branch was registered as a 501(c)(3) in Oregon. *Id.*

[901]*Id.*

[902]*Id.*

jihadi propaganda in the United States.[903] Also, CAIR,[904] ISNA,[905] and NAIT[906] have all been identified as supporters of Hamas or the Muslim Brotherhood.[907]

Such Islamic organizations not only knowingly provide material support to terrorists, but they also enable terrorist practices and may be held liable for such actions. For example, a U.S. district court held the Qur'anic Literacy Institute (QLI), an Illinois non-profit that translated and published Islamic texts,[908] civilly liable for the murder of David Boim by Hamas, based on QLI's intentional support of Hamas.[909] In 2008, after David Boim's family sued QLI in

[903]Press Release, Dep't of Justice, Former Officers of a Muslim Charity, Care International, Inc., Convicted (Jan. 11, 2008) (internal quotation marks omitted), *available at* http://www.justice.gov/opa/pr/2008/January/08_nsd_021.html ("'Today's verdict is a milestone in our efforts against those who conceal their support for extremist causes behind the veil of humanitarianism. For years, these defendants used an allegedly charitable organization as a front for the collection of donations that they used to support violent jihadists. This prosecution serves notice that we will not tolerate the use of charities as a means of promoting terrorism,' said Kenneth L. Wainstein, Assistant Attorney General for National Security.").

[904]*Our Vision, Mission and Core Principles*, CAIR.COM, http://www.cair.com/AboutUs/VisionMission CorePrinciples.aspx (last visited Mar. 21, 2011) ("The Council on American-Islamic Relations (CAIR) is a nonprofit 501(c)(3), grassroots civil rights and advocacy group. CAIR is America's largest Islamic civil liberties group . . . .").

[905]ISLAMIC SOCIETY OF NORTH AMERICA, ISNA STATEMENT OF POSITION: WHO WE ARE AND WHAT WE BELIEVE (Sept. 12, 2007), http://www.isna.net/Documents/ISNAHQ/ISNA-Statement-of-Position-Who-we-Are-and-What-We-Believe.pdf ("ISNA's mission and programs are largely supported through the generous donations of its thousands of members and other contributors from across North America, who are committed to the organization's ideals . . . .").

[906]*North American Islamic Trust*, NAIT.NET, http://www.nait.net/ (last visited Mar. 21, 2011) ("The North American Islamic Trust (NAIT) is a waqf, the historical Islamic equivalent of an American trust or endowment, serving Muslims in the United States and their institutions. . . . NAIT is a not-for-profit entity that qualifies as a tax-exempt organization under Section 501(c) (3) of the Internal Revenue Code.").

[907]Unindicted Co-conspirators, *supra* note 39, at 5 (CAIR was designated as an entity "who [is] and [was] [a] member[] of the US Muslim Brotherhood's Palestine Committee and/or its organizations."); *id.* at 8 (NAIT and ISNA were listed as "entities who are and or were members of the US Muslim Brotherhood.").

[908]Boim v. Holy Land Found. for Relief & Dev., 340 F. Supp. 2d 885, 924 (N.D. Ill. 2004).

[909]*Id.* at 511 F.3d 707, 710 (7th Cir. Ill. 2007) ("At the conclusion of a trial, a jury concluded that appellant Quranic Literacy Institute ('QLI') also was liable. The jury awarded damages of $52 million, which the district court trebled to $156 million."). In 1998, the federal government seized over $1 million of QLI's assets, United States v. One 1997 E35 Ford Van, No. 98-C-3548, 2010 U.S. Dist. Lexis 26909, at *2 (N.D. Ill. Mar. 22, 2010), upon learning that QLI had "knowingly" participated in money transfers intended to finance Hamas. United States v. One 1997 E35 Ford Van, 50 F. Supp. 2d 789, 792 (N.D. Ill. 1999) ("The United States government filed this civil forfeiture action seeking to forfeit all funds contained in seven bank accounts and two safe deposit boxes on the theory that these funds were transferred to financial institutions within the United States from abroad with the intent to support the international terrorist activities of the HAMAS organization in violation of the Money Laundering Control Act of 1986, 18 U.S.C. § 1956.").

Boim v. Holy Land Foundation, the United States Court of Appeals for the Seventh Circuit upheld a $156 million judgment for Mr. and Mrs. Boim[910] and against QLI for knowingly providing financial support to Hamas.[911] The Seventh Circuit stated the following regarding donor liability:

> Nor should donors to terrorism be able to escape liability because terrorists and their supporters launder donations through a chain of *intermediate* organizations. Donor A gives to innocent-appearing organization B which gives to innocent-appearing organization C which gives to Hamas. *As long as A either knows or is reckless in failing to discover that donations to B end up with Hamas, A is liable.* Equally important, however, if this knowledge requirement is not satisfied, the donor is not liable. And as the temporal chain lengthens, the likelihood that a donor has or should know of the donee's connection to terrorism shrinks. But to set the knowledge and causal requirement higher than we have done in this opinion would be to invite money laundering, the proliferation of affiliated organizations, and two-track terrorism (killing plus welfare). Donor liability would be eviscerated, and the statute would be a dead letter.[912]

This holding places Islamic charities, as well as financial institutions, on notice with regard to whom they designate to receive *zakat* donations. Indeed, if there is evidence to prove that a financial institution knowingly or recklessly gives to a charity which in turn gives to a terrorist organization, the financial institution would be held liable under federal law for funding terrorism.[913] U.S. banks that

---

[910]Boim v. Holy Land Found. for Relief & Dev., 511 F.3d 707, 710 (7th Cir. 2007).
[911]Boim v. Holy Land Found. for Relief & Dev., 549 F.3d 685, 705 (7th Cir. 2008) ("[T]he court had no choice but to enter summary judgment for the plaintiffs with respect to Hamas's responsibility for the Boim killing."), *cert denied*, Boim v. Salah, 130 S. Ct. 458 (2009).
[912]*Id.* at 701–02 (emphasis added).
[913]*E.g.*, 18 U.S.C. § 1956; *see also* 18 U.S.C. §§ 2339A–C.

are already *Shariah*-compliant or are seeking to become *Shariah*-compliant must be aware of these dangers. As mentioned, becoming *Shariah*-compliant requires that the bank place complete control of *zakat* funds in the hands of the *Shariah* board. Therefore, the *Shariah* board, which may have scholars following Mufti Usmani's authority, could be distributing the funds, either knowingly or recklessly, to charities that give to terrorist organizations. If this is the case, under the reasoning of *Boim*,[914] the bank may also be liable for funding terrorism.

Moreover, SCF proponents may even seek to use *Shariah* supervisory boards to limit U.S. financial institutions' compliance with federal agencies that aim to ferret out domestic institutions' funding of terrorist organizations. John Pistole, Former Deputy Director of the FBI, stressed that the FBI cannot successfully identify such institutions and charities that fund terrorist organizations "without the help and cooperation of the banking industry."[915] The industry's compliance with disclosure requirements and other FBI requests for information, Pistole said, "are absolutely vital to our efforts."[916] For this reason, Pistole emphasized the need to "tighten[] our financial systems," because "the threat is real, and the stakes are high."[917] With *Shariah* supervisory boards gaining a foothold in U.S. financial institutions, however, the FBI may be forced to address a decline in cooperation and transparency.

It is no surprise that Islamic charities support terrorist groups like Hamas and al-Qaeda. The *ummah* has specifically pledged to provide support for its "legitimate causes" for the "challenges faced by the Islamic world."[918] Economic cooperation among Islamic

---

[914]*Holy Land Found. for Relief & Dev.*, 549 F.3d at 701–02.
[915]Pistole, *supra* note 899.
[916]*Id.*
[917]*Id.*
[918]Organisation of the Islamic Conference Charter art. 1, § 2.

countries under the OIC's leadership resulted in the creation of the Islamic Development Bank, whose primary purpose is to "foster economic development and social progress of [OIC] member countries and Muslim communities individually as well as jointly in accordance with the principles of the Shari'ah."[919] To achieve its purpose of supporting Muslim communities living in non-member countries, the Bank created a "Special Fund."[920] One such Muslim community is "the Palestinian people."[921] The OIC Member States have pledged "to support the struggle of the Palestinian people, who [according to the OIC Charter] are presently under foreign occupation."[922] Islamic charities in the United States have funded Hamas to help end this "occupation," thereby fulfilling the common interest of the *ummah*. Whether by way of SCF or Islamic charities, financial *jihad*, in all its forms, is alive and well and poses danger to those countries that are willing to permit unchecked growth of *Shariah*-compliant institutions.

3. The Triumph of Political *Jihad*

Around the world, *Shariah* is successfully infiltrating countries that have recognized and accepted many of Islam's political goals and values. For example, in 1996, the United Kingdom created "Muslim Arbitration Tribunals," or "sharia courts."[923] In 2008, the British government "sanctioned the powers for sharia judges" to rule on cases between Muslims involving divorce, financial disputes,

---

[919]Islamic Development Bank Articles of Agreement art. 1.
[920]*Id.* arts. 10, 22.
[921]Organisation of the Islamic Conference Charter pmbl; *Aqsa Fund*, ISLAMIC DEVELOPMENT BANK, http://www.isdb.org/irj/go/km/docs/documents/IDBDevelopments/Internet/English/IDB/CM/About%20IDB/Organization/Aqsa_Fund.html (last visited Apr. 19, 2011) ("The emergency Arab Summit Conference held in Cairo during 21-22 October 2000 . . . decided to establish a fund with the name of Al-Aqsa Fund with a resources base of approximately US$ 800 million to be used for financing emergency and development projects and programs aimed at strengthening the internal capacity of the Palestinian economy and responding to the humanitarian needs of the Palestinian people during the crisis.").
[922]Organisation of the Islamic Conference Charter pmbl.
[923]Taher, *supra* note 451.

domestic violence, and other disputes involving *Shariah*.[924] In September 2008, a total of five *Shariah* courts had been established (in London, Birmingham, Bradford, Manchester, and with the headquarters in Nuneaton, Warwickshire), with plans to set up two more in Glasgow and Edinburgh.[925] Even before the government sanctioned the *Shariah* courts, Lord Chief Justice Phillips stated that *Shariah* "could be used to settle marital and financial disputes."[926] And, on February 7, 2008, the Archbishop of Canterbury stated that "incorporating some aspects of Shari'a law into the Common Law was inevitable."[927] Hence, despite its many differences and basic incompatibility with English Common Law, *Shariah* has become a binding source of law in the United Kingdom.

Similarly, *Shariah* has successfully infiltrated Ethiopia and Kenya through the creation of *Shariah* courts, which have been given jurisdiction in cases involving marriage, divorce, maintenance, guardianship of minors, and family relationships, provided that all parties are Muslims or the marriage under consideration was conducted under Islamic law.[928]

Although Islam often successfully masquerades as a political group on equal footing with any other ideology, these examples show that the political maneuverings of Islam have little to do with mere politics and are directly in line with every Muslim's religious

---

[924]*Id.*

[925]*Id.*

[926]*Id.*

[927]BUREAU OF DEMOCRACY, HUMAN RIGHTS AND LABOR, U.S. DEP'T OF STATE, INTERNATIONAL RELIGIOUS FREEDOM REPORT 2008: UNITED KINGDOM (Feb. 25, 2009), *available at* http://www.state.gov/g/drl/rls/irf/2008/108478.htm.

[928]Federal Courts of Sharia Consolidation Proclamation Act (Act. No. 188/1999) (Eth.), *available at* http://www.ethiopian-law.com/federal-laws/federal-justice-institutions/federal-courts/338-federal-courts-of-sharia-consolidation-proclamation-no-188-1999.html. The new Kenyan Constitution, adopted by referendum on August 27, 2010, expressly provides for the establishment of Islamic courts: "The jurisdiction of a Kadhis' court shall be limited to the determination of questions of Muslim law relating to personal status, marriage, divorce or inheritance in proceedings in which all the parties profess the Muslim religion and submit to the jurisdiction of the Kadhi's courts." CONST. art. 170(5) (2010) (Kenya).

duty to exert himself in Allah's path. Because fundamentalist Islam does not distinguish between religion and state, it is driven by a single, politico-spiritual agenda, which is nothing short of complete world domination. And, not only are political movements directed toward advancing this goal, but they represent only the second of three steps of pleasing Allah by making his law dominant over the entire world.

C. VIOLENT *JIHAD*

One of the most well-known ways the believer achieves the goal of Islamic *jihad* is through violent warfare. Some have attempted to define *jihad* completely in terms of personal religious duty and peaceful persuasion, and they claim that violent *jihad* is a mere misinterpretation of the *Qur'an* by so-called radical Muslims. The *Qur'an*, however, unambiguously commands *all* Muslims to commit themselves to violent war and to "fight for the faith, in the cause of Allah" because those who fight and "those who give (fighters) asylum and aid—these are (all) in very truth the believers: for them is the forgiveness of sins and a provision most generous."[929] Elsewhere, the *Qur'an* commands Muslims to "fight the Pagans all together,"[930] and to "[s]lay them wherever ye find them."[931]

These commands are not anomalous, but they are repeated in similar forms over and over again throughout the *Qur'an*: "Fight those who believe not in Allah nor the last day";[932] "slay them wherever ye catch them . . . . Such is the reward of those who suppress faith";[933] "fight and slay the pagans wherever ye find them, and seize them, beleaguer them, and lie in wait for them in every stratagem (of war)";[934] "fight the unbelievers who gird you

---

[929]QUR'AN, *supra* note 11, at *Surah* 8:74.
[930]*Id.* at *Surah* 9:36.
[931]*Id.* at *Surah* 4:89.
[932]*Id.* at *Surah* 9:29.
[933]*Id.* at *Surah* 2:191.
[934]*Id.* at *Surah* 9:5.

about, and let them find firmness in you: and know that Allah is with those who fear him."[935] Other passages in the *Qur'an* provide greater insight as to what type of *jihad* is promoted in these verses. For instance, the *Qur'an* allows Muslims to take women captured in *jihad*.[936] Similarly, Muhammad himself extolled the virtues and rewards of violent *jihad* to his followers:

> The person who participates in (Holy battles) in Allah's cause and nothing compels him to do so except belief in Allah and His Apostles, will be recompensed by Allah either with a reward, or booty (if he survives) or will be admitted to Paradise (if he is killed in the battle as a martyr). Had I not found it difficult for my followers, then I would not remain behind any [company] going for Jihad and *I would have loved to be martyred in Allah's cause and then made alive, and then martyred and then made alive, and then again martyred in His cause.*[937]

This *hadith* demonstrates that so-called radical Muslims do not misinterpret the *Qur'an*. The martyrdom referred to in the *hadith* is obviously literal, not spiritual, and Muhammad's esteem for it is unmistakable.

Although *jihad* may take many different forms, because Islam is in a constant state of war against the unbelieving world, *jihad* will always contain an ultimately violent element, no matter what kind of *imam* (Islamic spiritual leader), caliph (the head of the Islamic state), or secular leader presides. Despite changing political or social sensibilities or leadership, *jihad* always endures in an inherently violent form.[938]

---

[935]*Id.* at *Surah* 9:123.

[936]ASAD, *supra* note 432, at 124; QUR'AN, *supra* note 11, at *Surah* 4:25, 192 n.540 (expounding that "girls from among those whom your right hands possess," referenced in the passage, include "captives taken in Jihad").

[937]SAHIH BUKHARI, *supra* note 69, at Vol. 1, Bk. 2, No. 36 (emphasis added).

[938]*See* SAHIH MUSLIM, *supra* note 46, at Bk. 020, No. 4717 ("[T]he Holy Prophet (may peace be upon him) said: This religion will continue to exist, and a group of people from the Muslims will continue to fight for its protection until the Hour is established."); *id.*, at Bk. 041, No. 6985 ("Allah's Messenger

"Moderate" Muslims often argue that even though the *Qur'an* calls for violent *jihad*, the *Qur'an* also contains verses that promote peace, mercy, and tolerance. However, these Muslims ignore a very important fact. The verses that advocate violent *jihad* are present in sections of the *Qur'an* which were revealed *after* the verses that promote peace, and according to the doctrine of abrogation *(naskh)*,[939] the violent verses likely abrogate (i.e., supersede) the non-violent verses,[940] or at least remain authoritative because they were revealed later in time. Although the *Qur'an* is not organized chronologically, Muslim scholars, for abrogation purposes, divide the *Surahs* (chapters) into two categories—those verses revealed to Muhammad during his life in Mecca (Meccan verses) and those revealed after the *hijra* (Muhammad's migration from Mecca to Medina).[941] "Each verse that calls for forgiveness belongs to Mecca and each verse that encourages fighting belongs to Medina."[942] Additionally, those verses that advocate "a defensive military stance" are Meccan, while the "suras that contain a call to an offensive military stance" are Medinan.[943]

Specifically, verses advocating violent methods of *jihad* are predominately located in *Surahs* 2, 4, and 9, all of which are part of the Medinan revelations and were revealed *after* verses advocating

---

(may peace be upon him) [said]: The last hour would not come unless the Muslims will fight against the Jews and the Muslims would kill them until the Jews would hide themselves behind a stone or a tree and a stone or a tree would say: Muslim, or the servant of Allah, there is a Jew behind me; come and kill him; but the tree Gharqad would not say, for it is the tree of the Jews.").

[939]Abrogation is "the 'lifting *(raf)* of a legal rule through a legal evidence of a later date.' The abrogating text or evidence is called *nasikh*, while the repealed rule is called *mansukh*." NYAZEE, *supra* note 62, at 318. All four schools of *Sunni* thought generally accept the abrogation doctrine. *Id.*

[940]*See* QUR'AN, *supra* note 11, at *Surah* 2:106 ("None of our revelations do we abrogate or cause to be forgotten, but we substitute something better or similar: knowest thou not that Allah hath power over all things?"); *id.* at *Surah* 13:39 ("Allah doth blot out or confirm what he pleaseth: With him is the mother of the book."); *id.* at *Surah* 16:101 ("When we substitute one revelation for another—and Allah knows best what he reveals (in stages)—they say, 'thou art but a forger': But most of them understand not.").

[941]1 THE QUR'AN DILEMMA 66 (2011).

[942]*Id.* at 76.

[943]*Id.*

peace, tolerance, and non-violent methods of *jihad*.[944] These newer verses, because they came later in time, abrogate (i.e., supersede) the older peaceful verses, or at least remain authoritative.[945] Therefore, the *Qur'an* reinforces violent *jihad* as part of every Muslim's religious duty to exert himself for Allah's cause.

The validity of verses commanding violent *jihad* is evidenced by Muhammad's own life and practice. Muhammad, while acting under the peaceful revelation as a prophet in Mecca, was able to gain only a few followers in thirteen years.[946] But, when he migrated to Medina and had received the revelations commanding violent *jihad*, he became both a political leader and the commander-in-chief

---

[944]*See* QUR'AN, *supra* note 11, at 16 ("This [(*Surah* 2)] is in the main an early Madinah"); *id.* at 182 (stating that *Surah* 4 discusses principles for the community at Medina); *id.* at 435 (stating that *Surah* 9 was revealed during A.H. 9, during the Medinan period); ASAD, *supra* note 432, at 7 ("[*Surah* 2] is the first *sūrah* revealed in its entirety after the Prophet's exodus to Medina . . . . The reference, in verse 106, to the abrogation of earlier messages by that granted to the Prophet Muhammad is of the greatest importance for a correct understanding of this *sūrah*, and indeed of the entire Qur'ān. Much of the legal ordinances provided here (especially in the later part of the *sūrah*) – touching upon questions of ethics, social questions, and warfare, etc. – are a direct consequence of that pivotal statement."); *id.* at 116 ("A large part of the *sūrah* is devoted to practical legislation bearing on problems of peace and war, as well as to relations of believers with unbelievers" and "belongs in its entirety to the Medina period."); *id.* at 287 (*Sūrah* 9 encompasses both "*At-Tawbah* and *Al-Anfāl*" and is "largely devoted to problems of war between the believers and the deniers of the truth . . . . [It] was revealed shortly before, during and immediately after the campaign, and most of it at the time of the long march from Medina to Tabūk."); *see also* QUR'AN, *supra* note 11, at *Surah* 2:191 ("[S]lay them wherever ye catch them . . . . Such is the reward of those who suppress faith"); *id.* at *Surah* 9:41 ("Go ye forth (whether equipped) lightly or heavily, and strive and struggle, with your goods and your persons, in the cause of Allah"); *id.* at *Surah* 9:36 ("Fight the pagans all together as they fight you all together"); *id.* at *Surah* 9:29 ("Fight those who believe not in Allah nor the last day"); *id.* at *Surah* 9:5 ("fight and slay the pagans wherever ye find them, and seize them, beleaguer them, and lie in wait for them in every stratagem (of war).").

[945]QUR'AN, *supra* note 11, at 46 n.107 (discussing *Surah* 2:106).

> If we take it in a general sense, it means that Allah's message from age to age is always the same, but that its form may differ according to the needs and exigencies of the time. That form was different as given to Moses and then to Jesus and then to Muhammad. . . . There is nothing derogatory in this if we believe in progressive revelation. . . . There may be express abrogation, or there may be 'causing or permitting to forget.' How many good and wise institutions gradually become obsolete by afflux of time? Then there is the gradual process of disuse or forgetting in evolution. This does not mean that eternal principles change. It is only a sign of Allah's infinite power that his creation should take so many forms and shapes not only in the material world but in the world of man's thought and expression.

Id.

[946]SYED SAEED AKHTAR RIZVI, THE LIFE OF MUHAMMAD THE PROPHET, Chpts. 5–6, 8 (3d ed. 1999), *available at* http://www.al-islam.org/lifeprophet/.

of the army of believers.[947] After nine years of military expeditions as a prophet and political and military leader, Muhammad was able to conquer most of the Arabian Peninsula for Islam.[948] Muhammad's *Sunnah* (words and actions of Muhammad; essentially following Muhammad's footsteps) thus supports violent *jihad*, including *jihad* by war.

All the stages of *jihad* work together to create an integrated battle plan. One of the most horrific examples of this plan was the September 11th strike on the World Trade Towers and the Pentagon. One of the pilots, Hani Hanjour, integrated himself into U.S. society and took commercial pilot lessons before the attacks.[949] Despite being a terrorist, Hanjour succeeded in concealing his role in the plot and avoiding scrutiny.[950] According to Federal Aviation Administration (FAA) officials who checked the validity of Hanjour's license, they "observed nothing that warranted further action or suggested Hanjour would eventually hijack a plane. The inspector considered Hanjour just one of the many students that schools routinely seek FAA reviews on."[951] This tactic—becoming "just one of the many"—is part of Muslim fundamentalists' strategy to place themselves strategically in positions to engage in violent warfare when the opportunity presents itself.[952]

---

[947]*Id.* chpts. 12–20.

[948]*Id.*

[949]Associated Press, *FAA Probed, Cleared Sep. 11 Hijacker in Early 2001*, Fox News (May 10, 2002), http://www.foxnews.com/story/0,2933,52408,00.html.

[950]*Id.*

[951]*Id.*; *see also supra* notes 164–168 and accompanying text.

[952]Fiqh, *supra* note 305, at 528 (explaining that *jihad* is one of the obligations that is not subject to conditions of "time, place, person, justice or injustice").

CHAPTER SEVEN

THE WEST MUST OPPOSE ALL FORMS OF JIHAD, INCLUDING ATTEMPTS TO IMPLEMENT SHARIAH

Regardless of which method of *jihad* is used, the Muslim's duty to work toward Islamic dominance is unchanging, obligating believers across generations and across national borders to continue fighting until the entire world is brought into submission to Allah and his laws.[953] Therefore, no matter how sincere an individual Muslim may be in his claims that he desires to live peaceably with his non-Muslim neighbor and that he has no personal aspirations of imposing *Shariah*, individual Muslims lack authority to re-interpret the *Qur'an* to their liking. Further, many within Islam encourage other Muslims to lure non-Muslims into a false sense of security. Despite doctrinal disputes between so-called "moderate" Muslims and "radical" Muslims and between different sects of Islam, fundamental Islam teaches that *Shariah* is the supreme law and *jihad* is central to its promotion.

America must protect itself from religious laws that demonstrably contradict nearly every value that represents the American way of life. While the First Amendment provides freedom of religion, it does not allow for official recognition of a different set of laws that are wholly incompatible with the Constitution and laws of this country. The *jihad* of implementing *Shariah* is perhaps one of the most strategically coordinated and far-reaching politico-religious agendas in the world today, and Americans must recognize

---

[953]WAR AND PEACE IN THE LAW OF ISLAM, *supra* note 48, at 64.

it in order to protect America from such laws.

Western notions of law and justice have played a significant role in reforming the unjust laws and local cultural traditions— laws and traditions that are contrary to fundamental human rights and dignity—in many parts of the world. For instance, Western colonization in India, Central Asia, and Africa led to legal reforms that drastically modified or wholly replaced Islamic criminal law, jurisprudence, and procedure in those places.[954] The change resulted not only in more defined and consistent legal systems,[955] but also in the establishment of the rule of law in Islamic courts.[956] Colonization by the West resulted in the elimination of inhumane *Shariah* practices such as mutilation, crucifixion, stoning, and amputation.[957] Ultimately, Western colonial influence led to the codification of criminal law in places such as India (which included present-day Pakistan),[958] Nigeria,[959] and Egypt.[960]

While the beginning of the nineteenth century marked the initial "Westernization" of most Muslim countries, Western legal influence has waned in these countries.[961] Muslims who were discontented with Western political and cultural influences began to utilize Western political processes to impose their religious beliefs on their fellow citizens.[962] As discussed earlier, the religious belief

---

[954]PETERS, *supra* note 260, at 103–05; *see also* Jan Michael Otto, *Introduction: Investigating the Role of Sharia in National Law*, in SHARIA INCORPORATED: A COMPARATIVE OVERVIEW OF THE LEGAL SYSTEMS OF TWELVE MUSLIM COUNTRIES IN PAST AND PRESENT 17, 35 (Jan Michael Otto ed. 2010) [hereinafter "SHARIA INCORPORATED"]; U.S. TREASURY DEP'T-BUREAU OF STATISTICS, COLONIAL ADMINISTRATION, 1800–1900, 2679–84 (O.P. Austin ed. 1903) [hereinafter "COLONIAL ADMIN."].

[955]COLONIAL ADMIN., *supra* note 954, at 2679.

[956]PETERS, *supra* note 260, at 105–06, 109–10.

[957]*See id.* at 80–81; PETERS, *supra* note 260, at 104, 106, 108–09, 119–20; Philip Ostien and Albert Dekker, *Sharia and National Law in Nigeria*, in SHARIA INCORPORATED, *supra* note 954, at 553, 559–60.

[958]*Id.* at 110.

[959]Ostien and Dekker, *supra* note 957, at 589; PETERS, *supra* note 260, at 125.

[960]Maurits Berger and Nadia Sonneveld, *Sharia and National Law in Egypt*, in SHARIA INCORPORATED, *supra* note 954, at 51, 59.

[961]*See* PETERS, *supra* note 260, at 142–45; *see also* Otto, *supra* note 954, at 41; *see generally* RADICAL ISLAM'S RULES: THE WORLDWIDE SPREAD OF EXTREME *SHARI'A* LAW (Paul Marshall ed. 2005) [hereinafter "RADICAL ISLAM'S RULES"].

[962]PETERS, *supra* note 260, at 142–45; *see also* Paul Marshall, *Introduction: The Rise of Extreme*

motivating this movement to revert to pure *Shariah* comes from the *Qur'an*'s instruction that "Muslims, in order to be good Muslims, must live in an Islamic state, a state which implements the Shari'a."[963] The religious draw of Islamic law thus lies in the assumption that by implementing *Shariah*, the "community complies with [Allah's] wishes and [they] will be rewarded."[964]

The practical draw of *Shariah* lies in its deterrence component. Communities that are desperate to reduce crime often "welcome Islamic criminal law as a panacea for the cure of social evils" because of its powerful deterrent effects, swift verdicts, and harsh punishments.[965] Catering to these perceptions, advocates of *Shariah* specifically flaunt the application of "severe and painful punishments consisting of whipping, amputation and stoning to death."[966] For example, Iran's Ayatollah Khomeini stated that "Islamic justice is based on simplicity and ease. . . . All that is required is for an Islamic judge, with pen and inkwell and two or three enforcers, to go into a town, come to his verdict in any kind of case, and have it immediately carried out."[967] Responding to these arguments in favor of *Shariah*, many countries have moved to adopt and incorporate Islamic laws into the structures that were previously reformed by Western influence.

Libya is one such country.[968] When Muammar Gaddafi seized power in 1969, he implemented laws that were derived principally from Islamic *Shariah*.[969] Gaddafi banned alcoholic drinks,[970] changed

Shari'a, *in* RADICAL ISLAM'S RULES, *supra* note 961, at 1, 9.
[963] PETERS, *supra* note 260, at 144.
[964] *Id.* at 146.
[965] *Id.*
[966] *Id.*
[967] *Id.* at 147 (quoting KHOMEINI, SAYINGS OF THE AYATOLLAH KHOMEINI 30 (H. Salemson, trans. 1979)).
[968] PETERS, *supra* note 260, at 153.
[969] *Id.* at 153–54; *see also* Libyan Am. Oil Co. (LIAMCO) v. Gov't of the Libyan Arab Republic, 62 I.L.R. 140, 174 (Arb. of I.C.J. 1977) (stating that the "Revolutionary Command Council . . . provided that Islamic law shall be the principal source of Libyan legislation, and appointed special commissions to review existing laws and to amend them according to dictates of Islamic *Shari'a*").
[970] PETERS, *supra* note 260, at 154 (citing Law No. 89 of Nov. 20, 1974) (Libya)) (making the

the criminal law regarding theft,[971] criminalized extramarital sexual intercourse,[972] and organized a preparatory committee to Islamize the Libyan legal system.[973] Subsequently, the general punishment for illegal sexual intercourse was made to follow *Qur'anic* text (requiring flogging or incarceration for up to five years).[974] The laws additionally require amputation for certain offenses.[975] The first judicially imposed amputation was carried out on July 3, 2002,[976] and amputations continue to be imposed today.[977]

In 1979, General Zia-ul-Haq began the Islamization of Pakistan's legal system.[978] The reforms established a Federal Shariat Court[979] to "examine and decide the question whether or not any law or provision of law is repugnant to the injunctions of Islam . . . ."[980]

manufacture, consumption and possession of alcohol a punishable offense); KIMBERLY L. SULLIVAN, MUAMMAR AL-QADDAFI'S LIBYA 62 (2009).

[971]PETERS, *supra* note 260, at 154 (citing Law No. 148 of 1972 (Libya)); *see also* LIAMCO, 62 I.L.R. at 174.

[972]PETERS, *supra* note 260, at 154 (citing Law No. 70 of 1973 (Libya)); *see also* LIAMCO, 62 I.L.R. at 174; BUREAU OF DEMOCRACY, HUMAN RIGHTS & LABOR, U.S. DEP'T OF STATE, INTERNATIONAL RELIGIOUS FREEDOM REPORT 2009: LIBYA (2009), *available at* http://www.state.gov/g/drl/rls/hrrpt/2009/nea/136074.htm ("Sex outside of marriage is defined as adultery in Law 70 of 1973 and is a felony offense.").

[973]PETERS, *supra* note 260, at 154.

[974]*Id.*; *see also* QUR'AN, *supra* note 11, at *Surah* 24:2 ("The woman and the man guilty of adultery or fornication—flog each of them with a hundred stripes."); Summary prepared by the Office of the High Commissioner for Human Rights in accordance with paragraph 15(c) of the annex to Human rights Council resolution 5/1, Libyan Arab Jamahiriya, ¶¶ 10, 18, U.N. Doc. A/HRC/WG.6/9LBY/3 (July 15, 2010).

[975]PETERS, *supra* note 260, at 155 (citing art. 21, Law 148/1972) (though only under anesthesia and after appeal).

[976]AMNESTY INT'L, LIBYA: TIME TO MAKE HUMAN RIGHTS A REALITY 36 (Apr. 2004) (MDE 19/002/2004), *available   at*   http://www.amnesty.org/en/library/asset/MDE19/002/2004/en/0f0c0416-d631-11dd-ab95-a13b602c0642/ mde190022004en.pdf.

[977]Summary prepared by the Office of the High Commissioner for Human Rights in accordance with paragraph 15(c) of the annex to Human rights Council resolution 5/1, Libyan Arab Jamahiriya, ¶¶ 6–8, U.N. Doc. A/HRC/WG.6/9LBY/3 (July 15, 2010).

[978]Martin Lau, *Sharia and National Law in Pakistan, in* SHARIA INCORPORATED, *supra* note 954, at 373, 398; PETERS, *supra* note 260, at 155.

[979]President's Order 3 of 1979 amended the Constitution of Pakistan by inserting Part VII, Chapter 3A which created the Federal Shariat Court. Constitution (Amendment) Order, President's Order 3 of 1979, THE GAZETTE OF PAKISTAN EXTRAORDINARY, Feb. 7, 1979, *available at* http://www.pakistani.org/pakistan/constitution/orders/po3_1979.html; *see also* CONST. arts. 203A–203J (Pak.) (as amended); PETERS, *supra* note 260, at 155; Lau, *supra* note 978, at 400.

[980]CONST. art. 203D(1) (Pak.). "If any law or provision of law is held by the [Shariat] Court to be repugnant to the injunctions of Islam . . . such law or provision shall, to the extent to which it is held to be so repugnant, cease to have effect on the day on which the decision of the [Shariat] Court takes effect." *Id.* art. 203D(3).

The Islamization process "introduced Islamic criminal law for the first time since it had been gradually displaced during British colonial rule in [favor] of English criminal law."[981] This process continued in 1990 with the *qisas* (retaliation) and *diya* (blood money) ordinances which amended the Pakistan Penal Code to incorporate *Shariah* punishments for violent crimes.[982] Finally, in 1991, the Enforcement of Shari'ah Act, which declares that "Shari'ah . . . shall be the supreme law of Pakistan," was passed.[983]

Because of the incorporation of *Shariah* regarding *zina* (unlawful sexual intercourse) into Pakistan's Penal Code, rape victims in Pakistan who attempted to bring charges against their attackers were frequently charged with adultery.[984] In an attempt to remedy this injustice, the Protection of Women (Criminal Laws Amendment) Act was passed in 2006.[985] However, on December 22, 2010, Pakistan's Federal Shariat Court struck down numerous sections of the Act as unconstitutional because, under Pakistan's Constitution, *Shariah* is the supreme law.[986]

A further effect of Pakistan's re-establishment of criminal *Shariah* is the enforcement of blasphemy laws.[987] This re-Islamization movement in Pakistan led to the January 2011 assassinations of Pakistani Governor Salmaan Taseer and Federal Minister for Minorities Affairs Shahbaz Bhatti, both of whom

---

[981]Lau, *supra* note 978, at 398; *see also* PETERS, *supra* note 260, at 155.

[982]*See* PAK. PENAL CODE, ch. XVI (1860).

[983]Enforcement of Shari'ah Act, No. 10 of 1991, THE GAZETTE OF PAKISTAN EXTRAORDINARY (June 18, 1991), *available at* http://www.pakistani.org/pakistan/legislation/1991/actXof1991.html.

[984]UNITED STATES COMM'N ON INT'L RELIGIOUS FREEDOM, UNITED STATES COMMISSION ON INTERNATIONAL RELIGIOUS FREEDOM ANNUAL REPORT 2008: PAKISTAN, (May 1 2008), *available at* http://www.unhcr.org/refworld/docid/48556999c.html.

[985]*Id.*; *see also* PAK. PENAL CODE Act XLV of 1860, Protection of Women (Criminal Laws Amendment) Act (2006).

[986]PAK. PENAL CODE Act XLV of 1860, Protection of Women (Criminal Laws Amendment) Act (2006), *available at* http://www.pakistani.org/pakistan/legislation/2006/wpb.html. Notably, the Constitution of Pakistan explicitly empowers the Federal Shariat Court with the task of bringing "[a]ll existing laws . . . in[to] conformity with the Injunctions of Islam as laid down in the Holy Quran and Sunnah." CONST. art. 227 (Pak.).

[987]PAK. PENAL CODE, ch. XV (1860).

were assassinated for their outspoken opposition to the country's blasphemy laws.[988] Their deaths are further evidence that those who wish to reincorporate Islamic *Shariah* into modern legal systems will often stop at nothing, even death, to accomplish their radical political and religious goals.

Iran, too, underwent re-Islamization following the 1979 Islamic revolution.[989] Iranian courts have punished *hadd* crimes (offenses against Allah and those with fixed, severe punishments) with amputation, cross-amputation, and the death penalty.[990] As one example, Iranian law mandates death by stoning for "adultery while married."[991]

In Northern Sudan, where *Shariah* has been officially recognized since 1983,[992] apostasy (converting from Islam) is punishable by death.[993] Furthermore, Sudanese courts are permitted by law to convict for "acts that do not fall under the wording of the Penal Code, but are punishable under the Shari'a."[994]

The most recent Islamization movement in criminal law has taken place in Northern Nigeria, where, between 2000 and 2002, twelve northern states modified their criminal justice systems to

---

[988]*See Hada Messia, Pope Decries Attacks Against Religious Minorities, CNN (Jan. 10, 2011), http:// articles.cnn.com/2011-01-10/world/vatican.pope.speech_1_vatican-diplomatic-corps-pope-benedict-xvi-religious-intolerance?_s=PM:WORLD* ("'I once more encourage the leaders of [Pakistan] to take the necessary steps to abrogate [the blasphemy] law, all the more so because it is clear that it serves as a pretext for acts of injustice and violence against religious minorities.'"); Annabelle Bentham, *Shahbaz Bhatti Obituary*, THE GUARDIAN (Mar. 10, 2011), http://www.guardian.co.uk/world/2011/ mar/10/shahbaz-bhatti-obituary (reporting that Bhatti was assassinated for his "unrelenting opposition to Pakistan's blasphemy laws and the injustices and intolerance they encouraged").

[989]*See* PETERS, *supra* note 260, at 160; *see also* Ziba Mir-Hosseini, *Sharia and National Law in Iran, in* SHARIA INCORPORATED, *supra* note 954, at 319, 331.

[990]*See* PETERS, *supra* note 260, at 161; *see also* Mir-Hosseini, *supra* note 989, at 358–60.

[991]*See* AMNESTY INT'L, IRAN: EXECUTIONS BY STONING 2 (Dec. 2010) (MDE 13/095/2010), *available at* http://www.amnesty.org/en/library/asset/MDE13/095/2010en/968814e1-f48e-43ea-bee3-462d153fb5af/mde130952010en.pdf.

[992]Sudan: A Country Study (Helen Chapin Metz ed., GPO for the Library of Congress 1992), *available at* http://lcweb2.loc.gov/frd/cs/sdtoc.html#sd0111 (Chapter 4, The Legal System).

[993]Criminal Code of Sudan, art. 126 (1991); *see also* KEVIN BOYLE & JULIET SHEEN, FREEDOM OF RELIGION AND BELIEF: A WORLD REPORT 73 (1997); PETERS, *supra* note 260, at 168; Olaf Kondgen, *Shari'a and National Law in Sudan, in* SHARIA INCORPORATED, *supra* note 954, at 181, 213.

[994]PETERS, *supra* note 260, at 168–69.

comply with *Shariah*.[995] Similar to other countries under criminal *Shariah*, Nigerian *Shariah* penal codes have created significant uncertainty in the law by giving courts virtually unbridled discretion to punish any offenses under classical Islamic law.[996]

Re-Islamization of the law, however, is not limited to Islamic nations. *Shariah* courts in Britain and Kenya, the push for similar courts in Canada, and numerous examples discussed in this book where even United States courts have faced challenges to consider Islamic *Shariah*, show its universal reach. The same West that once helped Islamic nations to reform *Shariah* and restrict the application of laws that were incompatible with basic human rights is now being challenged to implement the very laws it once restricted. The United States, however, must recognize this challenge to protect not only one of its greatest values—liberty—but also its supreme law—the United States Constitution.

---

[995]Ostien & Dekker, *supra* note 957, at 553, 575; PETERS, *supra* note 260, at 169.

[996]*See, e.g.*, Shari'ah Penal Code of Zamfara art. 92 ("Any act or omission which is not specifically mentioned in this Shari'ah Penal Code but is otherwise declared to be an offence under the Qur'an, Sunnah and Ijtihad of the Maliki school of Islamic thought shall be an offence under this code . . . ."); *see also* PETERS, *supra* note 260, at 171; Ostien & Dekker, *supra* note 957, at 590.

APPENDIX A

PROPOSED LEGISLATIVE LANGUAGE

Although this book focuses on the dangers and incompatibility of Islamic *Shariah* with U.S. law, *Shariah* is only one of the world's legal systems that is incompatible with U.S. law. As such, the ACLJ proposes the following general language for state constitutional amendments or statutes to protect the liberties given to us by our Forefathers by prohibiting consideration and application of laws incompatible with our own.

* * * * *

AN ACT TO PROTECT INDIVIDUAL LIBERTIES GUARANTEED UNDER THE CONSTITUTION OF THE UNITED STATES OF AMERICA, THE CONSTITUTION OF THE STATE [COMMONWEALTH] OF [ ], LAWS MADE PURSUANT THERETO, AND THE COMMON LAW AS RECOGNIZED BY THIS STATE [COMMONWEALTH]

WHEREAS, the Constitution of the United States of America and the laws made pursuant thereto are the supreme law of the United States of America; and

WHEREAS, the individual rights and liberties guaranteed and protected by the Constitution of the United States of America and the Constitution of the State [Commonwealth] of [ ] are the envy of the world; and

WHEREAS, such liberties have encouraged individual genius to flourish in this Nation and State [Commonwealth] to the mutual benefit of all Americans and the world; and

WHEREAS, the principle of individual liberty is not simply a slogan for outside consumption but a reality for all Americans; and

WHEREAS, the role of elected officials of this State [Commonwealth] is to secure and protect for its citizens as well as subsequent generations the liberties provided to us by our Founders; and

WHEREAS, the existence of such liberties has been a beacon to draw immigrants from around the world yearning to live free; and

WHEREAS, there are other legal and political systems in the world whose principles and laws destroy individual liberty and lead to individual subservience to governing authorities to the dread and misfortune of the people so governed; and

WHEREAS, the people of the United States of America and the State [Commonwealth] of [ ] desire to preserve the blessings of liberty and the rule of law for themselves and their posterity and ensure that no foreign legal or political systems incompatible with our laws, traditions, and individual liberties are applied in this State [Commonwealth]; and

WHEREAS, it is the State [Commonwealth] legislature which sets the jurisdictional limits of its courts and other adjudicative bodies; and

THEREFORE, to protect and promote for ourselves and our posterity the individual rights and privileges granted by our Founders under the Constitution of the United States of America, the Constitution of the State [Commonwealth] of [ ], the laws made pursuant thereto, and the Common Law as recognized by this State [Commonwealth].

BE IT ENACTED BY THE [LEGISLATURE] OF THE STATE [COMMONWEALTH] OF [ ]:

Section 1. Prohibition of laws incompatible with the Constitutions of the United States and this State [Commonwealth].

The State [Commonwealth] of [ ], its political subdivisions, and any adjudicative bodies, including courts, judges, magistrates, arbitrators, mediators, city councils, administrative bodies, and the like shall not recognize or enforce any foreign law, religious law, custom, or practice that is contrary to or incompatible with the Constitution of the United States of America and the laws, rules, and regulations promulgated pursuant thereto; the Constitution of the State [Commonwealth] of [ ] and the laws, rules, and regulations promulgated pursuant thereto, or the Common Law as recognized in the State [Commonwealth] of [ ].

A. Foreign laws prohibited in this Section include any law, rule, or regulation of jurisdictions outside any state or territory of the United States of America and/or which does not provide the same or equivalent individual rights and liberties guaranteed under the Constitution of the United States of America and the Constitution of the State [Commonwealth] of [ ].

B. Religious laws, customs, or practices prohibited in this Section include any law, rule, or regulation constituting, implementing, or enforcing by civil authorities of this State [Commonwealth] a religious system, belief, code, or ethnic or tribal custom or practice.

C. Prohibited laws, customs, and practices, from whatever source they arise, include, but are not limited to, those which permit, enforce, or implement any of the following:

1. prejudicial treatment of women or persons of a particular race, religion, ethnicity, social class, or caste before the law;
2. prohibition of the right to leave, change, or renounce one's religion or belief;
3. prohibition of otherwise protected speech or assembly;
4. plural marriages;
5. marriages of convenience and/or contracts for sexual services;
6. forced or underage marriages;
7. violence against women and children, excluding reasonable parental discipline of children;
8. politically- or religiously-motivated physical violence and/or homicide;
9. cruel and unusual punishments as prohibited by the Eighth Amendment to the United States Constitution, including, but not limited to, punishments such as amputation, lashing, flogging, stoning, branding, or piercing;
10. female genital mutilation; or
11. human sacrifice.

Section 2. Ways in which incompatible laws may not be applied or enforced.

A. The courts, judges, magistrates, arbitrators, mediators, administrative agencies, or other adjudicative entities of this State [Commonwealth] shall not enforce contractual provisions or agreements that provide for the choice of law described in Section 1 to govern its interpretation, performance, or implementation, or to resolve any claim or dispute. This reflects the strong public policy of this State [Commonwealth].

B. The courts, judges, magistrates, arbitrators, mediators, administrative agencies, or other adjudicative entities of this State [Commonwealth] shall not recognize or enforce a decision rendered by any foreign court, administrative agency, arbitrator, mediator, or other adjudicative entity if that decision was governed by or applied laws described in Section 1. This reflects the strong public policy of this State [Commonwealth].

C. The courts, judges, magistrates, arbitrators, mediators, administrative agencies, or other adjudicative entities of this State [Commonwealth] shall not enforce contractual provisions or agreements that provide for forums in which courts, judges, magistrates, arbitrators, mediators, or other adjudicative entities are governed by or apply laws described in Section 1. This is the strong public policy of this State [Commonwealth].

D. The courts, judges, magistrates, arbitrators, mediators, administrative agencies, or other adjudicative entities of this State [Commonwealth] shall not grant a claim of *forum non conveniens* or a related claim in any litigation, arbitration, mediation, or any similar proceeding if the alternative forum is governed by or applies laws described in

Section 1. This is the strong public policy of this State [Commonwealth].

E. The courts, judges, magistrates, arbitrators, mediators, administrative agencies, or other adjudicative entities of this State [Commonwealth] shall not recognize or enforce any other motion, petition, or similar request for relief that they find violates Section 1. This is the strong public policy of this State [Commonwealth].

Section 3. Severability clause.

If any provision of this legislation [amendment] is found to be unconstitutional, it shall have no effect on the other provisions, which shall remain in full force and effect.

APPENDIX B

GLOSSARY

Transliteration of an Arabic word into English often leads to multiple spellings. Thus the spelling of the following terms may vary according to the source.

Accounting and Auditing Organization for Islamic Financial Institutions: an autonomous Islamic international non-profit corporate body that prepares accounting, auditing, governance, ethics, and *Shariah* standards for Islamic financial institutions.

Ahkam: commandments and/or decrees of Allah.

Aisha: one of Muhammad's wives; she was six years old when Muhammad married her and nine years old when the marriage was consummated.

Al Haramain Islamic Foundation: a charity headquartered in Saudi Arabia that registered a U.S. branch as a 501(c)(3); designated as a terrorist organization by the U.S. Department of the Treasury for funneling funds to *al-Qaeda*.

Al-Kitab: literally translated, "the Book"; a reference to the *Qur'an*, Islam's holy book and the primary source of *Shariah*.

Allah: the sole deity in Islam.

Al-Qaeda: sometimes spelled "Al-Qaida"; the terrorist organization that orchestrated and carried out the September 11th attacks and supports violent *jihad* for the global advancement of Islam.

Al-qat' min-khilāf: cross-amputation; severing a thief's right hand and left foot.

Benevolence International Foundation: an Illinois charity designated as a financier of terrorism by the United States Department of Treasury.

Burqa: traditional Islamic outer garment that covers women from head to toe and is worn in public by Muslim women; veil.

Cairo Declaration on Human Rights: a declaration adopted in 1990 and submitted to the United Nations by the Member States of the Organisation of the Islamic Conference (OIC); declares the official Islamic perspective on human rights and guarantees freedom and the right to dignified life only in accordance with *Shariah*.

Caliph: term referring to those who succeeded Muhammad and served as head of the Islamic community, or *ummah*; currently there is no official caliph.

Caliphate: divinely-instituted Islamic government run by a caliph.

Centre for Social Cohesion: London-based, non-partisan organization that researches radicalization and extremism within Britain.

Council on American-Islamic Relations (CAIR): an Islamic charity and advocacy group established in 1994 and headquartered in Washington, D.C.; also an unindicted co-conspirator in the *Holy Land Foundation* cases.

Dar al-harb: literally "territory of war"; constitutes all territories not under Islamic control.

Dar al-Islam: territory under Islamic control.

Da'wah: the invitation by Muslims to non-Muslims to convert to Islam and follow *Shariah*.

Diyat: blood money in physical injury and homicide cases; the compensation paid directly to an offender's victim or the victim's kin in exchange for pardon.

Fatwa: a religious edict or religio-legal opinion given by an Islamic cleric.

Fiqh: Islamic jurisprudence; the science of Islamic religious law.

Ghazwa: battles in which Muhammad participated.

Hadd (Hadood): offenses against Allah for which the *Qur'an* and *Sunnah* prescribe severe penalties that often involve loss of life or limb.

Hadith: the second primary source of Islamic law recounting the *Sunnah* (conduct and sayings of Muhammad); considered second in authority to the *Qur'an*.

Halal: that which is permitted or lawful according to Islam.

Hamas: Palestinian organization that maintains power in the Gaza Strip, is devoted to the destruction of Israel, and believes in violent Islamic conquest; regards peaceful solutions to be in contradiction to the Islamic Resistance Movement; designated a foreign terrorist organization by the U.S. Department of State.

Hanafi: the most prominent of the four schools of *Sunni* jurisprudence that purportedly takes a moderate approach in applying *Shariah* principles to contemporary legal issues but nonetheless calls for total subjugation of the world under *Shariah*; prominent in Pakistan and Afghanistan.

Hanbali: the most rigid of the four schools of *Sunni* jurisprudence; stresses the puritanical aspects of Islam and is uncompromising in its adherence to orthodoxy; forms the basis of *Shariah* in Saudi Arabia.

Haram: that which is forbidden by or unlawful in Islam.

Hezbollah: sometimes spelled "Hizbollah"; militant *Shi'ite* group in Lebanon that maintains strong ties with both Iran and Syria.

Hijab: a veil.

Hijra: Muhammad's migration from Mecca to Medina, which signifies the beginning of the Islamic calendar.

Holy Land Foundation cases: the Department of Justice's criminal prosecutions of the Holy Land Foundation; unveiled the names of numerous Islamic charities in the U.S. that dispersed funds to terrorist organizations.

Holy Land Foundation for Relief and Development (HLF): an Islamic charity, headquartered in Richardson, Texas, shut down by the U.S. government in 2001 for funding Hamas.

Ijarah: to give something on rent; to lease.

Ijmā: a consensus of Islamic jurists on Islamic legal issues arising after Muhammad's death.

Ijtihad: the hermeneutical efforts made by jurists in seeking knowledge of the *ahkām* (rules) of the *Shariah* through interpretation and to discover the intention of Allah, with respect to the rules of conduct.

Ikhwan al-Muslimin: Muslim Brotherhood.

Imam: the spiritual and religious leader of a mosque and Islamic community.

Islamic African Relief Agency: an Islamic charity headquartered in Sudan and having more than forty offices throughout the world, including the United States; designated by the U.S. Department of the Treasury as a terrorist organization in 2004 for directing funds to both Hamas and the Taliban.

Islamic Society of North America: a Muslim charity and outreach organization headquartered in Plainfield, Indiana; an unindicted co-conspirator in the *Holy Land Foundation* cases for its membership with the Muslim Brotherhood.

Ja'fari: the *Shi'ite* school of jurisprudence that was developed by Ja'far as-Sadiq.

Jald: flogging.

Jihad: holy struggle or holy war; its three distinct forms mandated by Islam include individual *jihad* (struggle against one's inner self), *da'wah* (non-violent methods of converting people to Islam), and violent *jihad* (violent conflict with all non-Muslims).

Jizyah: a poll tax that non-Muslims who live in the territory of Islam must pay to maintain practice of their own faith; otherwise, they must convert to Islam or fight and die.

Khul: legal separation; an alternative to divorce available to women if they voluntarily forfeit their dowers and can prove certain dissolution grounds.

Mahr: dower or marriage payment to women; serves as a sort of spousal support when a husband divorces his wife but generally must be forfeited when a woman initiates dissolution of her marriage.

Maliki: one of the four schools of *Sunni* jurisprudence; prioritizes Islamic tenets in applying *Shariah* but allows for some consideration of local customs and equitable and practical concerns; prevalent in northern and western Africa, including Sudan.

Muhammad: Islam's founder and prophet.

Mujahada: literally means "warfare to establish the religion"; a root term for *jihad*.

Murtadd: apostate; one who leaves Islam.

Musharakah: literally means "sharing"; denotes the profit-sharing relationship between lenders and debtors in Islamic banking.

Muslim: a believer in or follower of Islam; generally, Muslims identify themselves with either *Sunni* or *Shi'ite* Islam.

Muslim Brotherhood: a fundamentalist Islamic movement, also known as the *Ikhwan al-Muslimin*, dedicated to resurrecting the true Islamic caliphate (divinely-instituted Islamic government) based on *Shariah*; parent organization of *Hamas*; its political party was founded in Egypt in 1928 and introduced the party slogan, "Islam is the solution."

Muslim Students' Association: a student group that self-identifies as a moderate faith club at more than 600 college campuses throughout North America; believed to be a significant contributor to the rise of Islamic extremism and spread of fundamentalist Islam to a new generation of Islamic activists and sympathizers in North America.

Mufti: Islamic scholar.

Mutʿah: a legally permissible form of temporary, contract-based marriage with monetary payment as consideration; instituted by Muhammad but now endorsed only by *Shi'ite* Islam.

Naskh: abrogation or repeal of some earlier normative verses in the *Qur'an* that are now held as non-normative in view of some of its later verses. (**Nasikh:** abrogating rule; **Mansukh:** abrogated rule).

North American Islamic Trust: established in 1973 by the Muslim Students Association as a 501(c)(3); an unindicted co-conspirator in the *Holy Land Foundation* cases.

Occupied Land Fund: the original name for the Holy Land Foundation for Relief and Development.

Organisation of the Islamic Conference: the second largest international organization, second only to the United Nations; comprised of fifty-six Islamic nations; self-proclaimed purposes include "to safeguard and protect the interests of the Muslim world" at the United Nations and "to defend the universality of [the] Islamic religion."

Qadi: a *Shariah* judge.

Qisas: the equality in punishment; the "eye for an eye" retaliation prescribed by *Shariah*; the principle that the offender of a crime against a person should be punished in kind.

Qiyas: commonly recognized secondary sources of *Shariah*; the application of analogized rationalizations of *Shariah* principles to novel legal issues; limited to *Shariah* jurists throughout the Islamic legal tradition.

Qur'an: Islam's holy book and the primary source of *Shariah*; also transliterated "Quran" and "Koran."

Rajm: stoning.

Ridda: apostasy.

SAW (or PBUH): represents the Arabic phrase "salla Allah alaihi wa sallam," which is translated "peace be upon him"; Muslims should say or write this after Muhammad's name is spoken or written.

SWT: represents the Arabic phrase "subhanahu wa ta'ala," which is translated "glory to Allah"; a respectful way of saying or writing Allah's name that every Muslim is encouraged to use.

Sadqa: voluntary charity above and beyond *zakat* (obligatory charity).

Sahih: valid or authentic; generally applied to *hadith* as in Sahih Bukhari.

Sahih Bukhāri: one of *Sunni* Muslims' most trusted collections of *hadith*.

Shafi'i: likely the second most prominent school of *Sunni* jurisprudence; it is reluctant to create new legal principles for modern contexts and defers to those already existing in the *Qur'an* and *Sunnah*.

Shariah: the revealed or canonical law of Islam; considered supreme over all other legal systems for Muslims regardless of where they reside.

Shi'ite: one of the two major factions of Islam, accounting for approximately ten to fifteen percent of the world's Muslim population; follows the *Ja'fari* school of jurisprudence and has historically been at odds with all four schools of *Sunni* jurisprudence.

Shura Council: *Shura* is an Arabic term that denotes a consultative body.

Sunnah: the words, actions, approvals, silence, and customs ascribed to Muhammad; collected in *hadiths*.

Sunni: the more prominent of the two major factions of Islam, accounting for approximately eighty-five to ninety percent of the world's Muslim population.

Surah: the term for "chapters" in the *Qur'an*.

Talaq: divorce; Muslim husbands are permitted to divorce their wives by merely pronouncing three times that the wife is divorced.

Taliban: Islamic terrorists in Afghanistan who adhere to a strict interpretation of Islam.

Tazir: offenses against society; penalties are left to the discretion of the *qadi* (*Shariah* judge) because *Shariah* provides no specific punishment; distinct from *hadd* offenses and penalties.

Ummah: the global Islamic community that encompasses all Muslims, regardless of their geographical location or country of citizenship.

Zakat: one of the five pillars of Islam requiring Muslims to pay a percentage of their wealth for distribution to eight different categories of recipients, which include the poor, the indebted, and participants in violent *jihad*.

Zina: unlawful sexual intercourse, including adultery and fornication, for which *Shariah* prescribes harsh penalties (generally flogging or stoning).

APPENDIX C

MUSLIM BROTHERHOOD MEMORANDUM

Bate #<u>**ISE-SW/ 1B10/ 0000413**</u>

In the name of God, the Beneficent, the Merciful
Thanks be to God, Lord of the Two Worlds,
Prayers and peace be upon the master of the Messengers

An Explanatory Memorandum
On the General Strategic Goal for the Group
In North America
5/22/1991

Contents:
1- An introduction in explanation
2- The Concept of Settlement
3- The Process of Settlement
4- Comprehensive Settlement Organizations

Page 2 of 18

Bate #ISE-SW/ 1B10/ 0000414

In the name of God, the Beneficent, the Merciful
Thanks be to God, Lord of the Two Worlds
And blessed are the Pious

5/22/1991

The beloved brother/The General Masul, may God keep him
The beloved brother/Secretary of the Shura Council, may God keep him
The beloved brothers/Members of the Shura Council, may God keep them
God's peace, mercy and blessings be upon you.... To proceed,

I ask Almighty God that you, your families and those whom you love around you are in the best of conditions, pleasing to God, glorified His name be.

I send this letter of mine to you hoping that it would seize your attention and receive your good care as you are the people of responsibility and those to whom trust is given. Between your hands is an "Explanatory Memorandum" which I put effort in writing down so that it is not locked in the chest and the mind, and so that I can share with you a portion of the responsibility in leading the Group in this country.

What might have encouraged me to submit the memorandum in this time in particular is my feeling of a "glimpse of hope" and the beginning of good tidings which bring the good news that we have embarked on a new stage of Islamic activism stages in this continent.

The papers which are between your hands are not abundant extravagance, imaginations or hallucinations which passed in the mind of one of your brothers, but they are rather hopes, ambitions and challenges that I hope that you share some or most of which with me. I do not claim their infallibility or absolute correctness, but they are an attempt which requires study, outlook, detailing and rooting from you.

My request to my brothers is to read the memorandum and to write

what they wanted of comments and corrections, keeping in mind
that what is between your hands is not strange or a new submission
without a root, but rather an attempt to interpret and explain
some of what came in the long-term plan which we approved and
adopted in our council and our conference in the year (1987).
So, my honorable brother, do not rush to throw these papers away
due to your many occupations and worries. All what I'm asking of
you is to read them and to comment on them hoping that we might
continue together the project of our plan and our Islamic work in
this part of the world.
Should you do that, I would be thankful and grateful to you.
I also ask my honorable brother, the Secretary of the Council, to
add the subject of the memorandum on the Council agenda in its
coming meeting.

May God reward you good and keep you for His Daw'a
Your brother/Mohamed Akram

Page 3 of 18

Bate #**ISE-SW/ 1B10/ 0000415**

(1)

In the name of God, the Beneficent, the Merciful
Thanks be to God, Lord of the Two Worlds
And Blessed are the Pious

Subject: A project for an explanatory memorandum for the General
Strategic goal for the Group in North America mentioned in the
long-term plan

One: The Memorandum is derived from:
1- The general strategic goal of the Group in America which
was approved by the Shura Council and the Organizational
Conference for the year [1987] is "Enabled of Islam in North
America, meaning: establishing an effective and a stable Islamic
Movement led by the Muslim Brotherhood which adopts Muslims'
causes domestically and globally, and which works to expand the
observant Muslim base, aims at unifying and directing Muslims'
efforts, presents Islam as a civilization alternative, and supports the
global Islamic State wherever it is".
2- The priority that is approved by the Shura Council for the work
of the Group in its current and former session which is
"Settlement".
3- The positive development with the brothers in the Islamic Circle
in an attempt to reach a unity of merger.
4- The constant need for thinking and future planning, an attempt
to read it and working to "shape" the present to comply and suit
the needs and challenges of the future.
5- The paper of his eminence, the General Masul, may God keep
him, which he recently sent to the members of the Council.

Two: An Introduction to the Explanatory Memorandum:
-In order to begin with the explanation, we must "summon"
the following question and place it in front of our eyes as its
relationship is important and necessary with the strategic goal and
the explanation project we are embarking on. The question we are

facing is: "How do you like to see the Islam Movement in North America in ten years?", or "taking along" the following sentence when planning and working, "Islamic Work in North America in the year (2000): A Strategic Vision".

Also, we must summon and take along "elements" of the general strategic goal of the Group in North America and I will intentionally repeat them in numbers. They are:

[1- Establishing an effective and stable Islamic Movement led by the Muslim Brotherhood.

2- Adopting Muslims' causes domestically and globally.

3- Expanding the observant Muslim base.

4- Unifying and directing Muslims' efforts.

Page 4 of 18

Bate #**ISE-SW 1B10/ 0000416**

(2)

5- Presenting Islam as a civilization alternative
6- Supporting the establishment of the global Islamic State wherever it is].

- It must be stressed that it has become clear and emphatically known that all is in agreement that we must "settle" or "enable" Islam and its Movement in this part of the world.
- Therefore, a joint understanding of the meaning of settlement or enablement must be adopted, through which and on whose basis we explain the general strategic goal with its six elements for the Group in North America.

Three: The Concept of Settlement:
This term was mentioned in the Group's "dictionary" and documents with various meanings in spite of the fact that everyone meant one thing with it. We believe that the understanding of the essence is the same and we will attempt here to give the word and its "meanings" a practical explanation with a practical Movement tone, and not a philosophical linguistic explanation, while stressing that this explanation of ours is not complete until our explanation of "the process" of settlement itself is understood which is mentioned in the following paragraph. We briefly say the following:

Settlement: "That Islam and its Movement become a part of the homeland it lives in".
Establishment: "That Islam turns into firmly-rooted organizations on whose bases civilization, structure and testimony are built".
Stability: "That Islam is stable in the land on which its people move".
Enablement: "That Islam is enabled within the souls, minds and the lives of the people of the country in which it moves".

Rooting: "That Islam is resident and not a passing thing, or
                    rooted "entrenched" in the soil of the spot where it
                    moves and not a strange plant to it".

Four: The Process of Settlement:
- In order for Islam and its Movement to become "a part of the
homeland" in which it lives, "stable" in its land, "rooted" in the
spirits and minds of its people, "enabled" in the live of its society
and has firmly-established "organizations" on which the Islamic
structure is built and with which the testimony of civilization
is achieved, the Movement must plan and struggle to obtain
"the keys" and the tools of this process in carry out this grand
mission as a "Civilization Jihadist" responsibility which lies
on the shoulders of Muslims and - on top of them - the Muslim
Brotherhood in this country. Among these keys and tools are the
following:

**1-Adopting the concept of settlement and understanding its
practical meanings:**
The Explanatory Memorandum focused on the Movement
and the realistic dimension of the process of settlement and its
practical meanings without paying attention to the difference in
understanding between the resident and the non-resident, or who is
the settled and the non-settled

Page 5 of 18

Bate #<u>ISE-SW 1B10/ 0000417</u>

(3)

and we believe that what was mentioned in the long-term plan in that regards suffices.

2- Making a fundamental shift in our thinking and mentality in order to suit the challenges of the settlement mission.

What is meant with the shift - which is a positive expression - is responding to the grand challenges of the settlement issues. We believe that any transforming response begins with the method of thinking and its center, the brain, first. In order to clarify what is meant with the shift as a key to qualify us to enter the field of settlement, we say very briefly that the following must be accomplished:

- A shift from the partial thinking mentality to the comprehensive thinking mentality.
- A shift from the "amputated" partial thinking mentality to the "continuous" comprehensive mentality.
- A shift from the mentality of caution and reservation to the mentality of risk and controlled liberation.
- A shift from the mentality of the elite Movement to the mentality of the popular Movement.
- A shift from the mentality of preaching and guidance to the mentality of building and testimony
- A shift from the single opinion mentality to the multiple opinion mentality.
- A shift from the collision mentality to the absorption mentality.
- A shift from the individual mentality to the team mentality.
- A shift from the anticipation mentality to the initiative mentality.
- A shift from the hesitation mentality to the decisiveness mentality.
- A shift from the principles mentality to the programs mentality.
- A shift from the abstract ideas mentality the true organizations mentality [This is the core point and the essence of the memorandum].

3- Understanding the historical stages in which the Islamic

Ikhwani activism went through in this country:
The writer of the memorandum believes that understanding and comprehending the historical stages of the Islamic activism which was led and being led by the Muslim Brotherhood in this continent is a very important key in working towards settlement, through which the Group observes its march, the direction of its movement and the curves and turns of its road. We will suffice here with mentioning the title for each of these stages [The title expresses the prevalent characteristic of the stage] [Details maybe mentioned in another future study]. Most likely, the stages are:

A- The stage of searching for self and determining the identity.
B- The stage of inner build-up and tightening the organization.
C- The stage of mosques and the Islamic centers.
D- The stage of building the Islamic organizations - the first phase.
E- The stage of building the Islamic schools - the first phase.

Page 6 of 18

Bate #<u>**ISE-SW 1B10/ 0000418**</u>

(4)

F- The stage of thinking about the overt Islamic Movement - the first phase.

G- The stage of openness to the other Islamic movements and attempting to reach a formula for dealing with them - the first phase.

H- The stage of reviving and establishing the Islamic organizations - the second phase.

We believe that the Group is embarking on this stage in its second phase as it has to open the door and enter as it did the first time.

4- Understanding the role of the Muslim Brother in North America:

The process of settlement is a "Civilization-Jihadist Process" with all the word means. The Ikhwan must understand that their work in America is a kind of grand Jihad in eliminating and destroying the Western civilization from within and "sabotaging" its miserable house by their hands and the hands of the believers so that it is eliminated and God's religion is made victorious over all other religions. Without this level of understanding, we are not up to this challenge and have not prepared ourselves for Jihad yet. It is a Muslim's destiny to perform Jihad and work wherever he is and wherever he lands until the final hour comes, and there is no escape from that destiny except for those who chose to slack. But, would the slackers and the Mujahedeen be equal.

5- Understanding that we cannot perform the settlement mission by ourselves or away from people:

A mission as significant and as huge as the settlement mission needs magnificent and exhausting efforts. With their capabilities, human, financial and scientific resources, the Ikhwan will not be able to carry out this mission alone or away from people and he who believes that is wrong, and God knows best. As for the role of the Ikhwan, it is the initiative, pioneering, leadership, raising the banner and pushing people in that direction. They are then to work to employ, direct and unify Muslims' efforts and powers for this process. In order to do that, we must possess a mastery of the art of "coalitions", the art of "absorption" and the principles of "cooperation".

6- The necessity of achieving a union and balanced gradual merger between private work and public work:

We believe that what was written about this subject is many and is enough. But, it needs a time and a practical frame so that what is needed is achieved in a gradual and a balanced way that is compatible with the process of settlement.

Page 7 of 18

Bate #**ISE-SW 1B10/ 0000418** (Cont'd)

7- The conviction that the success of the settlement of Islam and its Movement in this country is a success to the global Islamic Movement and a true support for the sought-after state, God willing:
There is a conviction - with which this memorandum disagrees - that our focus in attempting to settle Islam in this country will lead to negligence in our duty towards the global Islamic Movement in supporting its project to establish the state. We believe that the reply is in two segments: One - The success of the Movement in America in establishing an observant Islamic base with power and effectiveness will be the best support and aid to the global Movement project.

Bate #**ISE-SW 1B10/ 0000419**
(5)

And the second - is the global Movement has not succeeded yet in "distributing roles" to its branches, stating what is the needed from them as one of the participants or contributors to the project to establish the global Islamic state. The day this happens, the children of the American Ikhwani branch will have far-reaching impact and positions that make the ancestors proud.

8- Absorbing Muslims and winning them with all of their factions and colors in America and Canada for the settlement project, and making it their cause, future and the basis of their Islamic life in this part of the world:
This issues requires from us to learn "the art of dealing with the others", as people are different and people in many colors. We need to adopt the principle which says, "Take from people… the best they have", their best specializations, experiences, arts, energies and abilities. By people here we mean those within or without the ranks of individuals and organizations. The policy of "taking" should be with what achieves the strategic goal and the settlement process. But the big challenge in front of us is: how

to connect them all in "the orbit" of our plan and "the circle" of our Movement in order to achieve "the core" of our interest. To me, there is no choice for us other than alliance and mutual understanding of those who desire from our religion and those who agree from our belief in work. And the U.S. Islamic arena is full of those waiting...., the pioneers.

What matters is bringing people to the level of comprehension of the challenge that is facing us as Muslims in this country, conviction of our settlement project, and understanding the benefit of agreement, cooperation and alliance. At that time, if we ask for money, a lot of it would come, and if we ask for men, they would come in lines. What matters is that our plan is "the criterion and the balance" in our relationship with others.

Here, two points must be noted; the first one: we need to comprehend and understand the balance of the Islamic powers in the U.S. arena [and this might be the subject of a future study]. The second point: what we reached with the brothers in "ICNA" is considered a step in the right direction, the beginning of good and the first drop that requires growing and guidance.

Page 8 of 18

Bate #<u>ISE-SW 1B10/ 0000419</u> (Cont'd)

9- Re-examining our organizational and administrative bodies, the type of leadership and the method of selecting it with what suits the challenges of the settlement mission:
The memorandum will be silent about details regarding this item even though it is logical and there is a lot to be said about it.

10- Growing and developing our resources and capabilities, our financial and human resources with what suits the magnitude of the grand mission:
If we examined the human and the financial resources the Ikhwan alone own in this country, we and others would feel proud and glorious. And if we add to them the resources of our friends and allies, those who circle in our orbit and those waiting on our banner, we would realize that we are able to open the door to settlement and walk through it seeking to make Almighty God's word the highest.

Bate #**ISE-SW 1B10/ 0000420**

(6)

11- Utilizing the scientific method in planning, thinking and preparation of studies needed for the process of settlement:
Yes, we need this method, and we need many studies which aid in this civilization Jihadist operation. We will mention some of them briefly:
- The history of the Islamic presence in America.
- The history of the Islamic Ikhwani presence in America.
- Islamic movements, organizations and organizations: analysis and criticism.
- The phenomenon of the Islamic centers and schools: challenges, needs and statistics.
- Islamic minorities.
- Muslim and Arab communities.
- The U.S. society: make-up and politics.
- The U.S. society's view of Islam and Muslims... And many other studies which we can direct our brothers and allies to prepare, either through their academic studies or through their educational centers or organizational tasking. What is important is that we start.

12- Agreeing on a flexible, balanced and a clear "mechanism" to implement the process of settlement within a specific, gradual and balanced "time frame" that is in-line with the demands and challenges of the process of settlement.
13- Understanding the U.S. society from its different aspects an understanding that "qualifies" us to perform the mission of settling our Dawa' in its country "and growing it" on its land.
14- Adopting a written "jurisprudence" that includes legal and movement bases, principles, policies and interpretations which are suitable for the needs and challenges of the process of settlement.
15- Agreeing on "criteria" and balances to be a sort of "antennas" or "the watch tower" in order to make sure that all of our priorities, plans, programs, bodies, leadership, monies and activities march towards the process of the settlement.

16- Adopting a practical, flexible formula through which our central work complements our domestic work.
[Items 12 through 16 will be detailed later].

17- Understanding the role and the nature of work of "The Islamic Center" in every city with what achieves the goal of the process of settlement:
The center we seek is the one which constitutes the "axis" of our Movement, the "perimeter" of the circle of our work, our "balance center", the "base" for our rise and our "Dar al-Arqam" to educate us, prepare us and supply our battalions in addition to being the "niche" of our prayers.

Page 10 of 18

Bate #**ISE-SW 1B10/ 0000421**

(7)

This is in order for the Islamic center to turn - in action not in words - into a seed "for a small Islamic society" which is a reflection and a mirror to our central organizations. The center ought to turn into a "beehive" which produces sweet honey. Thus, the Islamic center would turn into a place for study, family, battalion, course, seminar, visit, sport, school, social club, women gathering, kindergarten for male and female youngsters, the office of the domestic political resolution, and the center for distributing our newspapers, magazines, books and our audio and visual tapes. In brief we say: we would like for the Islamic center to become "The House of Dawa'" and "the general center" in deeds first before name. As much as we own and direct these centers at the continent level, we can say we are marching successfully towards the settlement of Dawa' in this country.

Meaning that the "center's" role should be the same as the "mosque's" role during the time of God's prophet, God's prayers and peace be upon him, when he marched to "settle" the Dawa' in its first generation in Madina. from the mosque, he drew the Islamic life and provided to the world the most magnificent and fabulous civilization humanity knew.

This mandates that, eventually, the region, the branch and the Usra turn into "operations rooms" for planning, direction, monitoring and leadership for the Islamic center in order to be a role model to be followed.

18- Adopting a system that is based on "selecting" workers, "role distribution" and "assigning" positions and responsibilities is based on specialization, desire and need with what achieves the process of settlement and contributes to its success.

19- Turning the principle of dedication for the Masuls of main positions within the Group into a rule, a basis and a policy in work. Without it, the process of settlement might be stalled [Talking about this point requires more details and discussion].

20- Understanding the importance of the "Organizational" shift in our Movement work, and doing Jihad in order to achieve it in the real world with what serves the process of settlement and expedites its results, God Almighty's willing:
The reason this paragraph was delayed is to stress its utmost importance as it constitutes the heart and the core of this memorandum. It also constitutes the practical aspect and the true measure of our success or failure in our march towards settlement. The talk about the organizations and the "organizational" mentality or phenomenon does not require much details. It suffices to say that the first pioneer of this phenomenon was our prophet Mohamed, God's peace, mercy and blessings be upon him, as he placed the foundation for the first civilized organization which is the mosque, which truly became "the comprehensive organization". And this was done by the pioneer of the contemporary Islamic Dawa', Imam martyr Hasan al-Banna, may God have mercy on him, when he and his brothers felt the need to "re-establish" Islam and its movement anew, leading him to establish organizations with all their kinds: economic, social, media, scouting,

Page 11 of 18

Bate #**ISE-SW 1B10/ 0000421** (Cont'd)

professional and even the military ones. We must say that we are in
a country which understands no language other than the language
of the organizations, and one which does not respect or give weight
to any group without effective, functional and strong organizations.

Bate #**ISE-SW 1B10/ 0000422**

(8)

It is good fortune that there are brothers among us who have
this "trend", mentality or inclination to build the organizations
who have beat us by action and words which leads us to dare
say honestly what Sadat in Egypt once said, "We want to build a
country of organizations" - a word of right he meant wrong with. I
say to my brothers, let us raise the banner of truth to establish right
"We want to establish the Group of organizations", as without it we
will not able to put our feet on the true path.
- And in order for the process of settlement to be completed, we
must plan and work from now to equip and prepare ourselves, our
brothers, our apparatuses, our sections and our committees in order
to turn into comprehensive organizations in a gradual and balanced
way that is suitable with the need and the reality. What encourages
us to do that - in addition to the aforementioned - is that we possess
"seeds" for each organization from the organization we call for
[See attachment number (1)].
- All we need is to tweak them, coordinate their work, collect their
elements and merge their efforts with others and then connect them
with the comprehensive plan we seek.
For instance,
We have a seed for a "comprehensive media and art" organization:
we own a print + advanced typesetting machine + audio and
visual center + art production office + magazines in Arabic and
English [The Horizons, The Hope, The Politicians, Ila Falastine,
Press Clips, al-Zaytouna, Palestine Monitor, Social Sciences
Magazines...] + art band + photographers + producers + programs

anchors + journalists + in addition to other media and art experiences".

Another example:

We have a seed for a "comprehensive Dawa' educational" organization: We have the Daw'a section in ISNA + Dr. Jamal Badawi Foundation + the center run by brother Hamed al-Ghazali + the Dawa' center the Dawa' Committee and brother Shaker al-Sayyed are seeking to establish now + in addition to other Daw'a efforts here and there…".

And this applies to all the organizations we call on establishing.

- The big challenge that is ahead of us is how to turn these seeds or "scattered" elements into comprehensive, stable, "settled" organizations that are connected with our Movement and which fly in our orbit and take orders from our guidance. This does not prevent - but calls for - each central organization to have its local branches but its connection with the Islamic center in the city is a must.

Page 12 of 18

Bate #**ISE-SW 1B10/ 0000422** (Cont'd)

- What is needed is to seek to prepare the atmosphere and the means to achieve "the merger" so that the sections, the committees, the regions, the branches and the Usras are eventually the heart and the core of these organizations.

Or, for the shift and the change to occur as follows:

Page 13 of 18

Bate #**ISE-SW 1B10/ 0000423**

(9)

1- The Movement Department + The Secretariat Department	- The Organizational & Administrative Organization - The General Center
2- Education Department + Dawa'a Com.	- Dawa' and Educational Organization
3- Sisters Department	- The Women's Organization
4- The Financial Department + Investment Committee + The Endowment	- The Economic Organization
5- Youth Department + Youths Organizations Department	- Youth Organizations
6- The Social Committee + Matrimony Committee + Mercy Foundation	- The Social Organization
7- The Security Committee	- The Security Organization
8- The Political Depart. + Palestine Com.	- The Political Organization
9- The Group's Court + The Legal Com.	- The Judicial Organization
10- Domestic Work Department	- Its work is to be distributed to the rest of the organizations
11- Our magazines + the print + our art band	- The Media and Art Organization
12- The Studies Association + The Publication House + Dar al-Kitab	- The Intellectual & Cultural Organization
13- Scientific and Medial societies	- Scientific, Educational and Professional Organization
14- The Organizational Conference	- The Islamic-American Founding Conference

15- The Shura Council + Planning Com.	- The Shura Council for the Islamic-American Movement
16- The Executive Office	- The Executive Office of the Islamic-American Movement
17- The General Masul	- Chairman of the Islamic Movement and its official Spokesman
18- The regions, branches & Usras	- Field leaders of organizations & Islamic centers

Five: Comprehensive Settlement Organization:

- We would then seek and struggle in order to make each one of these above-mentioned organizations a "comprehensive organization" throughout the days and the years, and as long as we are destined to be in this country. What is important is that we put the foundation and we will be followed by peoples and generations that would finish the march and the road but with a clearly-defined guidance.

Page 14 of 18

Bate #**ISE-SW 1B10/ 0000423** (Cont'd)

And, in order for us to clarify what we mean with the comprehensive, specialized organization, we mention here the characteristics and traits of each organization of the "promising" organizations.

1- From the Dawa' and educational aspect [The Dawa' and Educational Organization]: to include:

- The Organization to spread the Dawa' (Central and local branches).
- An institute to graduate Callers and Educators.
- Scholars, Callers, Educators, Preachers and Program Anchors.
- Art and communication technology, Conveyance and Dawa'.

Bate #<u>**ISE-SW 1B10/ 0000424**</u>

(10)

- A television station.
- A specialized Dawa' magazine.
- A radio station.
- The Higher Islamic Council for Callers and Educators.
- The Higher Council for Mosques and Islamic Centers.
- Friendship Societies with the other religions… and things like that.

2- Politically [The Political Organization]: to include:
- A central political party.
- Local political offices.
- Political symbols.
- Relationships and alliances.
- The American Organization for Islamic Political Action
- Advanced Information Centers….and things like that.

3- Media [The Media and Art Organization]: to include:
- A daily newspaper.
- Weekly, monthly and seasonal magazines.
- Radio stations.
- Television programs.
- Audio and visual centers.
- A magazine for the Muslim child.
- A magazine for the Muslim woman.
- A print and typesetting machines.
- A production office.
- A photography and recording studio
- Art bands for acting, chanting and theater.
- A marketing and art production office… and things like that.

Bate #<u>ISE-SW 1B10/ 0000425</u>

(11)

4- Economically [The Economic Organization]: to include:
- An Islamic Central bank.
- Islamic endowments.
- Investment projects.
- An organization for interest-free loans.... and things like that.

5- Scientifically and Professionally [The Scientific, Educational and Professional Organization]: to include:
- Scientific research centers.
- Technical organizations and vocational training.
- An Islamic university.
- Islamic schools.
- A council for education and scientific research.
- Centers to train teachers.
- Scientific societies in schools.
-An office for academic guidance.
- A body for authorship and Islamic curricula.... and things like that.

6- Culturally and Intellectually [The Cultural and Intellectual Organization]: to include:
- A center for studies and research.
- Cultural and intellectual foundations such as [The Social Scientists Society - Scientist and Engineers Society....].
- An organization for Islamic thought and culture.
- A publication, translation and distribution house for Islamic books.
- An office for archiving, history and authentication
- The project to translate the Noble Quran, the Noble Sayings....and things like that.

7- Socially [The Social-Charitable Organization]: to include:
- Social clubs for the youths and the community's sons and

daughters
- Local societies for social welfare and the services are tied to the Islamic centers
- The Islamic Organization to Combat the Social Ills of the U.S. Society
- Islamic houses project
- Matrimony and family cases office....and things like that.

Page 16 of 18

Bate #<u>ISE-SW 1B10/ 00004216</u>

(12)

8- Youths [The Youth Organization]: to include:
- Central and local youths foundations.
- Sports teams and clubs
- Scouting teams....and things like that.

9- Women [The Women Organization]: to include:
- Central and local women societies.
- Organizations of training, vocational and housekeeping.
- An organization to train female preachers.
- Islamic kindergartens…and things like that.

10- Organizationally and Administratively [The Administrative and Organizational Organization]: to include:
- An institute for training, growth, development and planning
- Prominent experts in this field
- Work systems, bylaws and charters fit for running the most complicated bodies and organizations
- A periodic magazine in Islamic development and administration.
- Owning camps and halls for the various activities.
- A data, polling and census bank.
- An advanced communication network.
- An advanced archive for our heritage and production....and things like that.

11- Security [The Security Organization]: to include:
- Clubs for training and learning self-defense techniques.
- A center which is concerned with the security issues [Technical, intellectual, technological and human]....and things like that.

12- Legally [The Legal Organization]: to include:
- A Central Jurisprudence Council.
- A Central Islamic Court.
- Muslim Attorneys Society.

- The Islamic Foundation for Defense of Muslims' Rights…and things like that.

And success is by God.

Page 17 of 18

Bate #**ISE-SW 1B10/ 0000427**

Attachment number (1)

A list of our organizations and the organizations of our friends
[Imagine if t they all march according to one plan!!!]

1- ISNA   = ISLAMIC SOCIETY OF NORTH AMERICA
2- MSA   = MUSLIM STUDENTS' ASSOCIATION
3- MCA   = THE MUSLIM COMMUNITIES ASSOCIATION
4- AMSS   = THE ASSOCIATION OF MUSLIM SOCIAL
             SCIENTISTS
5- AMSE   = THE ASSOCIATION OF MUSLIM
             SCIENTISTS AND ENGINEERS
6- IMA   = ISLAMIC MEDICAL ASSOCIATION

7- ITC=   ISLAMIC TEACHING CENTER
8- NAIT   = NORTH AMERICAN ISLAMIC TRUST
9- FID   = FOUNDATION FOR INTERNATIONAL
             DEVELOPMENT
10- IHC   = ISLAMIC HOUSING COOPERATIVE
11- ICD   = ISLAMIC CENTERS DIVISION
12- ATP   = AMERICAN TRUST PUBLICATIONS
13- AVC   = AUDIO-VISUAL CENTER
14- IBS   = ISLAMIC BOOK SERVICE
15- MBA   = MUSLIM BUSINESSMEN ASSOCIATION
16- MYNA   = MUSLIM YOUTH OF NORTH AMERICA
17- IFC   = ISNA FIQH COMMITTEE
18- IPAC   = ISNA POLITICAL AWARENESS COMMITTEE
19- IED   = ISLAMIC EDUCATION DEPARTMENT

20- MAYA   = MUSLIM ARAB YOUTH ASSOCIATION
21- MISG   = MALASIAN [sic] ISLAMIC STUDY GROUP
22- IAP   = ISLAMIC ASSOCIATION FOR PALESTINE
23- UASR   = UNITED ASSOCIATION FOR STUDIES AND
             RESEARCH
24- OLF   = OCCUPIED LAND FUND

25- MIA   = MERCY INTERNATIONAL ASSOCIATION

26- ISNA   = ISLAMIC CIRCLE OF NORTH AMERICA
27- BMI   = BAITUL MAL INC
28- IIIT   = INTERNATIONAL INSTITUTE FOR ISLAMIC
              THOUGHT
29- IIC   = ISLAMIC INFORMATION CENTER

Page 18 of 18

APPENDIX D

COMPARATIVE CHART

The following chart sets forth specific Islamic criminal and civil laws and compares them with U.S. laws, showing the inherent conflict between U.S. and Islamic standards of justice, punishments, and resolution of disputes.

Individual Rights (First Amendment)	Islamic *Shariah*	United States Law
Conversion from Islam (Apostasy)	Punished by death.[i]	Protected under the First Amendment's Free Exercise Clause.[ii]
Defaming Islam (e.g., blaspheming Muhammad, showing disrespect to the *Qur'an*, or defaming Allah)	Punished by death.[iii]	Protected under the First Amendment as free speech or expressive conduct.[iv]
Interfaith Marriage	Muslim women may only marry Muslim men; Muslim men may marry only Muslim, Jewish, or Christian women.[v]	With minor exceptions (e.g., age, consanguinity, etc.), everyone is free to marry the person of his or her choosing, regardless of religion, under the First and Fourteenth Amendments, and men and women must be treated equally by the law.[vi]

Criminal Law	Islamic *Shariah*	United States Law
Consuming Alcohol	Punished by flogging of forty lashes.[vii]	Allowed by state law upon reaching legal age.[viii]
Domestic Violence	Not punished if a wife is deemed to be rebellious or disobedient; the *Qur'an* allows a husband to beat his wife (or wives) to compel them to obey the husband's commands.[ix]	Punishable by imprisonment; state protection is offered to the victim.[x]
Female Genital Mutilation/Female Circumcision	Required for strict compliance with *Shariah*; generally done to promote women's chastity.[xi]	Illegal.[xii]
Marital Rape	A wife must have sex with her husband upon the husband's demand; if the wife refuses, the husband may take disciplinary steps (verbal admonition to physical beating).[xiii]	Forced sexual intercourse, even of a spouse, is punishable as domestic violence or marital rape.[xiv]
Short-term Contracted Sexual Relationships/ Prostitution (mut'ah)	Permitted under the *Shi'ite* school of Islamic thought.[xv]	Illegal in most states.[xvi]

Rape	If rape is proven, the rapist may either have to pay a marriage payment to the woman[xvii] or be punished as a fornicator or adulterer and receive lashes; women who are raped may be convicted of *zina* (unlawful sexual intercourse), punishable by stoning (if married) or lashes (if not married), unless they can produce four male Muslim eyewitnesses to prove they were raped.[xviii]	Perpetrator is punished by imprisonment; a woman's testimony is valid to establish rape, and the judge or jury decides based on all the evidence whether the sexual intercourse was forced or consensual; women are not punished for unlawful sexual intercourse if they cannot prove rape; evidence rules are designed to protect rape victims.[xix]
Theft	Punished by amputation.[xx]	Punished by fine or imprisonment.[xxi]
Family Law	**Islamic *Shariah***	**United States Law**
Adultery	Punished by stoning;[xxii] may be mitigated completely for *Shi'ites* by *mut'ah* (short-term sexual relationship); if a married woman is raped and cannot provide the necessary witnesses, she will likely be stoned as an adulteress.[xxiii]	Punished as a misdemeanor, if at all, in most states.[xxiv]
Child Custody	There is no "best interests of the child" standard; depending on whether the mother remarries or leaves Islam, custody will default to the father or mother.[xxv]	The child's interests are *the determining factor*;[xxvi] whatever is in the "child's best interests" will generally determine the outcome of the custody proceeding.

Divorce	Generally, husbands may divorce their wives without cause and without notifying them and may do so by merely declaring it audibly;[xxvii] women do not obtain legal divorces on their own initiative, but merely *dissolve* their marriages and become lawfully separated from their husbands.[xxviii] These dissolutions (*khul*) are limited to very particular grounds, and if women do choose to dissolve the marriage, they forfeit their financial security.[xxix]	Men and women have equal rights under the Fourteenth Amendment; both men and women may divorce each other and must do so through a judicial process that requires giving the other party notice and opportunity to be heard.[xxx]
Forced Marriage	Fathers and grandfathers have the power to force their minor daughters (in some cases as young as nine years old) to marry the men of the father's or grandfather's choosing.[xxxi]	Marriage is by the mutual consent of both parties (subject to a minimum age and consanguinity requirements prescribed by state law); marriages procured by force or duress are voidable.[xxxii]
Polygamy	Men may take up to four wives; women may only marry one man.[xxxiii]	Illegal.[xxxiv]

Miscellaneous	Islamic *Shariah*	United States Law
Shariah-Compliant Financing: Banking and Financial Markets	Financial institutions must become *Shariah*-compliant, involving saving, investing, and building wealth according to the teachings of the *Qur'an* and *Sunnah.*[xxxv]	The United States supports free markets and engages freely in various types of economic systems throughout the world.
Shariah-Compliant Financing: *Funding Jihad*	*Shariah*, and by extension *Shariah*-compliant financing, requires Muslims to give obligatory charitable contributions (*zakat*[xxxvi]), and part of such contributions must be given to "*those fighting for Allah*, meaning people engaged in Islamic military operations . . . ."[xxxvii]	Illegal; companies may not fund terrorist activities.[xxxviii]
Fornication	Punishable by 100 lashes;[xxxix] if an unmarried woman is raped but cannot provide the necessary witnesses, she will be lashed as a fornicator.[xl]	Under the Supreme Court's interpretation of the Due Process Clause, fornication is legal for consenting individuals (subject to certain age restrictions prescribed by the states);[xli] U.S. laws do not prescribe severe criminal penalties for unlawful fornication.

Homosexual Sodomy	Punished by death.[xlii]	Under the Supreme Court's interpretation of the Due Process Clause, homosexual sodomy performed in private is legal for consenting individuals (subject to certain age restrictions prescribed by state law).[xliii]
Honor Killings (killing women who dishonor their Islamic families through befriending or marrying non-Muslim men, refusing forced marriages, etc., or killing any family member who dishonors the family by converting to another religion, blaspheming Muhammad, etc.)	Certain offenses are justified under *Shariah*, e.g., killing a non-Muslim, killing an apostate, or killing one's own offspring.[xliv]	Illegal (murder).[xlv]
Testifying Witnesses: Men and Women	A woman's testimony is equal to half that of a man because of the supposed "deficiency of a woman's mind."[xlvi]	Men and women must be treated equally under the Fourteenth Amendment's Equal Protection Clause.[xlvii]

---

[i]Converting from Islam is a form of "apostasy" and is punishable by death. AHMAD IBN NAQIB AL-MISRI, RELIANCE OF THE TRAVELLER 595 (Nuh Ha Mim Keller, trans., Amana Publications rev. ed. 2008) (1368) [hereinafter RELIANCE OF THE TRAVELLER] ("When a person who has reached puberty and is sane voluntarily apostatizes from Islam, he deserves to be killed."); *see also* ABDULLAH YUSUF ALI, THE MEANING OF THE HOLY QUR'AN, *Surah* 5:33 (10th ed. 2001) [hereinafter QUR'AN] ("The punishment of those who wage war against Allah and His Messenger, and strive with might and main for mischief through the land is: execution, or crucifixion, or the cutting off of hands and feet from opposite sides, or exile from the land: That is their disgrace in this world, and a heavy punishment is theirs in the hereafter[.]"). Muhammad was recorded to have said, "If . . . (a Muslim) discards his religion, kill him." SAHIH BUKHARI, Vol. 4, Bk. 52, No. 260, *available at* http://www.usc.edu/schools/college/crcc/engagement/resources/texts/muslim/hadith/bukhari/092.sbt.html [hereinafter SAHIH BUKHARI] (internal citations omitted) (English translation of *hadith* of Sahih Bukhari *available at* http://www.usc.edu/schools/college/crcc/engagement/resources/texts/muslim/hadith/bukhari/) (official webpage of the Univ. of S. Cal.'s Center

for Muslim-Jewish Engagement).

[ii]U.S. CONST. amend. I ("Congress shall make no law respecting an establishment of religion, or prohibiting the free exercise thereof . . . ."); Cantwell v. Connecticut, 310 U.S. 296, 303 (1940) (The First Amendment "forestalls compulsion by law of the acceptance of any creed or the practice of any form of worship. Freedom of conscience and freedom to adhere to such religious organization or form of worship as the individual may choose cannot be restricted by law. On the other hand, it safeguards the free exercise of the chosen form of religion.").

[iii]QUR'AN, *supra* note 11, at *Surah* 4:140 ("Already has [Allah] sent you word in the book, that when ye hear the signs of Allah held in defiance and ridicule, ye are not to sit with them unless they turn to a different theme . . . ."; *see also* SAHIH BUKHARI, *supra* note 69, at Vol. 3, Bk. 46, No. 705 ("The Prophet said, 'Allah has accepted my invocation to forgive what whispers in the hearts of my followers, *unless* they put it to action *or utter it.*'" (emphasis added)); RUDOLPH PETERS, CRIME AND PUNISHMENT IN ISLAMIC LAW: THEORY AND PRACTICE FROM THE SIXTEENTH TO THE TWENTY-FIRST CENTURY 65 (2005) ("If the apostasy consisted in insulting the prophet (*sabb al-nabi*), according to most schools the apostate is not given an opportunity for repentance, but is killed immediately after the sentence."). Blasphemy is a form of apostasy. RELIANCE OF THE TRAVELLER, *supra* note i, at 596–98 ("Among the things that entail apostasy from Islam . . . are . . . to speak words that imply unbelief such as 'Allah is the third of three,' or 'I am Allah' . . . to revile Allah or His messenger . . . to be sarcastic about Allah's name . . . to deny any verse of the Koran or anything which by scholarly consensus belongs to it, or to add a verse that does not belong to it; [] to mockingly say, 'I don't know what faith is' . . . to describe a Muslim or someone who wants to become a Muslim in terms of *unbelief* . . . to revile the religion of Islam . . . to be sarcastic about any ruling of the Sacred Law; [] or to deny that Allah intended the Prophet's message . . . to be the religion followed by the entire world."). Apostasy is punishable by death, see *supra* note i, and therefore blasphemy is also punishable by death.

[iv]U.S. CONST. amend. I ("Congress shall make no law . . . abridging the freedom of speech."). Outside of the "uninhibited, robust, and wide-open" free speech protection of the First Amendment, *New York Times Co. v. Sullivan*, 376 U.S. 254, 270 (1964), only several narrow categories of speech are excepted from Constitutional protection, such as fighting words, *Chaplinsky v. New Hampshire*, 315 U.S. 568, 574 (1942); defamatory falsehoods, *Sullivan*, 376 U.S. 254, 279–80 (1964); and obscene materials, *Miller v. California*, 413 U.S. 15 (1973). The First Amendment also protects "expressive conduct," such as burning the American flag. Texas v. Johnson, 491 U.S. 397 (1989). The Supreme Court has continually held that in regulating expressive conduct, the "government may not prohibit the expression of an idea simply because society finds the idea offensive or disagreeable." *Id.* at 414.

[v]QUR'AN, *supra* note i, at *Surah* 5:5 ("This day are (all) things good and pure made lawful unto you. The food of the people of the Book is lawful unto you and yours is lawful unto them. (Lawful unto you in marriage) are (not only) chaste women who are believers, but chaste women among the People of the Book, revealed before your time . . . ."); *see also* RELIANCE OF THE TRAVELLER, *supra* note i, at 529 ("It is not lawful or valid for a Muslim man to be married to any woman who is not either a Muslim, Christian, or Jew; nor is it lawful or valid for a Muslim woman to be married to *anyone besides a Muslim.*" (emphasis added)).

[vi]U.S. CONST. amends. I, XIV. Specifically, in the landmark anti-miscegenation case, Loving v. Virginia, 388 U.S. 1 (1967), the U.S. Supreme Court held that "[t]he freedom to marry has long been recognized as one of the vital personal rights essential to the orderly pursuit of happiness by free men." *Id.* at 12. Further, "[t]o deny this fundamental freedom on so unsupportable a basis as . . . racial classifications . . . is surely to deprive all the State's citizens of liberty without due process of law." *Id.* Based on the reasoning of this case, any law forbidding interfaith marriages would be held unconstitutional in the United States.

[vii]QUR'AN, *supra* note i, at *Surah* 5:90–91 ("O ye who believe! Intoxicants and gambling . . . are an abomination—of Satan's handiwork; eschew such (abomination), that ye may prosper. Satan's plan is (but) to excite enmity and hatred between you, with intoxicants . . . , and hinder you . . . from prayer: will ye not then abstain?"). The punishment of forty lashes for consuming alcohol derives from *hadith*. SAHIH BUKHARI, *supra* note i, at Vol. 8, Bk. 81, Num. 764 ("The Prophet beat a drunk with palm-leaf stalks and shoes. And Abu Bakr gave (such a sinner) forty lashes."); *see also* RELIANCE OF THE TRAVELER, *supra* note i, at 617; PETERS, *supra* note iii, at 64.

[viii]*See* U.S. CONST. amend XXI (repealing prohibition); 18 PA.C.S. § 6308 (2010) (establishing the minimum age for consuming alcohol at twenty-one); *see also* South Dakota v. Dole, 483 U.S. 203,

211–12 (1987) (holding that Congress has authority under the Spending Clause to make receipt of federal funds conditional on whether a state's minimum drinking age was twenty-one).

[ix]QUR'AN, *supra* note i, at *Surah* 4:34 ("(Husbands) are the protectors and maintainers of their (wives) because Allah has given the one more (strength) than the other, and because they support them from their means. Therefore the righteous women are devoutly obedient . . . . As to those women on whose part ye fear disloyalty and ill-conduct, admonish them (first), (next,) refuse to share their beds, (and last) beat them (lightly) . . . ."). Each parenthetical, which collectively aim to soften the harshness of the text, was inserted by the translator's own initiative and is not in the original Arabic version of the *Qur'an*. *See* Int'l Inst. of Islamic Thought, *Preface to the New Edition*, in QUR'AN, *supra* note i, at ix–x; *see also* 2 MUHAAMAD SUBHI BIN HASAN HALLAQ, FIQH: ACCORDING TO THE QUR'AN AND SUNNAH 156 (2008) (Muhammad said: "[A]nd it is your right upon them that they do not allow any man whom you dislike to sit on your mattress; and if they do so, beat them, but not violently . . . .'") (citing *Hadiths* Narrated by Al-Hakim (2/189-190), Al-Baihaqi (7/293) and At-Tabarani) [hereinafter FIQH].

[x]*See, e.g.*, Violence Against Women Act (VAWA), 18 U.S.C. § 2261(a) (prohibiting anyone who "travels in interstate or foreign commerce" from "commit[ting] a crime of violence against [a] . . . spouse, intimate partner, or dating partner . . . .").

[xi]RELIANCE OF THE TRAVELLER, *supra* note i, at 59 ("Circumcision is obligatory (O: for both men and women. For men it consists of removing the prepuce from the penis, and for women, removing the prepuce (Ar. bazr) of the clitoris . . . ."); *see also* CENTRE FOR SOCIAL COHESION, CRIMES OF THE COMMUNITY: HONOUR-BASED VIOLENCE IN THE UK 69 (2d ed. 2010).

[xii]*See, e.g.*, 18 U.S.C. § 116(a) ("[W]hoever knowingly circumcises, excises, or infibulates the whole or any part of the labia majora or labia minora or clitoris of another person who has not attained the age of 18 years shall be fined under this title or imprisoned not more than 5 years, or both.").

[xiii]QUR'AN, *supra* note i, at *Surah* 2:223 ("Your wives are as a tilth unto you so approach your tilth when or how you will . . . ."); RELIANCE OF THE TRAVELLER, *supra* note i, at 525 (It is "obligatory for a woman to let her husband have sex with her *immediately* when: (a) he asks her; (b) at home . . .; (c) and she can physically endure it."). If a woman refuses her husband, she is deemed "rebellious" and the husband is permitted to force her to comply. *Id* at 542; *see also* QUR'AN, *supra* note i, at *Surah* 4:34.

[xiv]*E.g.*, N.J. STAT. ANN. § 2C:25-17 (2011) et. seq. ("Prevention of Domestic Violence Act of 1991"); OKL. ST. tit. 21, § 1111(B) (2010) ("Rape is an act of sexual intercourse accomplished with a male or female *who is the spouse* of the perpetrator if force or violence is used or threatened, accompanied by apparent power of execution to the victim or to another person." (emphasis added)).

[xv]QUR'AN, *supra* note i, at *Surah* 4:24 ("Also (prohibited are) women already married, *except* those whom your right hands possess. Thus hath Allah ordained (prohibitions) against you: Except for these, all others are lawful, provided ye seek (them in marriage) with gifts from your property— desiring chastity, not lust. Seeing that ye derive benefit from them, give them their dowers (at least) as prescribed; but if, after a dower is prescribed, ye agree mutually (to vary it), there is no blame on you." (emphasis added)). The typical *mut'ah* marriage resembles a short-term contractual relationship whereby a man gives something of value to a woman in exchange for the right to have sex with her for the duration of the contractual relationship. SHAUKAT MAHMOOD & NADEEM SHAUKAT, PRINCIPLES AND DIGEST OF MUSLIM LAW 55–58 (1993). The concept of Islamic *mut'ah* derives from Muhammad's early teachings and continues to be a commonly accepted practice by *Shi'ite* Muslims to this day. *See* Kelly McEvers, *Abuse of Temporary Marriages Flourishes in Iraq*, NPR (Oct. 19, 2010), http://www.npr.org/templates/story/story.php?storyId=130350678.

[xvi]Because prostitution is illegal in all states (with the exception of Nevada), see *U.S. Federal and State Prostitution Laws and Related Punishments*, PROCON ORG (Mar. 15, 2010), http://prostitution.procon.org/view.resource.php?resourceID=000119, contracts between parties for which the rendering of sexual services is consideration are unenforceable as a matter of public policy in most states because "such a contract is, in essence, an agreement for prostitution and unlawful for that reason." Marvin v. Marvin, 557 P.2d 106, 113, 116 (Cal. 1976) (holding that agreements between non-marital partners are unenforceable when they "rest upon a consideration of meretricious sexual services."); *see also* Wilcox v. Trautz, 427 Mass. 326, 332 (1998).

[xvii]RELIANCE OF THE TRAVELLER, *supra* note i, at 535 ("A man is obliged to pay a woman the amount typically received as marriage payment by similar brides . . . when a man forces a woman to fornicate with him," i.e., rapes her.).

[xviii]QUR'AN, *supra* note i, at *Surah* 4:15 ("If any of your women are guilty of lewdness, take the

evidence of four (reliable) witnesses from amongst you against them; and if they testify, confine them to houses until death do claim them, or Allah ordain for them some (other) way."); *see also* RELIANCE OF THE TRAVELLER, *supra* note i, at 638 ("If testimony concerns fornication or sodomy, then it requires four male witnesses (O: who testify, in the case of fornication, that they have seen the offender insert the head of his penis into her vagina).").

[xix]*E.g.*, OKL. ST. tit. 21, § 1111 (2010) (setting out various circumstances under which rape can occur); FED. R. EVID. 412(a)(1)–(2) (excluding evidence in criminal and civil cases (subject to minor exceptions) that is "offered to prove that any alleged victim engaged in other sexual behavior" or "to prove any alleged victim's sexual predisposition"). Rule 412 was explicitly instituted to protect women in rape proceedings and help bring offenders to justice by encouraging victim participation. FED. R. EVID. 412 advisory committee's note, *available at* http://www.law.cornell.edu/rules/fre/ACRule412.htm ("The rule aims to safeguard the alleged victim against the invasion of privacy, potential embarrassment and sexual stereotyping that is associated with public disclosure of intimate sexual details and the infusion of sexual innuendo into the factfinding process. By affording victims protection in most instances, the rule also encourages victims of sexual misconduct to institute and to participate in legal proceedings against alleged offenders.").

[xx]QUR'AN, *supra* note i, at *Surah* 5:38 ("As to the thief, male or female, cut off his or her hands: A punishment by way of example, from Allah, for their crime."). The *hadiths* explain that "[a] woman committed theft in the Ghazwa [(battle)] of the Conquest (of Mecca) and she was taken to the Prophet who ordered her hand to be cut off." SAHIH BUKHARI, *supra* note i, at Vol. 3, Bk. 48, Num. 816. In another instance, "[t]he Prophet cut off the hand of a thief for stealing a shield . . . ." *Id.* at Vol. 8, Bk. 81, Num. 788.

[xxi]*See, e.g.*, CAL. PEN. CODE §§ 489, 490 (2011) (specifying that punishment for larceny (theft without force or threat of force) should be fine or imprisonment, depending on the severity of the larceny); CAL. PEN. CODE § 213 (2011) (punishing robbery (theft by means of force or fear) by varying terms of imprisonment, depending on the severity of the robbery).

[xxii]According to *hadiths*, Muhammad prescribed stoning for adulterers. *See, e.g.*, SAHIH BUKHARI, *supra* note i, at Vol. 3, Bk. 49, Num. 860 ("go to the [adulterous] wife of this (man) and stone her to death"); *id.* at Vol. 7, Bk. 63, Num. 195 (After a married man confessed to the prophet that he had committed adultery, "the Prophet ordered him to be stoned to the death."); SAHIH MUSLIM, Bk. 017, Num. 4191, *available at* http://www.usc.edu/schools/college/crcc/engagement/resources/texts/muslim/hadith/muslim/ ("[I]n case of married male committing adultery with a married female, they shall receive one hundred lashes and be stoned to death."); *see also* Ishtiaq Ahmed, *View: Stoning to Death*, DAILY TIMES (Pak.) (Sept. 14, 2010), http://www.dailytimes.com.pk/default.asp?page=2010%5C09%5C14%5Cstory_14-9-2010_pg3_2 ("[A]ll the five schools of Islamic jurisprudence—Hanafi, Shafai, Maliki and Hanbali of the Sunnis and Ja'afri of the Shias prescribe stoning for adultery. On this point of law, there is complete unanimity of opinion.").

[xxiii]*See supra* note xviii; *see also, e.g.*, Seth Mydans, *In Pakistan, Rape Victims Are the 'Criminals,'* N.Y. TIMES (May 17, 2002), http://www.nytimes.com/2002/05/17/world/in-pakistan-rape-victims-are-the-criminals.html?scp=1&sq= (A Pakistani *Sharia* judge found the married rape victim, who could not meet the evidentiary requirements demanded of rape victims, guilty of adultery and subsequently sentenced her to death by stoning; the stoning sentence is rarely carried out in Pakistan, however, and female rape victims can typically expect ten to fifteen years in prison.).

[xxiv]*E.g.*, GA. CODE ANN. § 16-6-19 (2011) (punishing adultery as a misdemeanor). Many states still criminalize adultery as a misdemeanor, but prosecutions are rare. Jonathan Turley, *Adultery, in Many States, Is Still a Crime*, USA TODAY (Apr. 25, 2010), http://www.usatoday.com/news/opinion/forum/2010-04-26-column26_ST_N.htm.

[xxv]RELIANCE OF THE TRAVELLER, *supra* note i, at 550–53 (noting that "[a] woman has no right to custody . . . [if] she remarries" and the person who gets custody must also be a Muslim because a "non-Muslim has no right to authority and hence no right to raise a Muslim."); FIQH, *supra* note ix, at 201–202 ("The mother has more right to custody of her child, so long as she does not remarry[.]").

[xxvi]*See, e.g.*, *Ex Parte* Byars, 794 So. 2d 345, 347 (Ala. 2001) ("The controlling consideration in [an initial custody determination] is the best interest of the child."); Martin v. Martin, 74 A.D. 2d 419, 425 (N.Y. App. Div. 1980) ("It is familiar law that in a proceeding involving two natural parents custody is to be determined solely by what is in the best interest of the child . . . ."); *In re* Marriage of Harris, 499

N.W.2d 329, 330 (Iowa Ct. App. 1993) ("In child custody cases, the best interests of the child is the first and governing consideration."). As a general rule, neither the father nor the mother automatically has a paramount right to custody of their children; rather, both parents are deemed to have equal parental rights over their children. 27C C.J.S. *Divorce* § 994 (2005); *see also Ex Parte* Byars, 794 So. 2d at 347 ("Alabama law gives neither party priority in an initial custody determination."); *In re* Marriage of Harris, 499 N.W.2d at 330 ("Gender is irrelevant, and neither parent should have a greater burden than the other in attempting to gain custody in a dissolution proceeding."); *In re* Custody of Townsend, 427 N.E.2d 1231 (Ill. 1981); *In re* Marriage of Murphy, 592 N.W.2d 681 (Iowa 1999); In Interest of Cooper, 631 P.2d 632 (Kan. 1981); Park v. Park, 610 P.2d 826 (Okla. Ct. App. 1980).

xxviiRELIANCE OF THE TRAVELLER, *supra* note i, at 556–60 (noting that a valid divorce must come from the husband); FIQH, *supra* note ix, at 164; JOHN L. ESPOSITO, WOMEN IN MUSLIM FAMILY LAW 29–30 (2d ed. 2001) ("A husband's act of divorce in Hanafi law is unencumbered. A Muslim who has attained puberty and is of sound mind has the right to divorce his wife whenever he wishes without citing a cause. The fact that the wife has no part in the procedure is further indicated by the fact that she does not have to be present nor must she be informed. The divorce can be either revocable, which gives the man an opportunity to reconsider the decision, or irrevocable."). Esposito noted that at-will divorce— without court procedure or notice to the wife—is legally valid. *Id.* at 31.

xxviii*See* FIQH, *supra* note ix, at 171 (asserting that "*Al-Khul'* is dissolution, not divorce").

xxix*See* QUR'AN, *supra* note i, at *Surah* 2:229 (providing that in cases where a wife "fear[s] that [she] would be unable to keep the limits ordained by Allah" by remaining in a particular marriage, "there is not blame on either of [the spouses] if she give something for her freedom").

xxxU.S. CONST. amend. XIV ("No state shall . . . deny to any person within its jurisdiction the equal protection of the laws."). In the United States, "[a] divorce proceeding is generally a controversy between a *husband and a wife* to determine who is at fault in causing domestic difficulties," and a divorce is only available as an "extraordinary remedy" for "unavoidable and unendurable" circumstances affecting *either* spouse. 27C C.J.S. *Divorce* § 7 (2005) (emphasis added). However, most states have adopted some form of no-fault divorce laws. *E.g.*, CAL. FAM. CODE § 2310 (2011) (allowing divorce for "irreconcilable differences"); N.Y. DOM. REL. LAW § 170(7) (2011) (allowing divorce if "[t]he relationship between husband and wife has broken down irretrievably for a period of at least six months . . . ."). Also, a divorce proceeding requires adherence to due process requirements, which require giving both parties notice of the proceeding and opportunity to be heard. *See* Farid v. Farid, No. FA094011049S, 2010 LEXIS 2296, at *7–8 (Conn. Super. Sept. 10, 2010).

xxxiRELIANCE OF THE TRAVELLER, *supra* note i, at 522 (There are two types of guardians over women (and young girls), "those who may compel their female charges to marry someone, and those who may not." Guardians who may force the women or girls under their charge to marry include the girl's father or paternal grandfather.); *see also* Susan W. Tiefenbrun, *The Semiotics of Women's Human Rights in Iran*, 23 CONN. J. INT'L L. 1, 61 (2007).

xxxiiIn the United States, marriages procured by coercion or duress are voidable. *See, e.g.*, Newman v. Sigler, 125 So. 666, 666–67 (1930); Fluharty v. Fluharty, 193 A. 838, 839–40 (Del. Super. Ct. 1937); O'Brien v. Eustice, 19 N.E.2d 137, 140 (Ill. App. Ct. 1937); Norvell v. State, 193 S.W.2d 200, 200–01 (Tex. 1946). Valid marriages require the consent of both parties. *See, e.g.*, Madison v. Robinson, 116 So. 31, 35 (Fla. 1928); Elkhorn Coal Corp. v. Tackett, 49 S.W.2d 571, 573 (Ky. 1932); Davis v. Davis, 175 A. 574, 575 (Conn. 1934); Shonfeld v. Shonfeld, 184 N.E. 60, 60–61 (N.Y. 1933); Tice v. Tice, 672 P.2d 1168, 1170–71 (Okla. 1983); Garrison v. Garrison, 460 A.2d 945, 946 (Conn. 1983). Marriages may be proscribed under certain limited conditions, such as consanguinity, age of the parties, or special relationships between the parties. *See, e.g*, N.Y. DOM. REL. LAW § 5 (2011) (banning marriage between certain relatives); TEXAS FAM. CODE § 6.205 (2010) (proscribing marriage if either party is under 16 years of age and a court order has not been obtained); TEXAS FAM. CODE § 6.206 (2010) ("A marriage is void if a party is a current or former stepchild or stepparent of the other party.").

xxxiiiQUR'AN, *supra* note i, at *Surah* 4:3 ("[M]arry women of your choice, two or three or four; but if ye fear that ye shall not be able to deal justly (with them), then only one, or (a captive) that your right hands possess, that will be more suitable, to prevent you from doing injustice."); FIQH, *supra* note ix, at 128 ("'I embraced Islam and at that time, I had eight wives; I mentioned this to the Prophet and he said'": "'Choose four of them.'") (citing Abu Dawood (no. 2241) and Ibn Majah (no. 1952)). Muhammad himself was a polygamist, and among his wives was a girl, Aisha, whom he engaged when she just was six years old and with whom he had sexual intercourse when she was only nine years old. SAHIH BUKHARI, *supra* note i, at Vol. 5, Bk. 58, Num. 236 ("[Muhammad] married 'Aisha when she was a girl of six years of age, and he consumm[ated] that marriage when she was nine years old.").

xxxivReynolds v. United States, 98 U.S. 145 (1878). In *Reynolds*, the Supreme Court of the United States considered the question of whether a criminal charge against a man in a polygamous union would be excused on the basis of the man's Mormon faith. In holding that the criminal conviction would stand, the Court declared:

> Polygamy has always been odious among the northern and western nations of Europe . . . . [I]t is impossible to believe that the constitutional guaranty of religious freedom was intended to prohibit legislation in respect to this most important feature of social life. . . . [A]s a law of the organization of society under the exclusive dominion of the United States, it is provided that plural marriages shall not be allowed. Can a man excuse his practices to the contrary because of his religious belief? [To] permit this would be to make the professed doctrines of religious belief superior to the law of the land, and in effect to permit every citizen to become a law unto himself. Government could exist only in name under such circumstances.

Id. at 164-67.

xxxvTadashi Maeda, *Making Sense of the Fast-Growing Islamic Finance Market*, in CURRENT ISSUES IN ISLAMIC BANKING AND FINANCE: RESILIENCE AND STABILITY IN THE PRESENT SYSTEM 118 (Angelo M. Venardos ed., 2010). *Shariah*-compliant financing "is part of a wider agenda of jihad[] in accordance with the vision of Islamist ideologists of the overthrow of non-Islamic systems and the establishment of a pan-Islamic Caliphate that will rule the earth." PATRICK SOOKHDEO, UNDERSTANDING SHARI'A FINANCE 39 (2008).

xxxvi"Zakat is the prescribed share of one's wealth one owns, possesses and holds for one lunar year, provided the wealth is equal to or above a minimum amount called Nisab." *What is Zakat?*, ZAKATCHICAGO, http://www.zakatchicago.com/ (last visited Mar. 9, 2011). *Zakat* is considered to be "one of the pillars of Islam," a "duty toward Allah," and an obligation placed "on every Muslim who[se] wealth exceeds the value of Nisab." *Id.*; *see also* QUR'AN, *supra* note i, at *Surah* 2:43 ("[P]ractice regular charity[.]").

xxxviiRELIANCE OF THE TRAVELLER, *supra* note i, at 272. There are numerous documented instances of Islamic charitable organizations receiving *zakat* and using such funds to support terrorist organizations. *See, e.g.,* Press Release, U.S. Dep't of the Treasury, Treasury Designates Al-Aqsa International Foundation as Financier of Terror Charity Linked to Funding of the Hamas Terrorist Organization (May 29, 2003), *available at* http://www.treasury.gov/press-center/press-releases/Pages/js439.aspx; *Suspensions Pursuant to Code Section 501(p)*, IRS.Gov, http://www.irs.gov/charities/charitable/article/0,,id=141459,00.html (Mar. 10, 2011); U.S. DEP'T OF THE TREASURY, PROTECTING CHARITABLE GIVING—FREQUENTLY ASKED QUESTIONS 7–8 (2010), *available at* http://www.treasury.gov/resource-center/terrorist-illicit-finance/Documents/Treasury%20Charity%20FAQs%206-4-2010%20 FINAL.pdf. This has been termed "jihad with money." Alex Alexiev, *Jihad Comes to Wall Street*, NAT'L REVIEW ONLINE (Apr. 3, 2008), http://www.nationalreview.com/articles/223869/jihad-comes-wall-street/alex-alexiev; Press Release, BBC, Panorama: Faith, Hate, and Charity (July 30, 2006), *available at* http://www.bbc.co.uk/pressoffice/pressreleases/stories/2006/07_july/30/panorama.shtml.

xxxviii18 U.S.C. § 2339A–C (Prohibiting providing "material support" to terrorists).

xxxix*See* RELIANCE OF THE TRAVELLER, *supra* note i, at 610 ("If the offender is someone with the capacity to remain chaste, then he or she is stoned to death (def: o12.6), *someone with the capacity to remain chaste* meaning anyone who had sexual intercourse (A: at least once) with their spouse in a valid marriage, and is free, of age, and sane. . . . If the offender is not someone with the capacity to remain chaste, then the penalty consists of being scourged (def. o12.5) one hundred stripes and banished to a distance of at least 81 km./50 mi. for one year.").

xl*See supra* note xviii.

xliWhile some states still have laws prohibiting fornication, e.g., GA. CODE ANN. § 16-6-18 (2011), the Supreme Court, in *Lawrence v. Texas*, has interpreted the Due Process Clause to allow consenting adults to have sexual relations in private. 539 U.S. 558, 578 (2003) ("The State cannot demean their existence or control their destiny by making their private sexual conduct a crime. Their right to liberty under the *Due Process Clause* gives them the full right to engage in their conduct without intervention from the government.'").

xliiiSUNAN ABU-DAWUD, Bk. 38, No. 4447, *available at* http://www.usc.edu/schools/college/crcc/ engagement/resources/texts/muslim/hadith/abudawud/ [hereinafter ABU-DAWUD] ("[Muhammad] said: If you find anyone doing as Lot's people did (i.e., committing homosexual sodomy), kill the one who does it, and the one to whom it is done."); *see also* FIQH, *supra* note 143, at 442; RELIANCE OF THE TRAVELLER, *supra* note i, at 665 (recounting Muhammad's statement that Muslims should kill "the one who sodomizes and the one who lets it be done to him").

xliii*Lawrence*, 539 U.S. 558 (the Supreme Court interpreted the Due Process Clause of the Fourteenth Amendment to provide a right to engage in homosexual activity).

xlivRELIANCE OF THE TRAVELLER, *supra* note i, at 584 (listing certain types of homicides in which perpetrators cannot be prosecuted: a Muslim killing a non-Muslim; killing an apostate (convert from Islam); killing one's children); *see also* U.N. High Comm'r for Human Rights, Statement by Navi Pillay on International Women's Day (Mar. 8, 2010), *available at* http://www.un.org/en/events/women/iwd/2010/documents/HCHR_womenday_ 2010_statement.pdf. Navi Pillay noted that,

> [i]n the name of preserving family 'honour,' women and girls are shot, stoned, burned, buried alive, strangled, smothered and knifed to death with horrifying regularity.
>
> The reasons for these murders vary. They may be committed because the victim is considered to have breached family or community norms with respect to sexual conduct, or simply because a woman has expressed a desire to pick a husband of her own choice, or wishes to divorce or claim inheritance.

Id. Additionally, those who convert from Islam to another religion, like Christianity, are sometimes killed by their families for dishonoring the family. Because the punishment for apostasy is death, see *supra* note i, the families may go unprosecuted for murder. The *hadiths* continually reiterate that apostates should be killed, making the family even more justified in murdering an apostate son or "rebellious" daughter. *See* SAHIH BUKHARI, *supra* note i, at Vol. 9, Bk. 89, Num. 271; *id.* at Vol. 9, Bk. 84, Num. 57; *id.* at Vol. 9, Bk. 84, Num. 58; *id.* at Vol. 9, Bk. 83, Num. 37.

xlvPreserving "family honor" is never a valid justification for killing; it is murder.

xlvi*See* QUR'AN, *supra* note i, at *Surah* 2:282 ("And get two witnesses, out of your own men, and if there are not two men, then a man and two women, such as ye choose, for witnesses, so that if one of them errs, the other can remind her."). *Hadiths* explain that the testimony of a woman is equal to half that of a man because of a supposed "deficiency of a woman's mind." SAHIH BUKHARI, *supra* note i, at Vol. 3, Bk. 48, Num. 826 ("The Prophet said, 'Isn't the witness of a woman equal to half of that of a man?' The women said, 'Yes.' He said, 'This is because of the deficiency of a woman's mind.'").

xlviiU.S. CONST. amend. XIV, § I ("No state shall . . . deny to any person within its jurisdiction the equal protection of the laws.").